THE AUTHOR-CAT

Courtesy The Mark Twain Papers, University of California, Berkeley.

THE AUTHOR-CAT

Clemens's Life in Fiction

Forrest G. Robinson

Fordham University Press

New York   2007

Copyright © 2007 Fordham University Press

Library of Congress Cataloging-in-Publication Data

Robinson, Forrest G. (Forrest Glen), 1940–
    The author-cat : Clemens's life in fiction / Forrest G. Robinson.—1st ed.
        p.   cm.
    Includes bibliographical references and index.
    ISBN 978-0-8232-2787-7 (alk. paper)
    1. Twain, Mark, 1835–1910—Psychology   2. Twain, Mark,
1835–1910—Criticism and interpretation.   I. Title.   II. Title: Clemens's
life in fiction.
PS1331.R57   2007
818'.409—dc22

                                                                2007028547

Printed in the United States of America
09 08 07   5 4 3 2 1
First Edition

For Marie
—at last!

Autobiography is the truest of all books; for while it inevitably consists mainly of extinctions of the truth, shirkings of the truth, partial revealments of the truth, with hardly an instance of plain straight truth, the remorseless truth *is* there, between the lines, where the author-cat is raking dust upon it which hides from the disinterested spectator neither it nor its smell . . . the result being that the reader knows the author in spite of his wily diligences.

—Samuel Clemens to William Dean Howells, 14 March 1904

Contents

Preface and Acknowledgments

At Samuel Clemens's funeral, as he looked for a last time at the face he had known so long and so well, William Dean Howells was struck by the "silent dignity" of his friend's final "assent to what must be." Clemens in death seemed to have achieved the surrender and repose that had so eluded him in life. There was scant humor, Howells well knew, in the troubled "depths of a nature whose tragical seriousness broke in the laughter which the unwise took to be the whole of him." Howells goes on in the final sentence of *My Mark Twain* to describe his friend as "the Lincoln of our literature," a characterization that once again highlights the "tragical seriousness" of Clemens's "nature," and that hints quite aptly at his abiding preoccupation with the vexed question of American slavery. To the extent that it addresses itself to the intense moral gravity of our favorite humorist, and in its emphasis on the central importance of slavery in his life and work, *The Author-Cat* is squarely in the Howells tradition. I am indebted as well to the other really important first-hand treatment of Clemens's life, Albert Bigelow Paine's *Mark Twain: A Biography*. Though Paine was a grand progenitor of the genteel myth of Mark Twain, his fourth and final volume, which covers the late, most troubled years, when he enjoyed close daily contact with his subject, is a valuable source of insight into the darker reaches of the aging humorist's state of mind.

I am also inspired and edified by the work of a large handful of scholars who have more recently—and often against strenuous resistance—endeavored to come fully to terms with the elements in Clemens's life and personality that fail to conform to the preferred, iconic profile. Van Wyck Brooks (*The Ordeal of Mark Twain* [1920]) and Bernard DeVoto (*Mark Twain's America; Mark Twain at Work* [1942]) quarreled rather famously about Clemens, but agreed that he was a deeply troubled man. Despite its benign neglect of the late years, Justin Kaplan's brilliant, subtly shaded *Mr. Clemens and Mark Twain* (1966) is still the most coherent and psychologically penetrating life available. Hamlin Hill's *Mark Twain: God's Fool* (1975), which focuses exclusively on the final decade, is a bold, well-documented, painfully iconoclastic monument to a biographer's tough love for his subject. Though rather too clinical for some in its approach, Guy Cardwell's *The Man Who Was Mark Twain* (1991) develops balanced and plausible perspectives on a range of important—if delicate, and therefore frequently neglected—biographical issues. Pamela A. Boker's *The Grief Taboo in American Literature: Loss and Prolonged Adolescence in Twain, Melville, and Hemingway* (1996) is a psychoanalytic study that runs parallel in several ways to my own analysis. Recent, more narrowly focused studies by Philip Ashley Fanning (*Mark Twain and Orion Clemens: Brothers, Partners, Strangers* [2003]), Charles H. Gold ('*Hatching Ruin,' or Mark Twain's Road to Bankruptcy* [2003]), and Terrell Dempsey (*Searching for Jim: Slavery in Sam Clemens's World* [2003]) venture very profitably down hitherto less-traveled critical roads. Meanwhile, Jonathan Arac's *Huckleberry Finn as Idol and Target* (1997) substantially enhances our understanding of the cultural and ideological investments that have obstructed full critical access to Clemens and his writing. Finally, James M. Cox's *Mark Twain: The Fate of Humor* (1966) is an abiding model of lucid, incisive literary analysis.

The Author-Cat draws upon this impressive body of scholarship in arguing that Clemens's potent confessional impulse—to reveal what he regarded as the worst of himself to posterity—found its fruition not in his copious autobiographical writings, but rather in his travel books and major fiction. He was most free with the dark truth, I have found, when he was least aware that he was disclosing it. I have been prompted to explore these recesses of Clemens's interior life by his own evident fascination with them, and by a desire to understand better his lifelong, often exceedingly painful disenchantment with himself and the world. It should be understood that I am moved here not to judge Clemens, but to shed all possible light on his unsparingly harsh judgments of himself. I honor him in all the usual ways, but not least for his astonishing honesty about himself, coupled as it was with the intuitive certainty that the truth of the matter would inevitably elude him.

I am fortunate in my friends, many of whom have supported this project. Michael Cowan, the architect and guiding spirit of American Studies at UC Santa Cruz, has provided indispensable institutional support. John Dizikes, Americanist par excellence, commented very helpfully on the entire manuscript. Harry Berger, tireless scholar and friend, made key contributions to the development of my thinking on Clemens's habits of mind, and generously introduced me to Helen Tartar. European historian and sage observer of the passing human scene, Peter Kenez did his best to foster a balanced moral perspective. David Swanger, Bevil Hogg, Gabriel Brahm, James Christianson, Terrell Dempsey, Shelley Fisher Fishkin, and the late Ted Sarbin all read and commented usefully on portions of the work in progress. Special thanks to James M. Cox and Peter Messent for their interest and encouragement in the late going. I am grateful as well to Robert Hirst, Victor Fischer, Lin Salamo, and Neda Salem of the Mark Twain Papers for their unfailing generosity.

I draw in chapter 2 on my essay "The General and the Maid: Mark Twain on Ulysses S. Grant and Joan of Arc," which was published in the special issue on "Mark Twain at the Turn of the Century, 1890–1910," *Arizona Quarterly* 61 (2005): 41–56, and reprinted with permission. Portions of chapter 3 appeared as "Seeing the Elephant: Some Perspectives on Mark Twain's *Roughing It*," in *American Studies* 21 (1980): 43–64, reprinted with permission. Adapted passages from my essay "The Characterization of Jim in *Huckleberry Finn*," *Nineteenth-Century Literature* 43 (1988): 361–91, which appear in chapter 4, are reprinted with the permission of the University of California Press. Chapter 5 includes materials from "The Sense of Disorder in *Pudd'nhead Wilson*," *Mark Twain's Pudd'nhead Wilson: Race, Conflict, and Culture*, ed. Susan Gillman and Forrest G. Robinson (Durham: Duke University Press, 1990), 22–45, reprinted with permission of Duke University Press; and "Dreaming Better Dreams: The Late Writing of Mark Twain," *A Companion to Mark Twain*, ed. Peter Messent and Louis J. Budd (Oxford: Blackwell, 2005), 449–65, is reprinted with the permission of Blackwell Publishing.

I must end, as always, with my wife, Colleen, and my daughters, Grace, Renate, Emma, and Marie, whom I love even more than this work that fills so much of my time.

Abbreviations

AC   *The American Claimant.* The Oxford Mark Twain. New York: Oxford University Press, 1996.

AMT   *The Autobiography of Mark Twain.* Edited by Charles Neider. New York: Harper and Brothers, 1959.

CTSSE   *Collected Tales, Sketches, Speeches, and Essays.* 2 vols. New York: The Library of America, 1992.

CYA   *Connecticut Yankee in King Arthur's Court.* The Oxford Mark Twain. New York: Oxford University Press, 1996.

FE   *Following the Equator.* The Oxford Mark Twain. New York: Oxford University Press, 1996.

GA   *The Gilded Age.* The Oxford Mark Twain. New York: Oxford University Press, 1996.

HF   *Adventures of Huckleberry Finn.* Edited by Victor Fischer and Lin Salamo. Berkeley: University of California Press, 2003.

HH&T   *Mark Twain's Hannibal, Huck and Tom.* Edited by Walter Blair. Berkeley: University of California Press, 1969.

IA   *The Innocents Abroad.* The Oxford Mark Twain. New York: Oxford University Press, 1996.

JA   *Personal Recollections of Joan of Arc.* The Oxford Mark Twain. New York: Oxford University Press, 1996.

LM   *Life on the Mississippi.* The Oxford Mark Twain. New York: Oxford University Press, 1996.

MCMT   *Mr. Clemens and Mark Twain.* By Justin Kaplan. New York: Simon and Schuster, 1966.

MS   *The Mysterious Stranger.* Edited by William M. Gibson. Berkeley: University of California Press, 1969.

MTA   *Mark Twain's Autobiography.* 2 vols. Edited by Albert Bigelow Paine. New York: Harper and Brothers, 1924.

MTB   *Mark Twain: A Biography.* 4 vols. By Albert Bigelow Paine. New York: Harper and Brothers, 1912.

MTE   *Mark Twain in Eruption.* Edited by Bernard DeVoto. New York: Harper and Brothers, 1940.

MTFM   *Mark Twain's Fables of Man.* Edited by John S. Tuckey. Berkeley: University of California Press, 1972.

MTHL   *Mark Twain-Howells Letters.* 2 vols. Edited by Henry Nash Smith and William M. Gibson. Cambridge, Mass.: Harvard University Press, 1960.

MTL   *Mark Twain's Letters.* 2 vols. Edited by Albert Bigelow Paine. New York: Harper and Brothers, 1917.

MTN   *Mark Twain's Notebook.* Edited by Albert Bigelow Paine. New York: Harper and Brothers, 1935.

MTP   Mark Twain Papers

P&P   *The Prince and the Pauper.* The Oxford Mark Twain. New York: Oxford University Press, 1996.

PW   *Pudd'nhead Wilson and Those Extraordinary Twins.* Edited by Sydney E. Berger. New York: Norton, 1980.

RI   *Roughing It.* The Oxford Mark Twain. New York: Oxford University Press, 1996.

TA   *A Tramp Abroad.* The Oxford Mark Twain. New York: Oxford University Press, 1996.

TS   *The Adventures of Tom Sawyer.* The Oxford Mark Twain. New York: Oxford University Press, 1996.

WIM   *What Is Man? And Other Philosophical Writings.* Edited by Paul Baender. Berkeley: University of California Press, 1973.

WWD   *Mark Twain's Which Was the Dream? and Other Symbolic Writings of the Later Years.* Edited by John S. Tuckey. Berkeley: University of California Press, 1967.

THE AUTHOR-CAT

Never Quite Sane in the Night

I want to reflect at some length on the ways Samuel Langhorne Clemens thought about and represented his own life. The interest of the task is inseparable from its complexity, for my subject was fixed by a lifelong fascination with his myriad and finally ungraspable self, and with such kindred matters as human nature, the fathomless depths of the human mind, and the challenge of autobiography. The writer's thoughts never strayed for long from the events of his past. "Yes," he observed in 1886, "the truth is, my books are simply autobiographies."[1] Clemens's potent autobiographical impulse was the expression of an enduring need to come to terms with his remembered experience of life. Had those memories been as idyllic as some of the books he wrote about them, Clemens would have written a great deal less. For he wrote not so much to memorialize the past as to transform it; he was preoccupied, that is, not so much with fond memories as with things he could not forget. "I wonder why we hate the past so," his good friend William Dean Howells once asked him, to which the humorist replied, "It's so damned humiliating."[2] At the very center and focus of what Clemens could not forget was the tormenting image of what he took to be himself, a hopelessly flawed and profoundly guilty man. Remorse harried him relentlessly, not least of all because he was never able to acquiesce comfortably in his autobiographical self-constructions. Even as he felt compelled, and even morally obliged, to tell the truth about himself, Clemens came increasingly to recognize that the subtle lure of evasion was too strong to be resisted. Still, he never doubted that the truth was there, concealed in the massed records of his life, if one only knew how to look for it. This book is an attempt to bring that buried truth to light.

If we are what we most frequently and intensely think and feel, then it is Clemens's distinctive "self" that I would like to draw out. This was certainly the self as he understood it. "What a wee little part of a person's life are his acts and his words!" he wrote. "His real life is led in his head, and is known to none but himself. All day long, and every day, the mill of his

brain is grinding, and his *thoughts*, not those other things, are his history. . . .
The mass of him is hidden—it and its volcanic fires that toss and boil, and
never rest, night nor day. These are his life, and they are not written, and
cannot be written" (*MTA*, 1:2). I take the humorist at his word here,
though I regard his claims on the score of secrecy as a species of wishful
thinking. As we shall see, his need to conceal the "history" of his volcanic
interior life competed on nearly equal terms with his need to reveal it. And
so great was his fascination with that inner "life," and so pressing his felt
need to express it, that he wrote constantly, even compulsively, about himself. Whatever his intentions, then, the hot truth would out, willy-nilly.

Clemens wrote most, of course, about his childhood, the period in his
life, we may be sure, when his ceaseless inner fires were first ignited. It was
a deeply troubled time. Ron Powers, whose treatment of the early life is
aptly entitled *Troubled Waters*, foregrounds "the terrors, the griefs, the guilts,
the angers and the hallucinating obsessions that strung their path through
[Clemens's] boyhood."[3] According to Dixon Wecter, young Sam was his
mother's "problem child, with his illnesses, vivid imaginings, habits of wandering toward the nearest creek or river, and didos that seemed to multiply
as improving health increased his power for mischief." Unlike his siblings,
the boy "was fitful, idle, erratic, unpredictable."[4] His father, John Marshall
Clemens, was proud, taciturn, an ambitious but frustrated lawyer and judge
who shrank from personal intimacy, and who died suddenly in 1847, when
his most famous son was just eleven. Clemens remembered his father as a
stern, humorless, emotionally remote figure whose failure as a provider in-
stilled in his son a reflex acquisitiveness and fear of poverty. "My father and
I were always on the most distant terms when I was a boy," he recalled, "a
sort of armed neutrality, so to speak."[5] Relations with his mother, Jane
Clemens, a warm, vivacious woman who outlived her husband by nearly
half a century, were much more positive. To her the humorist traced his
energy and love of storytelling. She was also instrumental in his religious
and moral development. Jane joined the local Presbyterian church in 1843,
where her impressionable son was initiated into the dark mysteries of sin
and eternal damnation. Here, we may reasonably surmise, he developed his
early impressions of a ruthless, contradictory, punishing Christian God; here
as well, it seems likely, he first felt the sting of a conscience that hounded
him remorselessly through a long life.

Violence and death were pretty much business as usual in towns along
the river in frontier Missouri. Young Sam witnessed the deaths of his sister,
Margaret, in 1839, and of his brother, Benjamin, three years later. Dixon

Wecter observes that the Clemens "family took its losses hard, and, like most folk from the hills of Kentucky and the highlands of Tennessee, tended to clothe these griefs in the grim retrospection of certain dreams, visions, and premonitions, along with heartbreaking farewells and lingering touches of self-reproach."[6] One felt involved somehow in these tragedies, and vaguely responsible for them. In such times of distress, Sam had nightmares and terrified the family with his sleepwalking. He was even more traumatized by the postmortem performed on his father, which he witnessed through a keyhole. That appalling memory appears briefly, almost unspeakably, as "the autopsy" in "Villagers of 1840–43," Clemens's haunted 1897 reminiscences of his boyhood in Hannibal. Weirdly affectless in tone—as if stunned by the horrors it recalls—"Villagers" is host to a procession of catastrophes: madness, betrayal, untimely death, violent assault, murder. There is Ben, who "shot his thumb off, hunting"; the Hyde brothers, who tried to kill their uncle "with a pistol that refused [to] fire"; Roberta Jones, who "scared old Miss——into the insane asylum with a skull and a dough-face"; "The Stabbed Cal. Emigrant. Saw him"; Ouseley, the "prosperous merchant," who "killed old Smar"; and the Ratcliffe boy, the victim of a "religious mania," who chopped off his offending hand with a hatchet. He refused to wear clothes, and was chained up in a shed at the bottom of his family's yard, where he died (*HH&T*, 40, 30, 31, 32, 36, 37–38).

And of course there was slavery, popularly approved and justified, but quite evidently cruel and indefensible at the same time. The contradiction was manifest at firsthand in the Clemens household, where the slave girl Jennie was thought of as a member of the family, but also severely punished, and ultimately sold down the river. Her fate was sealed when she fell into the hands of the local "nigger trader," who bought slaves from people who "loathed" him for doing so. Nor was young Sam immune to the pervasive moral confusion. Insisting on one side that "there was nothing about the slavery of the Hannibal region to rouse one's dozing humane instincts to activity," he "vividly" recalls, on the other, "seeing a dozen black men and women chained to one another . . . and lying in a group on the pavement, awaiting shipment to the Southern slave market. Those were the saddest faces I had ever seen" (*MTA*, 1:124). It is scarcely a surprise that the confusion rubbed off on a youngster whose father earned widespread approval for his role in condemning three abolitionists to heavy prison sentences, but whose mother winced tearfully at the mere thought of a slave child's suffering. Such was life in the town Clemens later immortalized as the setting for his American boyhood idyll.

Some of the most prominent features of Clemens's adult personality—sensitivity, impulsiveness, need for approval, retreat from intimacy, acquisitiveness, radical mood swings, and a pronounced susceptibility to feelings of guilt—were already on display in his childhood. Others—notably a ferocious temper, a tendency to develop strong grudges against former friends and associates, and recurrent bouts of life-weariness—came clearly to view only as the years passed. Quite obviously, there was much of buoyancy and brilliance in Clemens's complex personality—curiosity, generosity, compassion, terrific energy, optimism, and resilience, along with vast and varied reserves of humor. Clemens was fully aware of the volatile contradictions at large in his personality. One of his earliest notebook entries, set down in 1855, is an extended outline of "The Sanguine Temperament" drawn from a published handbook on character analysis that Clemens modified at points to sharpen its alignment with his own personal qualities. Sanguinity, he writes, produces a "burning, flaming, flashing temperament."

> It gives activity, quickness, suppleness to all the motions of body and mind; great elasticity and buoyancy of spirit; readiness, and even fondness for change; suddenness and intensity to the feelings; impulsiveness, and hastiness of character; great warmth of both anger and love; it works fast and tires soon; runs its short race and gives over. It is fond of change; light, easy, active labor. . . . It loves excitement, noise, bluster, fun, frolic, high times. . . . It is always predominant in those active, stirring, noisy characters that are found in every community. It is very sensitive and is first deeply hurt at a slight, the next emotion is violent rage, and in a few moments the cause and the result are both forgotten for the time being. It often forgives, but never entirely forgets an injury. It loves with a wild intensity, but gets over it soon, when deprived of the stimulus afforded by the *presence* of its object. It feels grief and sorrow most bitterly, but soon becomes calm, and forgets it all. . . . It makes warm friends and fiery enemies, and they may be both friends and enemies in the same day, and be perfectly sincere. It has a ready tongue; is quick and sharp of speech; is full of eloquent flights and passionate appeals; is ardent, pathetic and tender, to the last degree: can cry and laugh, swear and pray, in as short a time as it would take some people to think once.[7]

We are in company here with a consciousness subject to constant, rapid swings between opposed moods and states of mind. Resilience is twinned with a penchant for sudden, precipitous descents into rage and depression. The balance between the extremes tilted toward the negative side as the years of adversity took their toll.

Of Clemens's leading biographers, Justin Kaplan provides the most discerning treatment of the troubles that plagued his subject's adult life. Kaplan's Clemens was an angry man. He was angry at the sanctimonious snobbery he encountered on board the *Quaker City*; angry at the deceit and greed in American business and politics; angry over the nation's imperial adventures at century's end. He was frequently incensed with those close to him—Bret Harte, Charles L. Webster, his brother Orion, and many others. In response to the imagined offenses of Whitelaw Reid, he flew into a revengeful rage that consumed energy and time for several weeks, and culminated in plans for an exposé of his enemy's manifold sins. At times, the rage spilled over in violence. On the lecture circuit in Iowa City in 1869, Clemens became so frustrated with the service at his hotel that he exploded in a furious temper tantrum. "The manager found him half naked," writes Kaplan, "abusive, out of control, and trying to kick the door off its hinges." There was a similar explosion, in similar circumstances, thirty years later, and many other blowups in the years between (*MCMT,* 88, 267). Anger was also a dread constant in the lives of Clemens's children, who learned to be wary of their father's sudden mood swings. "I found that all their lives my children have been afraid of me," he confessed to Howells in 1886; they "have stood all their days in uneasy dread of my sharp tongue & uncertain temper" (*MTHL,* 2:575).

Kaplan is attentive as well to numerous other wrinkles in his subject's makeup. Clemens the bachelor was a notorious drinker and carouser who had several run-ins with the law and once spent the night in a New York jail for brawling on the street. Though doubtless familiar with the demimonde, he was nonetheless a fastidious Puritan in sexual matters and reviled the French for their goatish degeneracy. A furious critic of greed and corruption in American business, Clemens was at the same time in thrall to a dream of fabulous personal wealth. "It is hard to think of another writer," observes Kaplan, "so obsessed in his life and work by the lure, the rustle and chink and heft of money." While Clemens "was notoriously reticent about depicting mature sexual and emotional relationships," Kaplan goes on, "he did write a kind of pornography of the dollar." Nor, when it served his interests to do so, was the scourge of the plutocrats at all hesitant to climb into bed with the enemy (*MCMT,* 35, 48, 96, 322–24).[8]

A much serener figure emerges from Andrew Hoffman's recent, very substantial biography, *Inventing Mark Twain.* Hoffman gives attention to the rages and contradictions, but with less frequency and emphasis than Kaplan. In place of the explosive, deeply divided subject of *Mr. Clemens and Mark*

Twain, Hoffman's protagonist is a rather more solitary and inwardly tormented human being—a man burdened by a "savage and perpetual dissatisfaction with himself" and self-condemned as "a failure and a coward."[9] By contrast, Hamlin Hill's *Mark Twain: God's Fool* follows—and rather notably exceeds—Kaplan in featuring the volatility, abrasiveness, and irrationality of his subject's outward behavior. Hill begins by emphasizing that the "rages, tantrums, and sorrows" featured in his narrative—which confines itself to the last decade of Clemens's life—were the excesses of an aging, frustrated, often desperate person. Leavening candor with compassion, Hill gives us a man of increasing "petulance and vanity" who is unwilling to accept responsibility for his failures and prone to "vindictive and occasionally alcoholic rages." Worn down by domestic and financial tribulations, Clemens was lonely, suspicious, and a failure as a husband and father.[10] Hill gathers up the pieces in a concluding portrait of a complex, profoundly troubled and unhappy human being. Clemens "was a man of contradictory impulses all his life. . . . An indisputable and almost overwhelming sense of inferiority competed inside him with a vanity and an aggressiveness that compelled him to seek the public spotlight whenever he could." Recoiling in fear from poverty, he indulged himself in excesses of wealth and foolish speculation. He was an insensitive tyrant with his family and a suspicious, often volatile friend. These character flaws, which became more prominent and severe in Clemens's late years, were increasingly erosive of his happiness and creativity.[11]

Torment is, of course, a dark mansion with many rooms. During his long, varied, and often tumultuous life, which of these rooms did Clemens most frequently inhabit? He was often very angry, it is true; and certain fears—of poverty, of disapproval—were staples of his interior life. By his own account, however, and by unanimous consensus among informed observers, Clemens's special curse was guilt. Without doubt, he was the most guilt-ridden of major American writers. "Guilt hung like a fog around Mark Twain's memories of his boyhood," observes Ron Powers.[12] His conscience, tireless in supplying reminders of personal shortcomings and grave offenses against others, was a permanent blight on his spirit. "Remorse was always Samuel Clemens's surest punishment," observed Albert Bigelow Paine. "To his last days on earth he never outgrew its pangs" (*MTB,* 1:65). The moral burden was compounded by his perverse habit of blaming himself on occasions when others were the victims of suffering for which he had no direct responsibility. Years after her father's death, Clara Clemens paused to comment on this peculiar feature of his psychological makeup.

"If on any occasion," she observed, "he could manage to trace the cause of some one's mishap to something he himself had done or said, no one could persuade him that he was mistaken. Self-condemnation was the natural turn for his mind to take, yet often he accused himself of having inflicted pain or trouble when the true cause was far removed from himself."[13] Little wonder that floating free and easy on a wide river, far removed from contact with others, was her father's idea of mortal bliss.

Clemens was given to representing his conscience as an independent agent, a malicious demon dedicated to inflicting the worst pain possible on all occasions. In "The Facts Concerning the Recent Carnival of Crime in Connecticut," read to the Hartford Monday Evening Club in 1876, his conscience is "a shriveled, shabby dwarf" who is "covered all over with a fuzzy, greenish mold." When asked why he persists in tormenting his host, the dwarf replies: "We do it simply because it is 'business.' It is our trade. The *purpose* of it *is* to improve the man, but *we* are merely disinterested agents. We are appointed by authority, and haven't anything to say in the matter" (*CTSSE* 1: 645, 652–53). The dwarf admits that he enjoys giving pain, and that he never misses an opportunity to intensify the sting of suffering. When Clemens finally captures and murders the loathsome creature, a blissful, conscience-free carnival of crime commences.

This humorous performance makes several things clear. Conscience is ferocious; it attacks frequently and with malice. Just as clearly, conscience cannot be killed. The dwarf's demise is as conspicuously a fiction as his insatiable ferocity is real. Nor is conscience content to confine itself to present offenses. To the contrary, it ranges widely over the past, dredging up old crimes which can never be permanently forgiven or forgotten. "It is my *business*—and my joy to make you repent of *everything* you do," boasts the dwarf. He torments his host with memories "of times when I had flown at my children in anger," of disloyalty to old friends, of the myriad "dishonest things which I had done," and even of "humiliations I had put upon friends since dead." Clemens's conscience is thus as potently resourceful as it is diabolically cruel. Finally, it bears emphasizing that it is indeed *his* conscience that afflicts him, and not, as the fiction would have it, a separate, independent being. Even as he execrates the dwarf, "this vile bit of human rubbish," Clemens concedes that he bears "a sort of remote and ill-defined resemblance to me!" In the dwarf's arrogant misdeeds, the humorist witnesses "an exaggeration of conduct which I myself had sometimes been guilty of in my intercourse with familiar friends" (*CTSSE*, 1:654, 648, 645).

"Myself am hell," pleads Satan;[14] and so it was for Clemens, whose guilty suffering commenced while he was still quite young. His warm memories of annual childhood visits to the farm of his uncle, John A. Quarles, are well known. "It was a heavenly place for a boy" (*AMT*, 4), he recalled in later life. Less familiar are his memories of his bedroom at that same farm on stormy summer nights. "I can remember how very dark that room was, in the dark of the moon, and how packed it was with ghostly stillness when one woke up by accident away in the night, and forgotten sins came flocking out of the secret chambers of the memory and wanted a hearing" (*MTA*, 1:113). Clemens's autobiographical reminiscences are replete with reports of similar episodes. Consider the drunken tramp who asked him for matches and later incinerated himself in the village jail. He "lay upon my conscience a hundred nights afterward," Clemens recalled,

> and filled them with hideous dreams—dreams in which I saw his appealing face as I had seen it in the pathetic reality, pressed against the window bars, with the red hell glowing behind him—a face which seemed to say to me, "If you had not given me the matches, this would not have happened; you are responsible for my death." I was *not* responsible for it, for I had meant him no harm, but only good, when I let him have the matches; but no matter, mine was a trained Presbyterian conscience and knew but the one duty—to hunt and harry its slave upon all pretexts and on all occasions, particularly when there was no sense nor reason in it. The tramp—who was to blame—suffered ten minutes; I, who was not to blame, suffered three months. (*MTA*, 1:130–31)

The pattern was clear right from the start: Clemens's conscience was no more relentless and punishing than it was seemingly arbitrary and vindictive in launching its attacks. In illustrating his assertion that "a boy's life is not all comedy," he goes on in his autobiography to describe "the shooting down of poor old Smarr in the main street" of Hannibal, the murder of a slave, and assorted bloody assaults. Not surprisingly, these horrific events gave him bad dreams; worse, they made him feel guilty. "My teaching and training," he observes, with rueful irony, "enabled me to see deeper into these tragedies than an ignorant person could have done. I knew what they were for. I tried to disguise it from myself but down in the secret depths of my troubled heart I knew—and I *knew* I knew. They were inventions of Providence to beguile me to a better life." He readily concedes the naive egotism of imagining that the moral weight of these dire events should have been focused exclusively on himself. And yet it was the perverse pattern of his conscience to heap the responsibility for all visible woe onto his own small shoulders. "It is quite true," he elaborates,

> I took all the tragedies to myself, and tallied them off in turn as they happened, saying to myself in each case, with a sigh, "Another one gone—and on my account; this ought to bring me to repentance; the patience of God will not always endure." And yet privately I believed it would. That is, I believed it in the daytime; but not in the night.
>
> With the going down of the sun my faith failed and the clammy fears gathered about my heart. It was then that I repented. Those were the awful nights, nights of despair, nights charged with the bitterness of death. After each tragedy I recognized the warning and repented; repented and begged; begged like a coward, begged like a dog; and not in the interest of those poor people who had been extinguished for my sake, but only in my *own* interest. It seems selfish when I look back on it now. My repentances were very real, very earnest; and after each tragedy they happened every night for a long time. But as a rule they could not stand the daylight. They faded out and shredded away and disappeared in the glad splendor of the sun. They were the creatures of fear and darkness, and they could not live out of their own place. The day gave me cheer and peace, and at night I repented again. In all my boyhood life I am not sure that I ever tried to lead a better life in the daytime—or wanted to. In my age I should never think of wishing to do such a thing. But in my age, as in my youth, night brings me many a deep remorse. I realize that from the cradle up I have been like the rest of the race—never quite sane in the night. (*MTA*, 1:130–34)

I quote this remarkable passage at length because it brings home in such a clear and vivid way the burden of guilt borne by young Sam Clemens, and the sharp contrasts already dominant in the texture and tempo of his interior life. As I have noted, the perversity and egotism of the affliction are not lost on him: he is contemptible in his own eyes for his suffering, and reproaches himself for what he regards as the selfishness of his repentance. He is thus guilty about his guilt! So complete is the tyranny of conscience that it exploits his native optimism as a foil, thereby intensifying the darkness of his nocturnal remorse. One wonders if he really believed that "the rest of the race" endured similar torments.

Evidence for the baleful authority of conscience in the early life of the future humorist is not far to seek. Dixon Wecter reviews the catastrophes that befell several of Clemens's boyhood friends, and the inexplicable assaults of guilt that followed. So deep was the boy's immersion in his mother's theology of redoubling sin and punishment that all the world's troubles seemed somehow traceable to his own wickedness.[15] As the "Turning Point of My Life" well illustrates, conscience attacked brutally at the time of his father's death in 1847. "The boy Sam was fairly broken down" by the tragedy, Paine reports, in an especially moving passage. "Remorse, which always dealt with him unsparingly, laid a heavy hand on him now. Wildness, disobedience, indifference to his father's wishes, all were remembered; a hundred things, in themselves trifling, became ghastly and heart-wringing in the knowledge that they could never be undone. Seeing his grief, his mother took him by the hand and led him into the room where his father lay." And there, alongside the coffin, she made him promise "to be a faithful and industrious man, and upright, like his father." We are struck, of course, with the utterly disproportionate weight of guilt in Clemens's grieving, and little surprised to learn that he "walked in his sleep several nights in succession after that" (*MTB*, 1:74–75).

When Sam Clemens left home in 1853, his mother placed his hand alongside hers on a Bible and made him swear to refrain from cards and drink while he was gone.[16] The figure of the obedient son, dutifully repeating his mother's earnest injunctions, is not one that comes readily to mind when we think of America's favorite humorist. He would in time break free from direct maternal authority; indeed, in the next decade he would develop a reputation as a hard-drinking, irreverent, bohemian womanizer with a pronounced allergy to the truth. This is not to suggest that advancing years brought with them a release from bondage to guilt. To the contrary, Clemens's dissolute behavior afforded his conscience an expanded field of operations and a tighter grip on his moral and emotional life. Justin Kaplan, who characterizes Clemens as "a lifelong guilt seeker," emphasizes that much of the anguish continued to attach to family. During the early years, Clemens dreaded returning home because of the inevitable complaints, especially from his melancholy sister Pamela, about his irreverence, his immoral habits, and his failure to provide financial support. He felt guilty as well for his impatience and anger with his idealistic but utterly improvident brother, Orion (*MCMT*, 149, 29).[17] While awaiting his departure on the *Quaker City* in early June 1867, Clemens wrote home about his restless eagerness to get underway. "Curse the endless delays! They always kill me— they make me neglect every duty & then I have a conscience that tears me like a wild beast. I wish I never had to stop *any*where a month. I do more mean things, the moment I get a chance to fold my hands & sit down than ever I can get forgiveness for." A week later, still waiting in New York, he went on in the same self-accusatory vein.

I am so worthless that it seems to me I never do anything or accomplish anything that lingers in my mind as a pleasant memory. My mind is stored full of unworthy conduct toward Orion & toward you all, & an accusing conscience gives me peace only in excitement & restless moving from place to place. If I could say I had done one thing for any of you that entitled me to your good opinions . . . I believe I could go home & stay there—& I *know* I would care little for the world's praise or blame. . . . You observe that under a cheerful exterior I have got a spirit that is angry with me & gives me freely its contempt. I can get away from that at sea, & be tranquil and satisfied.[18]

Discerning observers, even those who had not known him for long, glimpsed the torment that plagued the outwardly buoyant and famously humorous writer. Mrs. James T. Fields, a casual acquaintance, shrewdly observed of Clemens that "his whole life was one long apology."[19] Nor did settling into marriage and family life do much to ease the pain. He gave generously of his time during four-hour watches at the bedside of his father-in-law, Jervis Langdon, who died of stomach cancer in 1870. Yet Clemens later tortured himself with accusing memories of his failures to stay awake. "I can still see myself," he wrote, years later, "sitting by that bed in the melancholy stillness of the sweltering night, mechanically waving a palm-leaf fan over the drawn white face of the patient; I can still recall my noddings, my fleeting unconsciousness, when the fan would come to a standstill in my hand and I would wake up with a start and a hideous shock" (*MTA* 2:114). He was even more perversely self-lacerating over his imagined role in the death of his first child, the nearly two-year old Langdon, who succumbed to diphtheria in June 1872. Clemens convinced himself, against all the evidence, that his failure to keep the child warm during a morning coach ride brought on the end. "I have always felt shame for that treacherous morning's work and have not allowed myself to think of it when I could help it," he acknowledged, many years later (*AMT*, 190). Howells reports that his friend spoke to him only once about Langdon. "Yes, *I* killed him," he confessed, "with the unsparing self-blame in which he could wreak an unavailing regret."[20]

Though the tyranny of guilt persisted relentlessly during Clemens's middle years, the worst of the agony commenced with his decline into bankruptcy in 1893–94. Now he had himself to blame for making his family vulnerable to the hardship and stigma of poverty. The sudden death of his favorite daughter, Susy, in 1896 was perhaps the nadir, and brought him near to madness. "After a lifetime of hunting for a crime which he could say he had committed," observes Justin Kaplan, "his guilt had finally crystallized so massively around this real event that his grief at Livy's death eight years later hardly compared in intensity" (*MCMT*, 337). Susy's tragic passing accelerated Clemens's turn to god-hating, determinism, and assorted fragmentary dream stories preoccupied with failure and guilt. His characteristic mood swings persisted and afforded him intervals of outward relief. But his native resilience was no match for the tide of remorse that swelled periodically within him. When Livy's long battle with heart disease took a turn for the worse in 1902, the doctors barred Clemens from her room, insisting that his self-recriminations placed an added strain on his wife's wavering condition. Their forced separation, which persisted on and off until the time of Livy's death in 1904, intensified the resistless gnawing of conscience. In one of his many self-censuring notes to his wife, Clemens reproached himself for having undermined her religious convictions, and with them her health. "I do love you so, my darling," he wrote, "and it so grieves me to remember that I am the cause of your being where you are. I WISH—I WISH—but it is too late. I drove you to sorrow and heart-break just to hear myself talk. If ever I do it again when you get well I hope the punishment will fall upon me the guilty, not upon you the innocent."[21]

But of course the patient did not get well, though the punishment fell in ever greater portions on the stricken survivor. Clemens's guilt, which hounded him through the final years of his life, rose to one last crushing assault in December 1909, when his daughter Jean suffered an epileptic seizure in the bathtub and drowned. Jean's moodiness and erratic, sometimes violent behavior, exacerbated by her medical condition, led to her banishment from her father's midst to assorted homes and hospitals. She was, ventured Hamlin Hill, "the daughter Mark Twain wanted to forget."[22] The guilt that he must have suffered at the loss of this child he had pushed away seems to have been more than Clemens could bear. In trying to ease the pain, he recoiled from grief and remorse into the relief of resignation. "Would I bring her back to life if I could do it?" he asked. "I would not. . . . In her loss I am almost bankrupt, and my life is a bitterness, but I am content: for she has been enriched with the most precious of all gifts—that gift which makes all other gifts mean and poor—death."[23]

Oblivious death beckoned to the grieving father because it seemed to promise the silencing of conscience. "Ah, I have such a deep, grateful, unutterable sense of being 'out of it all,'" he wrote to Howells in 1878. "I think I foretaste some of the advantage of being dead. Some of the joy of it" (*MTHL*, 1:227). But the seductions of the grave went still further back with him, to his early years on the mining frontier. "I am utterly miserable," he complained to his brother Orion in 1865. "If I do not get out of debt in 3 months,—pistols or poison for one—exit *me*. (There's a text for a sermon on Self-Murder—Proceed.)"[24] Despondency over similar failures as a provider may have prompted a much closer brush with suicide in 1866. "I put the pistol to my head but wasn't man enough to pull the trigger," he recalled, more than four decades later. "Many times I have been sorry I did not succeed but I was never ashamed of having tried. Suicide is the only really sane thing the young or the old ever do in this life."[25]

"To the end," Justin Kaplan observes, Clemens was "an enigma and prodigy to himself" (*MCMT*, 388). I hasten to add that the mystery was largely of the subject's own making. Clemens did not lack a clear self-image; rather, he could not endure what he saw in himself, and so retreated to a host of partial and distorted self-fabrications. As Susan Gillman has shown, his speculations on dreams, spiritualism, and the new psychology were as intense and enduring as they were inconclusive.[26] This was so because his interest in human nature was in the service of a pressing but futile desire to win release from the burden of responsibility for what he regarded as his own hopeless degradation. Clemens was driven by a craving not so much for the truth as for freedom from the guilt that dogged his days. The accounts of human behavior that attracted him were widely varied in all respects save one, the certainty that because we do not choose our lives, we cannot be held morally liable for them.

Consider Clemens's 1898 letter to the British psychologist Sir John Adams, in which he elaborates at great length on the notion "that man's proudest possession—his mind—is a mere machine; an automatic machine; a machine which is so wholly independent of him that it will not even take a *suggestion* from him, let alone a command, unless it suits its humour; that both command and suggestion, when offered, originate not on the premises but must in all cases come from the outside." Professing to deplore the utter lack of human agency permitted by his mechanical construction of mind, Clemens goes on to claim "one consolation: my automatic mental machine is not one of the fine and good ones, but a lubberly and ill-made one which is always likely to combine its raw materials into foolish and mistaken patterns—but getting its scheme *from the outside* and therefore not personally blamable for its crazy work."[27]

Here, quite predictably, Clemens arrives at the magnetic pole toward which so much of his thinking tends: release from the burden of moral responsibility. Sir John Adams was alive to this dimension in his correspondent, as his published commentary clearly shows. He begins by tracing the letter's main argument back to *What Is Man?*, Clemens's philosophical indictment of human nature, privately printed in 1906, but already in draft in 1898, when the letter was written. Adams shrewdly observes that in the version of the argument advanced in *What Is Man?*, Clemens has no sooner "reduced us to machines" than he "sets about preaching to us," setting forth "in good pulpit fashion a summarized statement of his doctrine in the form of what he calls an 'Admonition.'" Adams reproduces the entire admonition ("Diligently train your ideas upward and still upward"), and then returns to the obvious question, "What justification has Mark to start preaching to us after having turned us into machines? . . . His argument tends to give us a comfortable feeling of irresponsibility. Being machines, and everything being determined from *outside*—note how fond Mark is of this word in the present argument—we were just feeling good when he stamps in with this disturbing admonition that we cannot but claim does not apply to us."[28] Adams is thus quick to recognize the glaring contradiction in Clemens's thought: on one side, a potent gravitation to determinism and the "comfortable feeling of irresponsibility" which it yields, and on the other, a moralistic bent issuing in righteous admonitions.

But the poles to which Adams quite properly draws attention appear much less fixed and tidy when viewed in the light of Clemens's seemingly offhand conclusion that he is "not personally blamable for [the] crazy work" of his mind. Are we to read this as the negligible, rather self-effacing jest that Clemens's tone seems to suggest? Or are we to look past the textual surface and confer full moral weight on the ideas advanced? How sharply conscious was Clemens, we wonder, of the implications of his apparent aside? There are no certainties here. But we may begin by noting that the mind-as-machine argument, though hardly compelling, seems to anticipate our question by conveniently tracing all thought to origins "outside" the mind. In the course of his reflections, Clemens pauses briefly over the question "*which is I, and which is my Mind? Are we two, or are we one?*" Unlike William James, who devotes a long chapter of *The Principles of Psychology* to this pivotal question, Clemens dismisses it as "not important, for if we say 'I will think,' neither I *nor* the mind originates the suggestion—it came from outside."[29] This veering away is apposite because it suggests that while Clemens was indeed thoughtful about the riddle of human consciousness, his consuming interest lay in securing freedom from blame for the "crazy work" going on inside his head. Thus he submerges the challenging philosophical question in a comforting determinism. And because the suggestion of the determinism comes from outside his mind, the responsibility for the denial of responsibility is itself denied. By such reasoning, Clemens cannot be held to account for the evidently self-interested espousal of an argument that exempts him from all moral reckoning, even if that is precisely what he has done.

Once the ambiguity of Clemens's intentions is acknowledged, an expanded range of interpretations opens to view. Let us suppose, for example, that he is entirely unaware of the fact that the "outside influence" argument exempts him from responsibility for contriving the patent impunity that the argument provides. Such a reading would render him doubly innocent, but it would also sit rather awkwardly with the skeptical turn of mind on display in the argument itself. This discrepancy might in turn prompt us to surmise that the straining after moral indemnity has an unconscious origin, and thus works to achieve its primary goal without surfacing in the consciousness of its putative beneficiary. But if the release from moral responsibility is as important as we suppose, then it is difficult to imagine its being sought and secured in an entirely unconscious way. If we go on to assume—as the ambiguity surely permits—that Clemens is aware of the immunity that his argument confers, then we must credit him with no little subtlety and showmanship, for he has seemed to back unconsciously into the very thing he craves. Once again he is doubly innocent, but in this interpretive instance the innocence is merely simulated; we may be fooled, but he is not, with the result that the all-important "comfortable feeling of irresponsibility" must necessarily elude him.

None of the interpretations so far entertained is as persuasive as we might like it to be. This is so because neither a fully conscious nor a fully unconscious approach to the desired goal makes real sense. Clemens seeks to arrive at a "comfortable feeling of irresponsibility" in an ingenious but evidently contrived manner. Because we know he regarded his conscience as an intolerable affliction, it is difficult to imagine his gaining release from it in an unconscious way. On the other side, consciousness of the artifice involved in approaching the goal makes its achievement impossible. If we suppose that Clemens really experienced, however briefly, the feeling of moral release that he describes at the end of his letter, then we are bound to conclude that during that serene interval he was profoundly self-deceived. This is to say that for a short time, at least, he successfully eclipsed from consciousness the knowledge that he was himself responsible for the denial that produced his "comfortable feeling of irresponsibility."

I dwell at length on the letter to Adams because it illustrates both the labyrinthine complexity of Clemens's flight from conscience, and the fact that it was principally his own disapproval, and not the world's, that he aimed to elude. Self-deception is a notorious conundrum. To define it narrowly is to assume that it is humanly possible to know and to not know the same thing at the same time. In *Nineteen Eighty-Four* George Orwell calls it doublethink, "the power of holding two contradictory beliefs in one's mind simultaneously, and accepting both of them"; or telling "deliberate lies while genuinely believing in them." Doublethink works, Orwell explains, because it can be turned on itself in successive acts of erasure that continue "indefinitely, with the lie always one leap ahead of the truth."[30] Clemens was similarly impressed with the virtually universal sway of self-deception— "how easily men are self-duped," he wrote in the early 1880s (*WIM,* 59)— though unlike Orwell, who conceived doublethink in the framework of totalitarian political regimes, he was inclined to view it as a servant of the characteristically human tendency to recoil from guilt into varieties of moral evasion. In this, I hasten to add, he drew deeply, and with some measure of self-awareness, on his own ceaseless struggle against the tyranny of conscience.

Clemens examined the ways and means of self-deception in two important essays on lying. In "On the Decay of the Art of Lying," first published in 1882, he playfully elaborates on the idea that "lying is universal—we *all* do it; we all *must* do it." Quite characteristically, the argument amounts to a plea for release from moral responsibility: because lying is universal and inevitable, it is also inculpable. Most deceit is conscious, though Clemens gives special attention to what he calls "the *silent* lie,—the deception which one conveys by simply keeping still and concealing the truth." Self-deception enters the picture at this point, among those who imagine "that if they *speak* no lie, they lie not at all." Such "obstinate truth-mongers" err not in lying, for that is universal, but in supposing that there is an alternative to deceit, and consequently a reward for veracity (*CTSSE,* 1:827–28). Such erroneous assumptions lead to self-deception: assent to the lie that lies are true.

The 1899 essay "My First Lie and How I Got out of It," once again proceeds from the premise "that all people are liars from the cradle onward, without exception." People begin "to lie as soon as they wake in the morning, and keep it up without rest or refreshment until they go to sleep at night." Deceitfulness is the very essence of human nature, and it is so by virtue of an "eternal law." Since man "didn't invent the law," he is not responsible for its effects; "it is merely his business to obey it and keep still." Clemens goes on to define this act of concealment as "the lie of silent assertion," the mute denial that humans are universally dishonest. The vast majority, he implies, come to believe this lie of lies, and actually imagine themselves honest, thereby quite ironically losing sight of the moral immunity conferred by the truth of their nature (*CTSSE* 2:439–40).

But not everyone is deceived in the same way. For side by side with the benighted masses, Clemens includes himself in an enlightened minority of perspicacious witnesses to "the lie of silent assertion." A member of this elite group—designated "we that know"—stands apart not only in the awareness that it is "the eternal law" of human nature to lie constantly, but also in bending to that law by deceiving "his fellow-conspirators into imagining that he doesn't know that the law exists. It is what we all do," Clemens observes, "we that know." Possessors of such secrets understand the dynamics and the awesome dominion of unacknowledged—and, for the vast majority of people, unrecognized—deception in human experience. This is knowledge of a unique weight and gravity, for it focuses not on the trivial deceits of everyday life, but rather on the ways in which "the lie of silent assertion" has "for ages and ages . . . mutely labored in the interest of despotisms and aristocracies and chattel slaveries, and military slaveries, and religious slaveries, and has kept them alive; keeps them alive yet, here and there and yonder, all about the globe; and will go on keeping them alive until the silent-assertion lie retires from business." Among his examples of modern crimes against humanity, Clemens gives first place to American slavery, an institution that fed deeply on lies. "It would not be possible," he insists,

> for a humane and intelligent person to invent a rational excuse for slavery; yet you will remember that in the early days of the emancipation agitation in the North the agitators got but small help or countenance from any one. Argue and plead and pray as they might, they could not break the universal stillness that reigned, from pulpit and press all the way down to the bottom of society—the clammy stillness created and maintained by the lie of silent assertion—the silent assertion that there wasn't anything going on in which humane and intelligent people were interested. (*CTSSE* 2:440–41)[31]

Following Clemens's lead, I have elsewhere defined such resistance to the truth as "bad faith," the deception of self and other in the denial of violations of public ideals of truth and justice. Such departures, as they appear in Clemens's work, are most frequently group phenomena, collaborative denials, and bear with them the clear implication that people will sometimes permit or acquiesce in what they cannot approve, so long as their complicity is submerged in a larger, tacit consensus. It is important to emphasize that bad faith is not always bad. In its benign and even beneficial phase, it enables a society to transcend the strict letter of its codes and the unanticipated limitations of its actors and circumstances. But it may also work to conceal problems of grave consequence. Clemens was sharply aware of the social unity and fellow-feeling to be derived from evasions of the truth, but he was equally attentive to the pathologies they foster. In either form, however, it is a telling feature of acts of bad faith that they incorporate silent prohibitions against the acknowledgment that they have occurred. Denial is itself denied.[32]

In previous discussions of bad faith, I have strongly emphasized its social dynamics as they are manifest in the characters, form, and reception of Clemens's fiction. In *Huckleberry Finn*, for example, bad faith is manifest in the behavior of people along the river, in the young hero himself, in his author's management of the story, and in the novel's enduring popular reception. At the root of this pervasive malady is race-slavery, an institution whose maintenance in a Christian democracy requires extraordinary bad faith denial. In the chapters that follow, I want to apply the notion of bad faith in a rather different way, to Clemens's theory and practice of autobiography. My approach will be broad-based, which is to say that I will accept my subject's invitation to treat all of his writing as autobiographical, and that I will draw inferences as seem warranted from his scattered reflections on such related topics as the mind, memory, dreams, the will, and human nature. The discussion will frequently turn, as it does in "My First Lie," on the topics of race and slavery. Just as often, as in the discussion of the 1898 letter to Sir John Adams, I will draw attention to the denial of denial in bad faith, and to Clemens's habit of betraying the fact that he is his own best laboratory for its analysis. In concluding his letter to Sir John Adams, for example, in which he has denied responsibility for the denial of responsibility, Clemens is moved to reveal the "one consolation" that he derives from his otherwise bleak argument, and thus hints at the unacknowledged motive driving his elaborate evasion. As if to confirm the hint, he goes on to add: this "is the longest letter I have written in ten years, I think; but I do not apologize, for that would make it even longer."[33] Apologize, indeed! There is no need for that, thanks to the "consolation" all but concealed in his comments. But Clemens knows better. There is no moral immunity, he seems almost jestingly to concede, only elaborate but ultimately fruitless attempts, such as his own deviously long letter, to deny that which he is ultimately driven, however obliquely, to affirm. This impulse to acknowledge his own bad faith registers quite frequently in Clemens's writing; it is as though he feels compelled at such moments to afford his audience a glimpse, however brief and uncertain, into the subtlety of his moral evasions.

The final movement of thought in "My First Lie" perfectly illustrates this persistent pattern of self-disclosure. As one of the "we that know," Clemens represents himself as having risen above the self-deception of "the lie of silent assertion." He knows, and admits that he knows, what the vast majority somehow contrive to deny: that the "lie of silent assertion" is "the support and confederate of all the tyrannies and shams and inequalities and unfairnesses" that modern civilization visits upon the world. But is he comfortable in the apparently superior moral position to which his knowledge elevates him? More to the point, perhaps, is he prepared to act constructively on what he knows? The answer to both questions is no. Instead, admitting that he is "satisfied with things the way they are," Clemens declines the role of reformer. "Let us be judicious," he advises, "and let somebody else begin" (*CTSSE*, 2:446).

But of course the essay is itself testimony both to the fact that its author is not satisfied with the world as he finds it, and that he is willing to do something about it. To the point of its sudden reversal, "My First Lie" reads like a reformist tract. But then, quite abruptly, the tone shifts, as earnest moral rumination gives way to ironic self-effacement. Clemens knows the worst, and acknowledges the responsibility to act; yet he retreats, and thereby seems to join the majority who acquiesce in "the lie of silent assertion." In fact, he has it both ways. The assault on bad faith stands, but so does his concluding declaration of complicity. True, the ironic tone of the disclaimer may suggest that Clemens has descended not to bad faith, but only to its ironic mimicry. Yet the disclaimer also stands, and produces no little ambiguity. Is Clemens ridiculing bad faith? Or, rather, does he mean to suggest that superior knowledge affords its possessor no protection against the irresistible pull of the impulse to conform? There is simply no way to decide. This much *is* clear, however: Clemens felt bound at least to hint at his own complicity in the world's denial of responsibility for the injustice in its midst. Indeed, his penetration into the insidious authority of bad faith is

nowhere more compelling than in this perfectly equivocal moral concession. Can we doubt that he is one of those who, in the years before the
Civil War, when the agitation for emancipation was most clamorous, denied
to others, and even to himself, that slavery was something in which humane
and intelligent people should be interested? No more than we can doubt
the depth of the aging humorist's regret for that unforgettable boyhood surrender to denial.

"In my schoolboy days," Clemens recalls in his *Autobiography,* "I had no
aversion to slavery. I was not aware that there was anything wrong about it.
No one arraigned it in my hearing; the local papers said nothing against it;
the local pulpit taught us that God approved it, that it was a holy thing, and
that the doubter need only look in the Bible if he wished to settle his mind"
(*MTA,* 1:101). Such was the dominant view in the slave-holding, frontier
state of Missouri in the decades just before the outbreak of the Civil War.
Slavery persisted at no apparent moral price to its white advocates; indeed,
in some quarters it was the source of considerable pride.[34]

But if young Samuel Clemens was at all representative of popular sentiment in Hannibal, then there was something else at large in the community,
a countercurrent of feeling running just below the settled surface of opinion.
For no sooner has Clemens recorded his lack of "aversion to slavery" than
he remembers "one small incident" of his boyhood, an incident, he writes,
that "must have meant a good deal to me or it would not have stayed in my
memory, clear and sharp, vivid and shadowless, all these slow-drifting
years." Suddenly, thought shifts direction and tone, as confident, unmingled
memories give way to their opposite. The mind may seem to wander, yet
it does so in predictable ways, following promising lines of recollection
until, almost invariably, they give way suddenly and sharply to darker currents laden with discord and remorse. In this case, he remembers a small
slave boy, "a cheery spirit, innocent and gentle," who was forever "singing,
whistling, yelling, whooping, laughing." Young Sam grew impatient with
the racket and went "raging" to his mother—"*wouldn't* she please shut him
up." Jane Clemens's response clearly suggests that she experienced an inner
"aversion to slavery," one that she communicated to her son in unforgettable terms. "The tears came into her eyes," he recalls, "and her lip trembled,
and she said something like this: 'Poor thing, when he sings it shows that
he is not remembering, and that comforts me; but when he is still I am afraid
he is thinking, and I cannot bear it. He will never see his mother again; if
he can sing, I must not hinder it, but be thankful for it" (*MTA,* 1:101–2).

Here surely is a memorable lesson in the uses of bad faith. Better the slave child should be deceived about his condition, for in his ignorance there is release for his captors from the truth of what they have done. In effect, Jane Clemens acknowledges the inhumanity of slavery, and her own complicity in it, but counsels willful self-deception; the damning reality of the situation, she suggests obliquely, is simply too much to bear. Her son registers no immediate response, but we must suppose—because he finds it all so vivid and memorable—that he is at some level attentive to what his mother's words imply. Nor is this entirely new ground to him. For what is it in the slave child's boisterous mood, we may wonder, that so enrages young Clemens? Is it not the unsettling awareness that the exultant behavior is utterly inappropriate to the slave child's actual condition? If the cheerful youngster is truly blind to reality, then his example suggests that humans have virtually unlimited tolerance for monstrous lies. The slave is grossly, pathetically deceived, but his oppressors may in turn be victims of even graver deceits, not least the evidently imperfect lie of their own innocence. More probably, perhaps, the child's wild outpourings of joy are expressions of a refusal or incapacity to endure the truth, a horrified recoil from intolerable deracination. The "singing, whistling, yelling, whooping, laughing" is marked by its weird excess as the dark opposite of joy. In either reading, the burden of guilt is heavy, and might be expected to produce, especially in one so sensitive as Clemens, a reflex surge of anger. Little wonder that this episode found a place in his memory, where it was borne along, "so clear and sharp, vivid and shadowless," during "all these slow-drifting years."

In this instance, as so frequently in Clemens's writing about himself, concealment signals an accompanying revelation. Forgetting what the poor slave boy has lost brings temporary relief, perhaps, but no protection against abrupt future intrusions of the harsh truth into consciousness. Nor, indeed, is the slave's real condition ever entirely obscured. The extremity of Clemens's anger bespeaks an unsettling presentiment of the damaging truth that surfaces rather less obliquely in his mother's anguished complaint. Thus concealment and revelation appear not so much in sequence as in simultaneous dialogue with one another, the relative volume and intensity of the voices varying, but never lapsing, at least for long, into mere monologue. Variations on this pattern of remembering and forgetting, knowing and not knowing, of denial, the denial of denial, and virtually simultaneous affirmations of both the fact of denial and the things denied—all fostering the suggestion that the mind is secretly familiar with what it has ostensibly

forgotten or denied—these will be staple ingredients of the biographical in-
quiries that follow.

Something approaching this complex mingling of the known and the
not-known may be observed in the extraordinary chapter 38 of *Following the
Equator*. The setting is Bombay. Clemens is at first wide-eyed with delight at
the physical beauty of the people and the brilliant "color, bewitching color,
enchanting color" that everywhere meets his eye. But before long "the land
of dreams and romance," with its "soft and gentle race," is painfully transformed. A burly German tourist, irritated at some minor offense, suddenly
strikes his Indian servant. "It seemed such a shame to do that before us all,"
Clemens observes, drawing back not so much from the deed itself as from
the knowledge of it. Better this had been done quietly and under cover.
The scene, and perhaps his own complicated response to it, precipitates a
startling recognition. "I had not seen the like of this for fifty years. It carried
me back to my boyhood, and flashed upon me the forgotten fact that this
was the *usual* way of explaining one's desire to a slave." Running darkly
through the memories, which descend in a rush, is a burden of guilt that he
strains to dispel. Striking slaves "seemed right and natural" when he was a
boy, "I being born to it and unaware that elsewhere there were other methods; but I was also able to remember that those unresented cuffings made
me sorry for the victim and ashamed for the punisher." He allows that his
father's physical abuse of slaves "proceeded from the custom of the time,
not from his nature." But such mitigating appeals to convention give way
under the memory of the brutal killing of a slave "for merely doing something awkwardly—as if that were a crime." Custom in this instance is not
enough to conceal the face of iniquity. "Nobody in the village approved of
that murder, but of course no one said much about it" (*FE*, 347, 351–52).

This furtive, troubled train of thought comes partially to rest in a reflexive turn inward on itself, as Clemens reflects on the mystery of his own
mental processes. "It is curious," he remarks rather coolly, "the space-annihilating power of thought. For just one second, all that goes to make the *me*
in me was in a Missourian village, on the other side of the globe, vividly
seeing again those forgotten pictures of fifty years ago, and wholly unconscious of all things but just those; and in the next second I was back in Bombay, and that kneeling native's smitten cheek was not done tingling yet!" In
a manner reminiscent of the letter to Sir John Adams, speculation on mental
processes here serves to distract attention from the deeper, more primary,
but largely submerged impulse to achieve moral immunity. The recourse in
this instance is not to the model of the mind-as-machine, but to a kind of

hyper-solipsism in which the "self," "the *me* in me," is dispersed and atten-uated between rapidly firing, apparently disconnected bursts of awareness. The pace is breathtaking, as the mind darts "back to boyhood—fifty years; back to age again, another fifty; and a flight equal to the circumference of the globe—all in two seconds by the watch!" (*FE*, 352). Clemens does not hint—as he does in the Adams letter—at the moral "consolation" to be de-rived from the model of mind on display, and yet his epistemological detour is manifestly driven along such lines. In this instance, the moral reprieve inheres in the clear suggestion that consciousness is so rapid and far-flung in its movements as to have no fixed place or center. In such a construction of subjectivity, there is no real "*me* in me," and thus no place for grief and remorse to take hold and fester.

Clemens doesn't draw this inference, and yet its weight is felt in the dra-matically reduced moral temperature of the passage that immediately fol-lows. The German tourist and the tingling in the native's cheek are forgotten; memories of slave murders in Hannibal recede from conscious-ness; a cacophony of sounds rises to his hotel bedroom from the street below, but the noise, while abrasive to the ear, represents no challenge to the spirit. And so, thanks to timely philosophical interventions—responsibility for the denial of responsibility is itself denied to a self with no center—an awakened sense of moral anguish is laid at least temporarily to rest. "Then," Clemens sighs, "came peace—stillness deep and solemn—and lasted till five" (*FE*, 353).

But of course the self does have a center of sorts, and so the silence is brief. The center is to be found along the line of association connecting Bombay to Hannibal, the British Empire to the antebellum American South, and the suffering Indian servant to the murdered slave. Those con-nections have their nexus in Clemens's mind, where they intersect and form a center to consciousness, "the *me* in me." At one level, the associations are evidence of nascent insights into continuities between New World slavery and Old World imperialism, into America's past and present entanglement in history. It is a story not so much of innocence lost as of an illusory inno-cence never possessed in the first place. A version of the same story links the youthful Sam Clemens of Hannibal to the aging sojourner in Bombay. In both settings, separated by half a world, half a century, and only "two sec-onds by the watch," he is witness to an uncanny repetition of events from which he draws back in horror. In both, stung by the hint of his own com-plicity, he retreats to the imagined moral shelter of youth, ignorance, and solipsism, only to find that in none of these is he truly, safely free from blame. The "shame" of the thing is obvious to him in Bombay, where he remembers that events in Hannibal made him "sorry for the victim and ashamed for the punisher." There is no final denying that he always already knew what was wrong, that the shame at the center of his consciousness defines him, anchors him in history, and denies him the moral repose he so longs for.

And so, at dawn, the noise "all broke loose again," signaling an oblique admission of responsibility for the denial of the responsibility previously denied. The raucous agent of discord is an Indian crow, a wonderful, protean rascal in whom Clemens catches a glimpse of himself, and who transports him at least halfway to moral self-reckoning. The remarkable portrait rewards a long, close look.

> I came to know him well, by and by, and [to] be infatuated with him. I suppose he is the hardest lot that wears feathers. Yes, and the cheerfulest, and the best satisfied with himself. He never arrived at what he is by any careless process, or any sudden one; he is a work of art, and "art is long"; he is the product of immemorial ages, and of deep calculation; one can't make a bird like that in a day. He has been re-incarnated more times than Shiva; and he has kept a sample of each incarnation, and fused it into his constitution. In the course of his evolutionary promotions, his sublime march toward ultimate perfection, he has been a gambler, a low comedian, a dissolute priest, a fussy woman, a blackguard, a scoffer, a liar, a thief, a spy, an informer, a trading politician, a swindler, a professional hypocrite, a patriot for cash, a reformer, a lecturer, a lawyer, a conspirator, a rebel, a royalist, a democrat, a practicer and propagator of irreverence, a meddler, an intruder, a busybody, an infidel, and a wallower in sin for the mere love of it. (*FE*, 353)

Once again, the staple elements of Clemens's "personal" bad faith surface together, not so much in sequence as in simultaneous combination, or "dialogue." They converge in the raucous crow, who is of course a figure, dimly glimpsed perhaps, of Clemens himself. His discordant croaking is at once an echo of the preceding day's strained apologetics and an indirect acknowledgment that the charges have not lost their force. On one side, Clemens complains, the bird is his antagonist and persecutor, belaboring "my clothes, and my hair, and my complexion, and probable character and vocation and politics, and how I came to be in India, and what I had been doing, and how many days I had got for it, and how I had happened to go unhanged so long, and when would it probably come off, and might there be more of my sort where I came from, and when would *they* be hanged,—and so on, and so on, until I could not longer endure the embarrassment of it." On the other, the crow points the way to redemption. For though the disreputable creature has in one incarnation or another been guilty of virtually all sins imaginable, he has in the process risen above moral responsibility into a condition of sublime if utterly brazen indifference. As the result, Clemens admiringly observes, "he does not know what care is, he does not know what sorrow is, he does not know what remorse is, his life is one long thundering ecstasy of happiness, and he will go to his death untroubled, knowing that he will soon turn up again as an author or something, and be even more intolerably capable and comfortable than ever he was before" (*FE*, 353–56).

Blithely fanciful as it may appear, the humor of the description is rooted in the questions about sin, guilt, and the mysteries of consciousness that surface more darkly in the preceding section on slavery. By the logic of the Indian crow's example, sin will disappear from the world only in the minds of those most immersed in it. Happiness, defined negatively as the immunity to sorrow and remorse, is the exclusive privilege of reprobates—writers prominent among them—so familiar with iniquity that it no longer disturbs their complacency. Clemens's esteem for the crow is, of course, a humorous simulation, a fantasy, wishful and half-conscious, of release from the remorseless gnawing of conscience. Clearly enough, the troubled American sojourner in Bombay is not the fabulous bird's most recent incarnation. He has none of the seasoned sinner's indifference to misery and guilt. To the contrary, the very extremity to which imagination transports him is an index to the depth and persistence of his affliction. It is integral to the brilliant economy of the passage that it compresses *multum in parvo*, dramatizing the simultaneous interplay of denial and assent in the face of relentless self-indictment. The entire process is briefly held up, half-acknowledged, and then set once again to rest. We have not heard the last of this.[35]

I like to think we hear an echo of the slave child's "singing, whistling, yelling, whooping, laughing" in the raucous Indian crow, who "is always chaffing, scolding, scoffing, laughing, ripping, and cursing, and carrying on about something or other" (*FE*, 354). Neither of these very vocal characters is conventionally articulate; both go on incessantly; in both, ebullient excess poses a challenge to tolerance; both are black; most crucially, both are self-deceived—the child in his happiness and the crow in his innocence. And in both we catch a glimpse of Clemens, a stranger in many ways to home and family, in his own eyes an incorrigible sinner, loudly at large in the world, laughing and scolding and cursing to the end. Like the child and the bird, Clemens sought relief on the wide world's stage from what inwardly ailed him. From boyhood on—whether in church, in parades, in the pilot house of a majestic riverboat, as a famous journalist, novelist, world traveler, lecturer and platform humorist, or as a high-profile globetrotter and pundit—he craved celebrity. At the same time, however, Clemens recognized that his public performances were at once glittering illusions carefully staged to conceal at least as much as they revealed. He was hiding in the bright lights. His formal evening outfit, in white broadcloth, and featuring a swallow-tail coat, was his "don'tcareadamn suit," he told his daughters, Clara and Jean, "a very beautiful costume—and conspicuous."[36] On one side, he insisted that his gorgeous suit expressed his desire "to be clean in the matter of raiment—clean in a dirty world" (*AMT*, 370); on the other, he recognized, with Howells, that his clothing concealed something darker within— that he was a "whited sepulchre."[37]

It was partly because of his distrust of public display that Clemens decided, when it came time to complete his autobiography, that the work would not be published in his own lifetime. "I speak from the grave rather than with my living tongue, for a good reason," he explains: "I can speak thence freely. When a man is writing a book dealing with the privacies of his life—a book which is to be read while he is still alive—he shrinks from speaking his whole frank mind; all his attempts to do it fail, he recognizes that he is trying to do a thing which is wholly impossible to a human being" (*MTA*, 1:xv). Clemens reported to Howells that he wanted the autobiography to "be a perfectly veracious record of his life and period; for the first time in literature there should be a true history of a man and a true presentation of the men the man had known."[38] Both were persuaded that the key to success lay in posthumous publication.

Clemens was also convinced that the fullest and most faithful record would emerge in spoken dictations rather than silent, solitary sessions with pen and paper. Assorted experiments with written autobiography— including childhood reminiscences, an account of his relationship with General Ulysses S. Grant, another of the disastrous Paige typesetting machine, and fond memories of his mother—had left him feeling unsatisfied. The results, he complained, were "too literary" (*MTA*, 1:237).[39] The enemy of free-flowing veracity was reflection, which produced self-conscious second thoughts and falsifying artifice. Much better that a competent stenographer should record his words as they emerged, unpremeditated, unobstructed, and unadorned from the well of memory. So pleased was Clemens with his dictations, he wrote to Howells in early 1904, that he planned to discard the earlier, written portions of his autobiography, "& do them over again with my mouth, for I feel sure that my quondam satisfaction in them will have vanished & that they will seem poor & artificial & lacking in color" (*MTHL*, 2:779).

Clemens worked with stenographers at brief intervals during the course of his long career, but made only two sustained attempts at dictating his autobiography. In Florence in early 1904, during the months just before Livy's death, he diverted himself by conducting dictations with his secretary, Isabel Lyon. These sessions dwell at length on the details of life in an Italian villa, but also feature portraits of John Hay and Henry H. Rogers, along with sketches of other famous friends. Of much greater interest are the nearly 250 autobiographical dictations undertaken between 1906 and 1909. Albert Bigelow Paine, who with Miss Lyon and a stenographer regularly sat in on the sessions, recalled that the setting and mood were entirely relaxed. "It was [Clemens's] custom to stay in bed until noon, and he remained there during most of the earlier dictations, clad in a handsome dressing-gown, propped against great snowy pillows. . . . Often he did not know until the moment of beginning what was to be his subject for the day; then he was likely to go drifting among his memories in a quite irresponsible fashion, the fashion of table conversation, as he said, the methodless method of the human mind" (*MTA*, 1:x).[40] Clemens was initially confident that simply by surrendering to the drift of mental associations as they surfaced in spoken language he would produce a narrative at once interesting and true. "In Florence, in 1904," he recalled, "I hit upon the right way to do an Autobiography: Start it at no particular time of your life; wander at your free will all over your life; talk only about the thing which interests you for the moment; drop it the moment its interest threatens to pale, and turn your talk upon the new and more interesting thing that has intruded itself into your mind meantime" (*MTA*, 1:193). Two years later, in a dictation on March 26, 1906, Clemens came back to the same idea. "Howells was here yesterday afternoon," he reports, "and I told him the whole scheme of this autobiography and its apparently systemless system—only apparently systemless, for it is not that. It is a deliberate system, and the law of the system is that I shall talk about the matter which for the moment interests me, and cast it aside and talk about something else the moment its interest for me is exhausted" (*MTA*, 2:245–46). The inevitable figure for such effortless, unimpeded discourse was of course free-flowing water. Ideally, Clemens believed, autobiographical "narrative should flow as flows the brook down through the hills and the leafy woodlands." It is like "a brook that never goes straight for a minute, but *goes*, and goes briskly," following the path of least resistance, "always *going*, and always following . . . the law of *narrative*, which *has no law*" (*MTA*, 1:237).

It will not come as a complete surprise, perhaps, that in practice the unrestrained current of Clemens's dictations led not to a flood, but rather to a striking paucity, of candid self-disclosures. The "natural," unregulated, "methodless method" of his mental drift was in fact a formula for easy avoidance. The channel of least resistance almost always veered away from those "privacies of his life" whose recollection gave him the greatest pain. The gentle, effortless flow of the dictations produced a mental state closely analogous to the one Clemens experienced when drifting down a great river. The "soft and peaceful beauty" of summertime in Germany is best appreciated, he writes in *A Tramp Abroad*, when one travels at a leisurely pace down a wide river. "The motion of a raft is the needful motion; it is gentle, and gliding, and smooth, and noiseless; it calms down all feverish activities, it soothes to sleep all nervous hurry and impatience; under its restful influence all the troubles and vexations and sorrows that harass the mind vanish away, and existence becomes a dream, a charm, a deep and tranquil ecstasy" (*TA*, 126). Ten days of rafting down the Rhone in 1891, he wrote to his close friend, Joseph Twichell, left his "conscience in a state of coma, and lazy comfort, and solid happiness. In fact there's *nothing* that's so lovely" (*MTL*, 2:558). The easeful moral undercurrent in the pull of great rivers surfaces to view in the title of Clemens's unpublished manuscript *The Innocents Adrift*, which Albert Bigelow Paine abridged for posthumous publication in *Europe and Elsewhere*. "To glide down the stream in an open boat, moved by the current only," and thereby to experience a "strange absence of the sense of sin, and the stranger absence of the desire to commit it,"[41] this was for Clemens the height of attainable mortal bliss.

But though remote from the world, rivers nonetheless flow through it, and virtually all journeys end on shore. Just after his escape from the feuding Grangerfords and Shepherdsons, Huck rejoins Jim on the raft, where for a time he feels "mighty free and easy and comfortable." But that time is brief. The solitude of the river is easeful, but it also produces "lonesomeness," as Huck more than once observes. Nor is the solitude proof against reminders of human perversity along the shore. The sight of a log cabin at dawn reminds Huck of the "cheats" in wood-yards who pile wood "so you could throw a dog through it anywheres." A "nice breeze springs up," but the fresh air is mingled with the stench of "dead fish" left by thoughtless people to rot on the banks (*HF*, 155–57). In fact, the stretches of water separating the raft from land are slender, and do little to screen out regular reminders of what awaits Huck on shore. He is a fugitive, pursued, he believes, by his father, and in increasingly breathless retreat from what he regards as the potential threat in all humans, especially white people, and including himself. Much of the trouble, it is clear, is rooted in race and slavery. Alone with Jim on the raft, Huck is at a safe distance from that trouble, even as it operates within his own psyche. But when they leave the raft, the destructive potential in his ambivalent feelings about Jim is increasingly a factor in the developing action. So long as he keeps to the middle to the stream, Huck is relatively safe from the world, and from that world in himself. On shore, he is a part of the problem.[42]

The same is generally true of the autobiography. There is no little selfishness and cruelty at large in the world that falls open to Clemens's memory and imagination, but such things are generally held at arm's length in the flow of his dictations. The "sense of sin" and "the desire to commit it," though prominently on display, are almost always assigned to others, almost never to himself. The more one explores the published and unpublished pages of the autobiography, the more one is impressed with their relative freedom from the varieties of guilt and self-loathing so often found in Clemens's writing. "An autobiography is the most treacherous thing there is," he wrote in 1907. "It lets out every secret its author is trying to keep" (*WIM*, 266). How perfectly ironic, in light of these sentiments, that his own autobiography should have revealed so little. As Bernard DeVoto observed many years ago, though Clemens is "one of the most autobiographical of writers, he is least autobiographical when he seriously tries to be and does not carry his attempt to reveal himself very far or very deep" (*MTE*, xiv). James M. Cox takes the same view, observing that "despite Mark Twain's vast claims about the revelation he was about to make, the *Autobiography* is singularly tame."[43] Several others have concurred.[44] This surprising blandness is directly traceable to the "methodless method" of Clemens's meandering narrative.

In his novels—*Huckleberry Finn* and *Pudd'nhead Wilson* come most readily to mind as examples—the unfolding logic of his plots often forced Clemens to confront painful moral issues, or to engage in elaborate evasions as a way of avoiding them. I will come back in due course to this pattern in his fiction, though for now it will be enough to observe that the autobiographical dictations made it easy to avoid such dilemmas. In the brief, unstructured oral sessions, Clemens could begin and end where he liked. If snags seemed to threaten, he could change course immediately and without explanation.

He described his approach in 1906 as "a system which is a complete and purposed jumble—a course which begins nowhere, follows no specified route, and can never reach an end while I am alive" (*MTA*, 2:246). Freed of all plot constraints and navigating along the lines of least resistance, it was easy enough to keep trouble at a distance and to maintain relative serenity at the center. As the result—and with scant awareness that he was doing so—Clemens steered clear of the scandalous self-revelations that the project was ostensibly designed to produce. There was indeed a method at work in the "methodless" dictations, but not one that he could readily identify. To him, at least initially, the easy flow of the talk seemed "natural," unpremeditated, unreflecting, and therefore free of distortion. It felt *true*. It also almost invariably left him occupying the moral high ground. Little wonder, then, that he found the dictations so pleasurable, and that he continued with them even after his memory had run dry and the talk had dwindled to little more than news and gossip.

This is not to deny that there is discord in the autobiography. Discord is plentiful, but it almost invariably attaches to others. Bret Harte is surely the most famous of Clemens's targets. "He hadn't a sincere fiber in him," wrote the humorist. "I think he was incapable of emotion, for I think he had nothing to feel with. I think his heart was merely a pump and had no other function. I am almost moved to say I *know* it had no other function" (*MTE*, 265). And so it goes, remorselessly, for dozens of pages. Theodore Roosevelt comes in for some heavy shelling, as do Jay Gould ("the mightiest disaster which has ever befallen this country"), Andrew Carnegie ("he is just like the rest of the human race but with this difference, that the rest of the race try to conceal what they are and succeed, whereas Andrew tries to conceal what he is but doesn't succeed"), and other famous and not so famous plutocrats and politicians (*MTE*, 77, 36). Clemens is venomous as well in his treatment of his publishers, most especially Elisha Bliss and Charles L. Webster.

Still, it is easy to exaggerate the extent of the bitterness on display in the dictations. Albert Bigelow Paine left much of the personal vitriol out of his edition of the autobiography, but both Bernard DeVoto and Charles Neider more than corrected the imbalance in theirs. In DeVoto's edition most especially—it is tellingly entitled *Mark Twain in Eruption*—we are in company with a very angry man. When DeVoto's selections are read in sequence with the many unpublished—and almost invariably good-humored—dictations that surround them, however, the impact of the eruptions is much less pronounced. Harsh feelings are even further diluted when Clemens's many positive portraits (of Grant, Kipling, Henry H. Rogers. Rev. Joseph Twichell, Captain Ned Wakeman, and the members of his family, among many others), along with his loving evocations of Hannibal, are brought into the reckoning. This is not to deny that assaults on human nature reminiscent of *What Is Man?* and *The Mysterious Stranger* occasionally turn up in the autobiography. Nor is it to overlook the sadness that overtakes the narrative when Clemens turns to the deaths of his wife and daughter. But, again, the bitterness in the dictations is generally directed outward toward other people, and not inward upon the character of Clemens himself. That he once described the self-portrait emergent from the autobiography as "degraded"[45] is testimony to his strange failure to recognize how relatively benign the picture really was.

Similarly occluded gestures toward scandalous self-revelation are on display in Clemens's earliest experiments with autobiography. *Mark Twain's (Burlesque) Autobiography and First Romance* appeared in 1871. The first section of the slender booklet, which features a transparent send-up of conventional autobiography, traces the Twain surname through a copious rogues' gallery of felons and frauds, beginning in the Middle Ages and ending at the time of the American Revolution. As for his own life, the putative subject of the work, the narrator Mark Twain sets it aside, insisting belatedly that "it is simply wisdom to leave it unwritten until I am hanged."[46] Critics at the time and since have dismissed the book as a failure, scarcely worthy of comment.[47] Clemens himself promptly arrived at this view, and even tried to destroy the plates of the ill-fated volume. Perhaps he was put off, as others have been, by the strange misfiring of his humor. At one level, Clemens's chronicle of degenerate forebears makes a jest of the autobiographical enterprise. As Justin Kaplan has observed, however, the would-be humorist's "self-hatred" is "so nakedly displayed" in the piece "that what was meant to be a joke ends up being genuinely unpleasant" (*MCMT*, 124).

Crosscurrents of a similar variety surface in Clemens's "An Autobiography," published in *Aldine*, a journal of art and typography, also in 1871. "I was born November 30th, 1835," he begins. "I continue to live, just the same." And there the story ends. The rest is a brief explanation for the even greater brevity of the preceding narrative.

> Thus narrow, confined and trivial, is the history of a common human life!— that part of it, at least, which it is proper to thrust in the face of the Public. And thus little and insignificant, in print, becomes this life of mine, which to me has always seemed so filled with vast personal events and tremendous

consequences. I could easily have made it longer, but not without compromising myself. Perhaps no apology for the brevity of this account of myself is necessary. And besides, why should I damage the rising prosperity of *The Aldine*? Surely *The Aldine* has never done me any harm.[48]

Once again, the impulse to explore personal history is no sooner broached than abandoned; and the manner of the withdrawal betrays an undercurrent of self-abasement which works to deflate the presumptive joke. To be sure, the tone here is a shade or two lighter than in *Mark Twain's (Burlesque) Autobiography*, but the reflex self-diminishment is the surest evidence that the two pieces are cut from the same cloth. In both, the clearest message of all is the admission, "I am not worthy."

Confronted with the prospect of describing his life publicly and for print, Clemens's instinctive response was retreat into humorous denial. True, he had some success with autobiographical sketches of his childhood in Missouri, and with accounts of his business affairs. He was also comfortable composing brief portraits of friends and family members. As Michael J. Kiskis has observed, the best of this work was produced during periods of emotional stress, and reflects Clemens's characteristic recourse to writing as a stay against confusion. For example, the evocation of "Early Days" in Missouri, written just after the death of his daughter, Susy, was undertaken, Kiskis points out, "as a deliberate attempt to gain solace and peace from memory."[49] A heavy glaze of nostalgia insulates the piece against the brutal memories of Hannibal that surface elsewhere in Clemens's writing, most notably in "Villagers of 1840–43." But the vast majority of the early autobiographical experiments were not written with publication in mind. A few of them, it is true, subsequently appeared as "Chapters from My Autobiography," published serially by the *North American Review* in 1906–7, but the selections for this very profitable venture were designed to preserve the image of Clemens the family man and fast friend. As if to acknowledge the ruse, the final installment concludes: "Now, then, that is the tale. Some of it is true."[50]

In sum, Clemens wrote and dictated thousands of pages of explicit autobiography. This material is inherently interesting, of course, but it is almost never as deeply and damagingly self-revealing as its author believed it would be. It may be that Clemens took a lesson from the abortive autobiographies of 1871: that writing for publication about his background and character triggered an impulse toward self-denigration that he felt bound to resist. Once the threat of public exposure was removed, he reasoned—when he wrote, that is, without seeking publication, or "from the grave"—the censors would relax, permitting the harsh truth to come to the fore. In fact, however, just the opposite occurred. Nonetheless, the compulsion to reveal the worst of himself, and the assumption—a reasonable assumption, on the face of things—that autobiography was the likely site for such revelations, persisted in Clemens's thinking; witness his numerous references to the shocking revelations and personal degradation putatively on display in the early reminiscences and subsequent dictations. It was as though he felt compelled to tell, and even thought he was telling, damaging personal truths that in practice failed to come to light. This failure occurred because the "methodless method" of autobiography enforced pursuit of the line of least moral resistance. At the slightest hint of impending trouble, the mind simply veered off into more promising avenues. In fact, what Clemens regarded as the guilty truth about himself was least likely to surface in that mode of writing most closely associated in his mind with damaging personal revelations. The secret method of the "methodless method" rendered evasion obligatory.

It is important to emphasize that the impulse to reveal himself—in effect, to confess—was an important element in what attracted Clemens to autobiography. In this light alone are we able to properly appreciate his answering impulse to conceal the very things he felt moved to expose. To remorseless inward accusations of guilt, and the irresistible compulsion to confess, he responded with an array of subterfuges, including veiled philosophical disavowals (as in the letter to Sir John Adams), pleas of nolo contendere (as in the abortive autobiographies of 1871), and evasive narrative techniques (such as the "methodless method" of his autobiographical dictations). But while Clemens's urgent confessional impulse was invariably blocked when he wrote with conscious autobiographical intentions, the same impulse, working much less consciously in his travel writing and fiction, produced numerous and startling, if oblique, self-revelations. This is quite clearly the case, as we have seen, in the extraordinary Bombay section of *Following the Equator*, where the thought of confession had no part at all in his conscious intentions.

As they commenced the autobiographical dictations in 1906, Albert Bigelow Paine took Clemens at his word that they were embarking on a personal narrative of unprecedented candor. "I felt myself the most fortunate biographer in the world," Paine exults, delighted at the copious flow of his subject's memories and reflections. After "several weeks," however, Paine came around to a less credulous perspective. "I began to realize," he concedes, "that these marvelous reminiscences bore only an atmospheric relation to history; that they were aspects of biography rather than its veritable narrative, and built largely—sometimes wholly—from an imagination that, with age, had dominated memory, creating details, even reversing them, yet with perfect sincerity of purpose on the part of the narrator to set down the literal and unvarnished truth" (*MTB*, 4:1268). But Clemens was not deceived about his lapses. "I have been dictating this autobiography of mine daily for three months," he observed on April 6, 1906; "I have thought of fifteen hundred or two thousand incidents of my life which I am ashamed of, but I have not gotten one of them to consent to go on paper yet. I think that that stock will still be complete and unimpaired when I finish this autobiography, if I ever finish it" (*MTA* 2:331). "As to veracity," he told Howells, the autobiography "was a failure; he had begun to lie, and . . . if no man ever yet told the truth about himself it was because no man ever could."[51]

But Clemens knew something more. He knew that if he was powerless to tell the damaging personal truth, he was just as powerless to conceal it. He was fascinated, he wrote to his brother Orion, with the idea of a "story of an abject coward who is *unconscious* that he is a coward; & . . . of an unsuccessful man who is blissfully unaware that he was unsuccessful & does not imagine the reader sees he was unsuccessful."[52] He attributes similarly inadvertent self-revelations to "his Grace Mark Twain, Bishop of New Jersey," the ancient historian whose works are extensively drawn upon in *The Secret History of Eddypus*, Clemens's darkly satirical vision of a world overtaken by the religion of Mary Baker Eddy. Though the Bishop is a rather shadowy figure, the narrator of *The Secret History* is adept at drawing out the shameful secrets of the old reprobate's life. This is possible, he says, because "as a rule we get as much information out of what [history] does not say as we get out of what it does say. . . . History consists of two equal parts; one of these halves is statements of fact, the other half is inference, drawn from the facts" (*MTFM*, 338). Applying this rule to his subject's life, the narrator concludes that he must have had a harem! He goes on to applaud his Grace Mark Twain's candor in describing the flaws of his friends—who "stand before us absolutely naked"—but adds that while the Bishop "was intending to wear clothes himself . . . many and many is the time that they slipped and fell in a pile on the floor when he was not noticing." As the result, "we know him naked as intimately as we know him clad. Indeed, we know him better than he knew himself" (*MTFM*, 342).

Clemens recognized that his autobiographical drive to confess was in tension with a drive to conceal the dark truth. He recognized as well that he was driven to conceal things not only from others, but from himself as well, and then to conceal those acts of concealment. And he saw that his memory was tacitly in league with this bad-faith dynamic. Such, I take it, is the thrust of the irony in his familiar declaration: "When I was younger I could remember anything, whether it happened or not . . . but I am getting old, and soon I shall remember only the latter" (*MTB* 1:xvii). Knowing all of this, he allowed that there were things about himself—almost certainly unpleasant things—that he had obscured from consciousness, but that were apparent nonetheless to others. How, after all, could he contrive to conceal from the world the personal flaws that he had thrust out of his own sight and mind? Self-deception, Clemens rightly intuited, made him vulnerable to inadvertent self-exposure.

He knew all of this, though he never arranged the elements of his knowledge systematically, as I have here. To have done so would have been to draw the ornate mechanism of his bad faith fully into consciousness, and thereby to jeopardize the fragile stay against self-loathing that his multiple deceptions afforded him. But if he successfully avoided articulation of the elaborate ways and means of his bad faith—if, that is, he successfully denied denial—he also acknowledged it, though always obliquely and in bits and snatches. His expressed fascination with the "unsuccessful man who is blissfully unaware" of what his autobiography reveals is one such acknowledgment. His humorous observations on the derelictions of memory are another. There are dozens more scattered through his writings. Consider the following 1898 entries in his notebook: "Truth is more of a stranger than fiction"; "The unspoken word is capital. We can invest it or we can squander it"; "When people do not respect us we are sharply offended; yet deep down in his heart no man much respects himself" (*MTN*, 315, 317) He comes even closer to a full reckoning with the mechanisms of his denial in his treatment of his Grace Mark Twain, who makes a point of placing the flaws of his friends on public display, but fails to recognize that he is himself just as nakedly exposed, and thus better known to others than to himself. The Bishop is quite obviously unaware of his ignominious self-betrayal. Just as obviously, Clemens's treatment of his alter ego is a clear if oblique acknowledgment that his writings revealed to others degrading personal truths that he had strained to hide from himself.

Clemens makes the same acknowledgment, only more directly, in two very revealing passages written in Florence in 1904. In an autobiographical dictation devoted to "A Memory of John Hay" he reports that his subject believed that an autobiographer could not fail to be interesting if he comes as near to telling the truth about himself as he can. And he *will* tell the truth in spite of himself, for his facts and his fictions will work loyally together for the protection of the reader; each fact and each fiction will be a dab of paint, each will fall in its right place, and together they will paint his portrait; not the portrait *he* thinks they are painting, but his real portrait, the inside of him, the soul of him, his character. Without intending to lie, he will lie all the time; not bluntly, consciously, not dully unconsciously, but half-consciously—consciousness in twilight; a soft and gentle and merciful twilight which makes his general form comely, with his virtuous prominences and projections discernible and his ungracious ones in shadow. His truths will be recognizable as truths, his modifications of facts which would tell against him will go for nothing, the reader will see the fact through the film and know his man. There is a subtle devilish something or other about autobiographical composition that defeats all the writer's attempts to paint his portrait *his* way. (*MTA*, 1:235–36)

The autobiographer will invariably improve his self-portrait with half-conscious lies, but "his real portrait" will nonetheless be visible. Though Clemens declines to elaborate on the dynamics of this inevitable, inadvertent self-betrayal, the passage clearly illustrates his understanding that the autobiographer's bad-faith denial does not deceive a discerning reader, for whom "the inside" of the subject is an open book.

A virtually identical assessment surfaces in a 1904 exchange of letters between Clemens and Howells. The latter wrote in support of his good friend's enthusiastic experiment with autobiographical dictations, and to commend him for his veracity. "I fancy you may tell the truth about yourself," Howells declares. "But *all* of it? The black truth, which we all know of ourselves in our hearts, or only the whity-brown truth of the pericardium, or the nice, whitened truth of the shirtfront? Even *you* wont tell the black heart's-truth. The man who could do it would be famed to the last day the sun shone on" (*MTHL*, 2:781). Taking his cue from Howells' anatomical figure, Clemens replies

that an Autobiography is the truest of all books; for while it inevitably consists mainly of extinctions of the truth, shirkings of the truth, partial revealments of the truth, with hardly an instance of plain straight truth, the remorseless truth *is* there, between the lines, where the author-cat is raking dust upon it which hides from the disinterested spectator neither it nor its smell . . . the result being that the reader knows the author in spite of his wily diligences. (*MTHL*, 2:782)

Once again, the impulse to reveal what Howells calls the "black truth" is discovered in tension with an impulse to conceal the same thing. But even as the "author-cat" attempts to bury the offal of his life, the "remorseless truth" is nonetheless discernible to "the disinterested spectator."

In effect, then, Clemens knew that he could not hide. Somewhat paradoxically, however, autobiography, undertaken with the express intent of revealing the worst, was the mode of composition in which Clemens revealed the least. It is a kindred paradox that he came closest to revealing the truth about himself in his travel and fiction writing, where the pressure to tell the personal truth was much reduced. Autobiography was "safe" because it made evasion easy. Fiction was "safe," he assumed, because it wasn't "true"; evasion therefore had no part to play in it. But of course he was wrong in that assumption. And we have his error to thank for the fact that Clemens revealed in his fiction a great deal of what he regarded as the dark truth about himself.

The bad faith in Clemens's writing appears with special frequency and intensity at a few flashpoints in his consciousness, at sites of intersection between memory and painful self-reproach. His creativity was in thrall to a short list of self-accusing themes—race-slavery most prominent among them—repressed, but also mobilized by conscience to elude the censors and rise at opportune intervals into the flow of consciousness, there no sooner glimpsed than denied, but in denial obliquely acknowledged. What may most claim our attention is not the fact that Clemens was inclined to press certain "dangerous" topics out of sight and mind. Rather, it is the volatility of the proscribed elements that stands out, and the regularity and ease with which they breached the barriers erected to contain them. Guilt made him wince and turn away, but then came around to catch his eye all over again, often when he least expected it. The movement back and forth helps to account for Clemens's marked tendency to contradict himself, and for his suspicion, especially in his later years, that life was a bad dream, or that he had lost his mind. It also contributed to his extraordinary honesty, the need to acknowledge—alternately, the inability to conceal—what he regarded as his moral degradation. Little wonder that he gravitated to the "methodless method" of the autobiographical dictations—which minimized his vulnerability to unforeseen assaults of conscience—or that the dark truth found its way to the surface in less guarded narrative settings. He had lived long enough to know where the danger lay, and how best to avoid it. He knew as well that guilty self-betrayal was inevitable, and that his only recourse was to scratch the dirt a little and move on.

2   *The General and the Maid*

In his *Colors of the Mind: Conjectures on Thinking in Literature*, Angus Fletcher makes the case for what he calls "noetics," critical inquiry into "the precise activity occurring when the poet introduces thought as a discriminable dimension of the form and meaning of the poem." He continues: "If poetics shows us the ways by which the poet arranges his poem so that it will cohere poetically, as a thing made, then noetics shows us how thoughts, ideas, reflections, memories, judgments, intuitions, and visions are involved in the fundamental process of the making of the poem." Fletcher's interest falls squarely on texts in which "the active *process* of thinking is a dimension of meaning." Indeed, he goes on to insist that in noetic analysis, "as distinct from thematics or the history of ideas," the emphasis falls upon the *process* of thinking as an aspect of literary (or other) discourse."[1] Because he is most especially interested in thought as it gathers toward moments of clarity, Fletcher is drawn to writers, and more narrowly to poets—Spenser, Shakespeare, Donne, Marvell, Milton, Coleridge, and Stevens—whose work displays a markedly meditative, reflective, or argumentative trajectory. But he is careful to make room as well for the study of literature that dramatizes the less tidy, less consciously purposive phases of mental behavior. These are most readily observed in "fictions," which often feature "the experience of vague, unclear thought which may have been engendered by confusion and frustration. Fictions can show how one thinks through an issue or problem, while revealing the conflicts within the mind as the mental struggle proceeds. . . . Fictions can show what seems in life to be the vital *necessity* of incomplete, inconsistent, nonsystematic thinking."[2]

The relevance of Fletcher's ideas to present purposes must be obvious. The noetic analysis of Clemens's writing leads invariably to the discovery of confusion, frustration, mental struggle and, ultimately, in the pervasive operations of bad faith, to what amounts to the "vital *necessity* of incomplete, inconsistent, nonsystematic thinking." "My First Lie and How I Got Out of It" is a justification on deterministic grounds for full-blown, pathological bad faith, the widespread denial, itself denied, that race-slavery is inconsistent with the ideals of Christian democracy. To be sure, Clemens clearly deplores "the lie of silent assertion" even as he includes himself among those who inevitably surrender to its authority. "My First Lie" is thus remarkable not only for the potency of its cultural analysis, but also as an interval of striking lucidity in Clemens's understanding of himself and his art. In good part because of its determinism on the score of human deceitfulness, the essay frees the guilt-ridden writer to acknowledge his own profound immersion in the cultural pathology he so skillfully anatomizes. It is much more characteristic of Clemens, as the letter to Sir John Adams and the chapter from *Following the Equator* well illustrate, to lapse into bad faith without recognizing that he has done so. In this he joins company with the majority in "My First Lie," whose denial of their complicity in "the lie of silent assertion" confirms the "vital *necessity*" for pervasive bad faith. Clemens, I am arguing, had a deep but rarely acknowledged investment in the evasions enacted by his own "incomplete, inconsistent, nonsystematic thinking."

Angus Fletcher gives special emphasis in his outline of noetics to *anagnorisis* or recognition, which, he reasons, "may well be the central modality of thinking, for literary purposes." Recognition "is thought in the fullness of life; as such, it seeks to make sense of the enigmatic pattern of a described, narrated, or dramatized existence." Moreover "it is the larger purpose of each *final* recognition to organize a story into a signifying whole, whose gradual shaping is articulated through smaller, partial recognitions," and whose unfolding "directly influences and controls the shaping of the narrative form."[3] While this model of thought in literature applies in obvious ways to the highly self-conscious works featured in *Colors of the Mind*, it falls short when applied to the mental operations on display in the writings of Samuel Clemens. Consider, for example, the Bombay chapter in *Following the Equator*. To be sure, there is a movement of mind here toward recognition; but there is a simultaneous and competing movement in the opposite direction, toward evasion. This double movement occurs because the recognition toward which the narrator's consciousness tends is an acknowledgment of moral complicity that he is loath to own. The tension between the impulses to know and not to know produces a highly charged liminal impasse in which energy is expended not in the achievement of recognition, but rather in its indefinite deferral. Both here and elsewhere in Clemens's writing about his own life, it is this virtually simultaneous attraction and aversion to the final disclosure of emergent moral implication that, in

Fletcher's words, "directly influences and controls the shaping of the narrative form." Noetically speaking, bad faith is the fundamental "process of
thinking" manifest in Clemens's autobiographical writing.

The authority of guilt in Clemens's early life is well illustrated by a minor
episode that serves at the same time to advance my larger argument about
the autobiographical significance of his fiction and travel writing. In a long
letter to his old friend, Will Bowen, written in February 1870, less than a
week after his wedding to Olivia Langdon, Clemens was overtaken by the
powerful pull of boyhood nostalgia. In the midst of a flood of memories,
Clemens recalls for Bowen the time "you had the measles & I went to your
house purposely to catch them."[4] Why he engaged in such dangerous folly
is not explained, at least in this version of the story. The account set out
in the autobiography is much more detailed. Clemens there recalls that an
epidemic of measles descended on Hannibal in 1845. The disease "made a
most alarming slaughter among the little people," necessitating "a funeral
almost daily," and striking fear into the hearts of local mothers. Jane Clemens took steps to isolate her children, but failed as usual to restrain her most
wayward and willful son. "I cannot remember now whether I was fright-
ened about the measles or not," Clemens reports, "but I clearly remember
that I grew very tired of the suspense I suffered on account of being contin-
ually under the threat of death. I remember that I got so weary of it and so
anxious to have the matter settled one way or the other, and promptly, that
this anxiety spoiled my days and nights." And so he slipped out to the
Bowen house and climbed into bed with young Will, who was "dangerously ill." Mrs. Bowen angrily intervened and sent him home, but he
returned a second time, and thereby contracted the disease. "It was a good
case of measles that resulted," Clemens exults:

> It brought me within a shade of death's door. It brought me to where I no
> longer felt any interest in anything, but, on the contrary, felt a total absence
> of interest—which was most placid and tranquil and sweet and delightful and
> enchanting. I have never enjoyed anything in my life any more than I
> enjoyed dying that time. I was, in effect, dying. The word had been passed
> and the family notified to assemble around the bed and see me off. . . . They
> were all crying, but that did not affect me. I took but the vaguest interest in
> it, and that merely because I was the center of all this emotional attention
> and was gratified by it and felt complimented. (*MTA*, 2:219–21)

Clemens's inclination to cast the episode in a humorous light, as an instance of vain and romantic boyish excess, is indisputably clear. This said,

we cannot fail to be struck by what his reminiscence reveals: that even as a child his interior life was so troubled that the release from consciousness seemed attractive; and that the tranquility he experienced at "death's door" was substantially enhanced by the attention and approval it drew from those closest to him. We are amused, of course, when Clemens relates that his doctor, "very much to his astonishment—and doubtless to my regret . . . dragged me back into this world and set me going again" (*MTA*, 2:221). But the acknowledgment of his childish attraction to oblivion, with all that implies of unforgotten anguish, infuses the humor with unmistakable gravity.

This version of the measles episode reveals that when he was about ten years old, Clemens craved the release from inner turmoil that he imagined death would bring. What the account does not reveal is the precise nature of the feelings that so troubled him. What in particular made oblivion so appealing? He comes no closer to an explanation in "The Turning Point of My Life," an essay written in 1909 on commission for *Harper's Bazar*, and published just before his death the following year. The measles figure in the narrative is the first in a series of incidents that finally result in his becoming a writer. Once again, Clemens emphasizes the deadliness of the disease, the dread that it produced in the village, and his decision to make himself sick rather than endure continued fear and uncertainty. He notes in passing that his neighbors took an interest in his affliction, but makes no mention of the inner serenity brought on by the disease and his subsequent dismay at returning from "death's door" to ordinary life. It is of interest, however, that in this version of the story Clemens is twelve and a half years old, and that his father has recently died. His errant behavior exacerbates an already stressful situation to such an extent that his mother decides to take him out of school and commence his apprenticeship as a printer. "She was tired of trying to keep me out of mischief," he concludes, "and the adventure of the measles decided her to put me into more masterful hands than hers" (*WIM*, 458).

Dixon Wecter notes that the actual measles epidemic occurred in 1844, well before the death of Judge Clemens, when Sam was still a young boy.[5] In imagining himself older, Clemens casts the episode into a more unsettled period in his family life, and heightens the significance of his own intractable behavior. He is a bigger boy in this version, and more of a burden on his poor mother, who is forced by his rebelliousness to take extreme steps. The gravity of the situation is even clearer in an earlier, unpublished draft of "The Turning Point of My Life," in which Clemens describes himself as "a difficult boy" prone to "foolish and troublesome mischief." It is perhaps telling that in this earlier, discarded version the measles episode arises in the context of a discussion of temperament, the inflexibly fixed and determined part of an individual's make-up. Circumstances may modify temperament, but they cannot change it. Thus, in Clemens's words, "No Circumstances can get anything more than a modified magnanimity out of a mean temperament, nor anything more than a modified warmth out of a cold one." He goes on that an individual is *"not* responsible for his temperament, which was *born* to him—like the color of his eyes and as unchangeable" (*WIM*, 526–27). Framed in this way, the self-inflicted bout with the measles invites interpretation as the behavior of a temperamentally troubled, difficult, and impulsive person who is disinclined to accept responsibility for what his compromising disclosure clearly reveals.[6]

There are several points to be made about the versions of the measles outbreak consulted so far. The most damaging version, in which Clemens is oldest, most difficult and troubled, and most evidently concerned about the moral significance of his behavior, is the rejected draft of "The Turning Point of My Life." The two versions completed for publication—in the autobiography and in *Harper's Bazar*—give much less evidence of such concern. It is obvious that Clemens felt compelled to tell this story; but it is nearly as obvious that the more the telling revealed about the darker implications of the episode, the less he was inclined to release it into the light of day. Thus quite in spite of his commitment to self-revealing candor in his dictations, the version in the autobiography is the least revealing of all. Indeed, so benign is this rendering of the episode that Clemens decided to include it in the carefully selected "Chapters from My Autobiography," published in the *North American Review* in 1906 and 1907.

All of the versions of the measles episodes so far discussed are nonfictional and explicitly autobiographical; despite their differences in detail and tone, they all offer themselves as faithful accounts of Clemens's life. The three versions are alike as well in their common failure to illuminate the question, previously posed, about the evident craving for oblivion on display in the boy's self-initiated brush with death. What in particular attracted young Clemens to "the total absence of interest—which was most placid and tranquil and sweet and delightful and enchanting"—that accompanied his approach to the grave? The closest thing to an answer surfaces not in anything overtly autobiographical, but in *Tom Sawyer*, where Clemens drew copiously on personal experience, but under the liberating premise of fiction.

We enter the story as Tom and Huck look on from their hiding place in the village graveyard as Injun Joe fatally stabs Dr. Robinson and then persuades Muff Potter (who is unconscious at the time of the killing) that he is the murderer. Moved by their fear of the dread half-breed, the boys take a solemn oath to "keep mum" about what they know, even though their silence virtually ensures that Potter will be tried and convicted of a crime he did not commit. Huck is so mortally terrified of Injun Joe that his fear is all-consuming. For Tom, however, fear gradually gives way to guilt over his failure to speak out on Potter's behalf. We follow the curve of his emotions through more than a dozen chapters in which he labors to conceal the saving truth from himself and others. It is an extended but ultimately futile exercise in textbook bad faith that takes its course through assorted distractions—joining the Cadets of Temperance, keeping a vacation diary, a minstrel show, the Fourth of July, a circus, a phrenologist, and a mesmerist. Finally, all ingenuity for self-deception having failed, the boy is helpless to resist the ceaseless sting of conscience. "The dreadful secret of the murder," he admits to himself, "was a chronic misery. It was a very cancer for permanency and pain." Tom is overwhelmed by guilt, but nonetheless postpones the inevitable confession in order to venture one last, positively life-threatening distraction. For "then," the text continues, "came the measles. During two long weeks Tom lay a prisoner, dead to the world and its happenings. He was very ill, he was interested in nothing" (*TS*, 178–79).

It is the clear message of this revealing passage that because they jeopardize his life and render him "dead to the world," the measles are as close as Tom can get to a cure for the guilt that afflicts him. The element so conspicuously missing from the other, nonfictional accounts—a plausible explanation for the relief that the disease confers—is here, in the fictional version, clearly in evidence. The boy embraces the mortal disease because it renders him oblivious to his conscience. Looking past the text to its foundation in Clemens's experience of life, we can hardly doubt the anguish that guilt must have caused him, even as child. Indeed, the extremity of the relief serves as an index to the extremity of the suffering. Quite evidently, it was the painful sting of conscience that made the measles episode memorable, and yet it was also the feature of the episode that most resisted telling. To put it another way, the guilt makes scant appearance in those versions of the story that profess to be true, but dominates the ostensibly fictional treatment of the same events. The approach to the painful truth of his interior life was thus eased for Clemens when veracity was at no apparent premium in the telling. Under such circumstances, the ordinarily vigilant author-cat relaxed his guard.

I want to be perfectly clear: his self-induced bout with the measles was a meaningful experience for Clemens. We know this both because of the gravity of the situation as he describes it, and because he comes back to it so frequently in his writing. This was a story he felt compelled to tell. And yet analysis of the several versions of the story reveals that telling it completely, with conscious attention to its painful deeper meaning, was very difficult for Clemens. The impulse to tell was thus in tension with an impulse not to tell, which helps to explain why he produced so many incomplete versions of the story. It also helps to explain why the most complete telling, with its emphasis on the oppressive guilt that motivated the otherwise inexplicable behavior, surfaces not in an autobiographical setting, but in a novel. Clemens, it is clear, responded to a lifelong impulse to tell the dark truth about himself, but answered that impulse with evasions and half-truths except when veracity ceased to be an issue, in fiction.

It is a good question, of course, what precise species of guilt drove young Sam Clemens to seek relief in the measles. Clearly, it was not anguished concern for the fictional Muff Potter (though Tom's guilty concern for the captive derelict is reminiscent in obvious ways of Clemens's similarly charged feelings about the tramp who incinerated himself in the Hannibal jail). Almost certainly, the youngster's unforgettable misery had its foundation in the stern religious and moral sentiments fostered in him by his mother. The evidence on this score is perfectly clear in Clemens's vivid memories of boyhood fear and trembling during long, remorseful nights when sanity itself seemed in doubt. We must imagine that Jane Clemens's sternly Calvinistic system of belief informed the disciplinary standards she brought to bear on her children, and most especially on restless, troubled, difficult Sam. Indeed, the suggestion arises in more than one of the versions of the measles episode that maternal disapproval had a part to play in triggering the child's self-destructive behavior. In "The Turning Point of My Life," for example, it is clear that Jane has despaired of controlling her "difficult boy," and has been driven to the extreme step of removing him from the household into the "more masterful hands" of a local printer.

A strikingly similar interplay of oppressive guilt, autobiographical evasion, and oblique fictional resolution characterizes Clemens's response to the death of his brother Henry in 1858. Indeed, it is to this tragic event and its aftermath that Clara Clemens turns to illustrate her father's reflex "self-condemnation," his habit of blaming himself for human suffering he could not possibly have caused.[7] The facts of the case are fairly straightforward.[8] In mid-June 1858, just south of Memphis, the boilers on the steamboat *Pennsylvania* exploded. Among the injured was Henry Clemens, who worked on board as a "mud" clerk. Henry's brother, Sam, who happened to be just a day away on another steamboat, reached Memphis in time to witness Henry's final agony. A local newspaper reported that he rushed "to see his brother, and on approaching the bedside of the wounded man, his feelings so overcame him, that he sank to the floor overpowered." The article goes on to note that the surviving brother "had been pilot on the Pennsylvania, but fortunately for him, had remained in New Orleans when the boat started up."[9] The extremity of Clemens's response, and his feelings about his good fortune at not being on the *Pennsylvania* when it exploded, are registered in a letter of 18 June 1858 to his sister-in-law, Mollie Stotts Clemens.

> Long before this reaches you, my poor Henry,—my darling, my pride, my glory, my *all*, will have finished his blameless career, and the light of my life will have gone out in utter darkness. O, God! this is hard to bear. Hardened, hopeless,—aye, lost—lost—lost and ruined sinner as I am—I, even *I*, have humbled myself to the ground and prayed as never man prayed before, that the great God might let this cup pass from me,—that he would strike me to the earth, but spare my brother—that he would pour out the fulness of his just wrath upon my wicked head, but have mercy, mercy, mercy upon that unoffending boy. The horrors of three days have swept over me—they have blasted my youth and left me an old man before my time. Mollie, there are grey hairs in my head to-night. For forty-eight hours I labored at the bedside of my poor burned and bruised, but uncomplaining brother, and then the star of my hope went out and left me in the gloom of despair. Then poor wretched me, that was once so proud, was humbled to the very dust,—lower than the dust—for the vilest beggar in the streets of Saint Louis could never conceive of a humiliation like mine. Men take me by the hand and *congratulate* me, and call me "lucky" because I was not on the Pennsylvania when she blew up! My God forgive them, for they know not what they say.[10]

At first glance, this may strike us as an outpouring of conventional, appropriately Biblical grief. But closer inspection reveals that something quite remarkable is going on. Henry's death is acknowledged, but the tone is florid, rhetorical, and rather detached in its literary allusiveness. Indeed, the rhetorical hyperbole ("my darling, my pride, my glory, my *all* . . . the light of my life") sits rather oddly with (and compensates for) the fact that Henry is virtually forgotten in the remainder of the passage. What follows is not the celebration of Henry's estimable human qualities, and the stunned expression of great personal loss, that we might have expected. At first, the subject is Clemens's depravity, not his deceased brother's virtue. "That unoffending boy" is mentioned, but merely to highlight the manifold, if obscure, transgressions of his older brother. Self-reproach then gives way to something like self-pity. For example, we cannot fail to be struck by the contrast between Henry, the "burned and bruised, but uncomplaining brother," and Sam, "poor wretched me," who vents "the gloom of despair" by straining for examples of degradation adequate to a "humiliation like mine." Finally, gloomy self-scrutiny issues in a paradox. Sam insists that he was not fortunate to have stayed behind when the *Pennsylvania* sailed from New Orleans. Had he been aboard, it is suggested, he would have perished, and death would have been preferable to the intolerable circumstances of survival.

To summarize the passage in this fashion does little to exhaust its range of implication. For example, one cannot too much emphasize its dominant and conspicuous—though hardly conscious—egocentrism. Henry's death is important primarily because of its consequences for the surviving brother. As perceived and articulated by Sam, these consequences are complex and closely related. On one side, there is a question: Why is it that I, the sinful one, have been spared, while my "blameless" brother has been swept away? The question is freighted with an unmistakable burden of guilt—the sense that the disaster was Sam's responsibility, and that Henry has been his victim. But in the absence of evidence to substantiate this implicit self-accusation, we may suppose that the guilt is the result of a prior and unconscious fratricidal wish that achieved harrowing actualization in the *Pennsylvania* disaster. Otherwise, how are we to explain Sam's extraordinary overreaction?

Guilty self-reproach has an impulse toward self-defense as its complement and sequel. The mourner's emphasis on his own anguish and humiliation is a movement in this direction. His implied readiness to change places with his brother goes a step or two further, for it bears the clear suggestion that the survivor is, in fact, the victim. The biblical echoes serve to complete the reversal of roles. "Let this cup pass from me" recalls Christ's agony in the garden, and the concluding appeal, "My God forgive them," is the familiar prayer from the cross. More obliquely, the assurance that "the vilest beggar in the streets of Saint Louis could never conceive of a humiliation like mine" is reminiscent of Lamentations 1:12: "Behold, and see if there be any sorrow like unto my sorrow, which is done unto me, wherewith the Lord hath afflicted *me* in the day of his fierce anger." Such allusions are more than an assertion of guiltlessness. Working in precise counterpoint to declarations of guilt, they place the survivor in the role of sacrificial cross-bearer. Ironically—and exquisitely so—he becomes the victim of Henry's death, for as its consequence he must suffer death-in-life.

I have paused at some length over this passage because it so richly illustrates the subtleties of Clemens's relationship with his brother. To be sure, others have been here before me. With Clara Clemens, numerous critics have noted Clemens's pronounced tendency toward self-condemnation, and several have pointed to the *Pennsylvania* episode as evidence.[11] But no one has advanced the discussion as far as Coleman O. Parson, who in a venerable essay argues that "Samuel Clemens's guilt complex was rooted in his relations with Mother Jane and Brother Henry." In support of this view, Parsons surveys a number of familiar anecdotes involving the two brothers, concluding with a summary of the way things were between them.

> What was wrong with Henry? What trait aroused a hostility, strangely coupled with love, a hostility which, translated into other terms, was to make Sam suffer ages of remorse? Henry was, I am afraid, one of Burns's "unco-guid," a moral prig. . . . Without being vicious, Henry had a way of tattling, of capitalizing on his mother's preference, of letting the blame fall on Sam's head."
>
> Sam Clemens had a sensitive eagerness for love—especially for the approving love of his mother. But "sturdy, industrious, dependable" Henry, his complete antithesis, stood in his way, basked in the maternal sunshine, and irritatingly came off with a favorable verdict whenever he and Sam took their dispute to the domestic tribunal. Even when Sam was punished for a rare misdeed of Henry's, his tardily enlightened mother considered the thrashing one on account. In retaliation, Sam tried to get Henry into trouble with Mrs. Clemens—but never succeeded. Hence the resentment, mingled with love, the shame for feeling hostile to good people, the sense of rejection, unworthiness, and guilt.[12]

In a word—one that Parsons approaches, but never uses—Clemens's feelings toward his younger brother were charged with ambivalence. Nor does Parsons point out that this mingling of love and hate must have been rooted in a sibling jealousy that was born, with Henry, when Sam was just midway in his third year. The ensuing competition for Jane Clemens's attention and approval was intense, but not apparently abnormal. It was not until 1858, when the fatal steamboat accident gave horrifying expression to his repressed resentment and hostility, that the disruptive potential of Sam's fraternal ambivalence began to surface. The psychological result was strikingly similar to an affliction that Freud describes and analyzes in his study of *Mourning and Melancholia.*

Freud's treatise develops a distinction between mourning, the "normal" reaction to the loss of a loved person or idea, and melancholia, the pathological response to similar circumstances. The key and outstanding difference between the two conditions is that the melancholiac, unlike the mourner, experiences "an extraordinary diminution in his self-regard, an impoverishment of his ego on the grand scale. In mourning it is the world which has become poor and empty; in melancholia it is the ego itself. The patient represents his ego to us as worthless, incapable of any achievement and morally despicable; he reproaches himself, vilifies himself and expects to be cast out and punished."[13]

The application of this analysis to Clemens, the bereaved bother— especially in its emphasis on what Freud describes as "dissatisfaction with the ego on moral grounds"[14]—is perfectly obvious. The likeness appears even closer in the light of Freud's observation that "melancholia contains something more than normal mourning. In melancholia the relation to the object is no simple one; it is complication by the conflict due to ambivalence."[15]

Yet the temptation to apply the term "melancholia" to Clemens's condition is probably best resisted. Freud's subsequent analysis of the dynamics of the pathology is much too elaborate and complex, and our knowledge of Clemens's suffering too slender, to permit such a step. We are on safer ground, however, if we turn to what Freud describes as "pathological mourning," a condition in which "the conflict due to ambivalence gives a pathological cast to mourning and forces it to express itself in the form of self-reproaches to the effect that the mourner himself is to blame for the loss of the loved object, i.e., that he has willed it."[16] Quite evidently, in pathological mourning, as in melancholia, there is a dynamic relationship between repressed hostility and conscious feelings of guilt. There is, in Freud's words, "a satisfaction of trends of sadism and hate which relate to an object, and which have been turned round upon the subject's own self."[17] Indeed, so potent was Clemens's guilt in the matter of his brother's death that it triggered a retreat to the sense of martyrdom that surfaces toward the end of the passage from his letter home. The guilty survivor thus takes refuge in the role of abused victim. I hated him, Sam seems to admit, but I had good cause. Henry's self-righteousness and moral gamesmanship made my hostility inevitable, with the result that I now bear the burden of intolerable guilt.

Clemens's letter to his sister-in-law was hardly his last word on the *Pennsylvania* disaster. Freighted as it was with unresolved ambivalence, the very vital memory of Henry's final days made periodic assaults on the survivor's consciousness for the remaining half-century of his life. Of course, memory was not entirely reliable. It could hedge, amend, fabricate, or, as the following passage from *The Autobiography* suggests, it could be perfectly wrong and unwittingly just as right all at the same time. "I used to remember my brother Henry walking into a fire outdoors when he was a week old. It was remarkable in me to remember a thing like that and it was still more remarkable that I should cling to the delusion for thirty years that I *did* remember it—for of course it never happened; he would not have been able to walk at that age" (*AMT,* 3). The fact that Henry *did* accidentally hurt himself in a fire—an event whose charged memory Sam seems to have repressed, and subsequently recalled as an utterly implausible, and therefore harmless, "delusion"—does nothing to obscure the unconscious wish on display in this remarkable recollection.[18] "Of course it never happened"; but of course, quite unforgettably, it did.

As we have seen, contrasting impulses toward self-accusation and self-defense are already at work in the first paragraph of Clemens's 1858 letter to his sister-in-law. The case for the defense is resumed in the second paragraph, where the awkward and implicitly suspicious matter of personal good fortune is raised. "Mollie you do not understand why I was not on that boat—I will tell you." Clemens goes on to explain that he was one of the steersmen on the *Pennsylvania* during the trip south from St. Louis to New Orleans. While en route, the pilot, one Mr. Brown, made an unprovoked attack on Henry, striking him in the face. Sam was "wild from that moment. I left the boat to steer herself, and avenged the insult—and the Captain said I was right—that he would discharge Brown in N. Orleans if he could get another pilot."[19] Since another pilot could not be found, the Captain elected to ease the tension on board the *Pennsylvania* by requesting that the elder Clemens brother return to St. Louis on another boat.

The coincidental separation of the brothers permitted more than one interpretation. It could of course serve as an example of virtue (the gallant defense of Henry, approved by the Captain) receiving its just reward. But the simple fact that Clemens took such pains to explain his absence from the *Pennsylvania* suggests that he was morally uneasy with his survival. The rueful irony of his conclusion—"Had another pilot been found, poor

Brown would have been the 'lucky' man"[20]—points in the same direction. In its defensiveness, its appeal to virtuous motives, and its ironic dismissal of apparent good fortune, the passage protests too much. Beneath its surface we hear another voice, one which acknowledges that Henry's demise had a place in the unconscious wishes of the surviving brother.

Nearly twenty-five years later, Clemens returned to the Mississippi to revisit the scenes of his childhood and youth, and to gather information for a new travel book. One of the entries in his notebook for the trip is a reminder to "Tell, now, the events preceding & following the Pennsylvania's explosion."[21] The set-to with Brown figures prominently among "the events" mentioned, as it does again in *Life on the Mississippi*, where the story is reproduced in full dramatic detail. The notebook entry also contains two items that furnish new evidence in Clemens's developing case against himself. The first of these has to do with "the prophetic talk on the levee between Henry & me that night in N. O. before Pa. sailed on her fatal journey."[22] That conversation, as Clemens recounts it in *Life on the Mississippi*, was prophetic in especially grim fashion, for it turned on the subject of steamboat disasters. The brothers "decided that if a disaster ever fell within our experience we would at least stick to the boat, and give such minor service as chance might throw in the way. Henry remembered this afterward, when the disaster came, and acted accordingly" (*LM*, 236). It is probably fair to assume that the older and more experienced brother took the lead in formulating this noble resolution. Its fatal sequel, which followed with stunning immediacy, must have reinforced Sam's sense of complicity in his brother's undoing. And doubtless the sting of self-indictment was sharpened by the knowledge that Henry's heedless valor rendered him insensible to the severity of his own injuries. As the result, *Life on the Mississippi* reports, "he believed he was not hurt, (what an unaccountable error!) and therefore" returned to "help save the wounded" (*LM*, 241). But while Henry's impetuosity may have contributed to his death, his behavior was hardly the mystery that his brother makes it seem. After all, the larger narrative provides clear evidence that Henry's "error" was inspired by the heroic counsel of his older brother. Viewed in this light, Clemens's professed incredulity—"what an unaccountable error!"—may seem puzzling, or even disingenuous. On the other hand, it may be a telling sign of his pathology that the account of Henry's death should manifest guilt and repressed hostility that fail to register in the teller's conscious awareness.

The second item of new evidence in the notebook is an admonition to "*Leave out* that wonderful dream."[23] The dream referred to, we learn from an autobiographical dictation made nearly twenty-five years later, occurred in St. Louis shortly before the *Pennsylvania* disaster. It was a vision of Henry lying in an unusual metallic coffin. He was dressed in a suit of his brother's clothing; a bouquet of white roses, with a red rose in the center, rested on his chest. "In the morning, when I awoke," Clemens recalls, "I had been dreaming, and the dream was so vivid, so like reality, that it deceived me and I thought it *was* real." As events were to prove, the vision was all too accurate. A few days after the explosion, when he entered the "dead-room" in Memphis, Sam found Henry in a metallic coffin, "dressed in a suit of my clothing. I recognized instantly that my dream of several weeks before was here exactly reproduced" (*AMT*, 99–101). Quite in spite of the hostility and guilt at large beneath the surface of the dream, Clemens pursues his account with remarkable *sang-froid*. Since they are repressed, such feelings do not figure in the foreground of the narrative to which, ironically, they may be said to give rise. Once again, then, we catch the humorist at a moment of simultaneous concealment and disclosure.

Clemens prefaces the account of his premonition by explaining why, when he was planning *Life on the Mississippi*, he cautioned himself to pass over his "wonderful dream." "It is not likely that I told the dream in that book," he reflects. "It is impossible that I can have published it, I think, because I never wanted my mother to know about that dream" (*AMT*, 98). But why did he choose to keep the dream a secret from his mother? Ostensibly, of course, he was moved by a protective impulse. On reflection, however, we may wonder why he assumed that knowledge of his dream would add to his mother's suffering. Or was it something else that moved him to silence? Was it, perhaps, an unconscious intuition that his mother would be able to plumb the dream's deeper significance? This seems quite probable. Fittingly enough, his professed desire to keep the secret was itself ambivalent. His uncertainty as to whether he had made the dream public is an indirect acknowledgment that his mother *may* indeed have known about it. In fact, she did know about it. According to his niece, Annie Moffett Webster, Clemens was quite open about "the dream he had of seeing Henry dead before they started on the fatal trip. He says that my grandmother never knew about it, but she did, and often talked about it." So potent was Clemens's ambivalence that it overflowed into memory, leaving him with contradictory versions of the same story. Viewed as psychological phenomena, both versions were "true." On one side, Clemens felt moved to confess to the dimly perceived implications of his "wonderful dream." On another side, in retreat from the same implications, he tried to abolish the fact of the disclosure from memory. The parties to the struggle, it is evident, were responding to the same guilt in diametrically opposite ways, and the result was uncertainty and considerable anguish. Meanwhile, in a deplorable irony, "the family were not impressed; indeed they were amused that he took it so seriously."[24]

The surface calm of the autobiographical dictation is stirred by yet another tremor of repressed guilt. About a week after the accident, the doctor in charge predicted that Henry "was out of danger and would get well." In the event that the muttering of other patients kept him awake, however, the doctor suggested that Clemens ask the assistants on duty to administer an eighth grain of morphine. "Oh, well," the autobiography continues, "never mind the rest of it. The physicians on watch were young fellows hardly out of the medical college and they made a mistake—they had no way of measuring the eighth of a grain of morphine, so they guessed at it and gave him a vast quantity heaped on the end of a knife blade, and the fatal effects were soon apparent" (*AMT*, 101).

It is striking that this, the most overt of the elements in Clemens's self-indictment, should have been so belated in coming to light. It may be that his direct involvement in the administration of a lethal overdose was more than he could bear to reveal. On the other hand, our credulity may balk at the idea of such gross medical incompetence, and we may be inclined to view the story as the fabrication of a diseased conscience. In either case, the tone of weary resignation—"Oh, well"—does little to disguise the resonances of culpability that play through the passage. Whatever its veracity, this final memory finds Clemens casting himself as an accomplice in yet another fatal mischance.[25]

Clemens's innocence in the matter of Henry's death is perfectly obvious. It is equally apparent that the mourning that overtook him after the *Pennsylvania* disaster was rooted in unconscious feelings of hostility toward his brother. The result, in the years that followed, was the erection of an elaborate scenario in which Clemens gave imaginative expression to submerged feelings of guilt. Without quite knowing it, he built a case against himself. To this point, I have focused on the *how* of that case—on the circumstances, some remembered, some obviously distorted, some undoubtedly fabricated, that worked to substantiate his self-indictment. It remains to investigate the *why* of the case. In the fitful elaboration of his unconscious case against himself, what, if anything, did Clemens provide in the way of a motive?

The first recorded treatment of Henry's death occurred, as we have seen, during Clemens's return to the Mississippi in 1882. The trip stirred memories that turn up in the final two-thirds of *Life on the Mississippi*, published the following year. The first third of the new book is an elaborated version of "Old Times on the Mississippi," a series of essays written for the *Atlantic Monthly* in 1875. The contrast between the parts of the volume is quite striking. The opening chapters, centering on the education of the "cub" pilot, are warmly nostalgic; those "Old Times," as remembered in 1875, were very good times. The new material, the product of a much more recent and intimate look at the past, is generally much darker in tone. Appropriately enough, the transition from old to new is the account of the *Pennsylvania* explosion. And the main transitional figure, as James M. Cox has observed, is Brown, the pilot who appears in the "Old Times" chapters as a garrulous but utterly harmless old fool. "In the new episode, however, he becomes a ruthless brute who takes pleasure in humiliating his cub."[26]

The memory of Henry's death—irresistible, no doubt, because of its freight of unresolved ambivalence—is the key to the transformation of Brown. On one side, Clemens's unconscious hostility toward his brother is projected on to the pilot, who becomes a sadistic villain. On the other, Brown's apparently gratuitous aggression makes him a convenient target for repressed feelings of self-reproach and thus the object of righteous wrath. "I often wanted to kill Brown, but this would not answer," Clemens recalls. "However, I could *imagine* myself killing Brown. . . . I threw business aside for pleasure, and killed Brown. I killed Brown every night for months" (*LM*, 223–24). This initial resurgence of threatening and barely contained emotion sets the tone for much of what follows in *Life on the Mississippi*. Quite suddenly, and for no apparent reason, the narrator's consciousness is overtaken by memories of long-forgotten horrors and catastrophes. For example, a long and decidedly purple description of a Mississippi sunrise—"one of the fairest and softest pictures imaginable"—is followed without transition by the memory of a man who, in attempting to save his wife's life, inadvertently crushes her skull (*LM*, 332). This pattern grows much more pronounced as the narrator's attention turns to Hannibal, and to episodes from his childhood. Standing on a hill overlooking the sleeping village, he is struck by an intimation that his nostalgic feelings for the place may themselves be vulnerable to sudden and disturbing transformations. As James M. Cox points out, the memories that emerge when he descends from the hill, like the earlier memory of Henry, are "essentially guilt fantasies cast in the form of nostalgic recollections and boyhood adventures."[27]

The erosion of Clemens's nostalgia commences when he engages an old Hannibal gentleman in conversation. He learns that some of his childhood acquaintances have succeeded in life, that more have failed, and that one poor girl, the victim of a cruel practical joke, has spent the past thirty-six years in an insane asylum. News of this tragedy in the dim past triggers the memory of Lem Hackett, a friend who drowned one Sunday when Clemens was a boy. That night "a ferocious thunder-storm" caused the surviving boys of the village to "lay awake, repenting." Clemens's suffering was particularly acute, for he felt that the story would draw attention to those "among us who might otherwise have escaped notice for years. I felt that I was not only one of those people, but the very one most likely to be discovered." He goes on at considerable length, describing "agonies of remorse for sins which I knew I had committed, and for others which I was not certain about" (*LM*, 530–32). The key features of the account—intense feelings of guilt in the absence of direct responsibility, and oppressive fear of discovery—form what is by now a familiar pattern. Very similar elements figure in the next story, an account of the accidental drowning of a German boy who, like Henry, "was exasperatingly good" (*LM*, 533–36). Both episodes conclude with broadly ironic glances at the gullibility of the superstitious village children, and at the fickleness of their resolutions to reform. But the humor seems peripheral to the dominant, genuinely traumatic mood of the stories. Indeed, the mere fact that these tales come so readily to mind is good evidence that they could not be laughed away.

Memories of childhood anguish and guilt give way, however briefly, to an anecdote in which humor arises from the themes of death and gullibility. As a child, Clemens recalls, he was once in awe of a local carpenter who represented himself as the Mysterious Avenger, a remorseless killer. Though evidently cognate with the stories that precede it, the account of the child's deflated credulity does provide an interval of comic relief. The chapter ends less than comically, however, as Clemens is reminded of a Hannibal citizen who entombed his deceased daughter in a copper cylinder filled with alcohol. "The top of the cylinder was removable; and it was said to be a common thing for the baser order of tourists to drag the dead face into view and examine it and comment upon it" (*LM*, 547).

The macabre image of that dead face has the memory of the burning tramp as its almost inevitable sequel. As he does years later in his autobiography, Clemens here recalls the circumstances leading up to the outbreak of the fire. He insists that he fled from the scene before its fatal climax, but it is nonetheless "the face . . . pleading through the bars" that fixes his memory. "I saw that face, so situated, every night for a long time afterward; and I believed myself as guilty of the man's death as if I had given him the matches purposely that he might burn himself up with them. I had not a doubt that I should be hanged if my connection with this tragedy were found out." Though he claims to find the episode amusing in retrospect, there is scant humor in Clemens's deadly serious account. Rather, there is horror and terror and an abundance of guilt. "If anybody spoke of that grisly matter, I was all ears in a moment, and alert to hear what might be said, for I was always dreading and expecting to find out that I was suspected; and so fine and so delicate was the perception of my guilty conscience, that it often detected suspicion in the most purposeless remarks, and in looks, gestures, glances of the eye which had no significance, but which sent me shivering away in a panic of fright, just the same" (*LM*, 549–50).

The weight of guilt and the fear of discovery enforced a commitment to absolute secrecy upon the young sufferer. This worked well enough in waking hours, but at night there were dreams and, worse yet, there was

> the fact that I was an inveterate talker in my sleep. One night I awoke and found my bed-mate—my younger brother—sitting up in bed and contemplating me by the light of the moon. I said:
> "What is the matter?"
> "You talk so much I can't sleep."
> I came to a sitting posture in an instant, with my kidneys in my throat and my hair on end.
> "What did I say? Quick—out with it—what did I say?"
> "Nothing much."
> "It's a lie—you know everything!"
> "Everything about what?"
> "You know well enough. About *that*" (*LM*, 550).

Apparently by design ("Nothing much"), Henry's disclaimers create excruciating uncertainty in the mind of his brother. The only way to relief, Clemens decides, is to "probe him with a suppositious case." Henry is promptly roused from sleep and urged to pass judgment on a hypothetical episode that quite transparently parallels the circumstances of the tramp's death. Would it be murder to loan a loaded pistol to a drunken man who accidentally killed himself with it? "Yes," Henry replies, it is "probably murder, but I don't quite know." Again, we suspect that Henry's response is subtly designed to produce painful uncertainty and further disclosures. This is most certainly its effect. Neglecting to mention his own involvement in the incident, Clemens goes on "to set out the real case," once again requesting a judgment.

> There was a long pause. Then came this heavy verdict:—
> "If the man was drunk, and the boy knew it, the boy murdered the man. This is certain."
> Faint, sickening sensations crept along all the fibres of my body, and I seemed to know how a person feels who hears his death sentence pronounced from the bench.

Despite its apparent drift, however, the incriminating discussion ends with a reprieve. Henry declares that the guilty party is Ben Coontz, a member of the local gang. Limp with unexpected relief, Clemens quite naturally agrees. But how, he asks, did Henry know? "You told me in your sleep," is the reply. In the upshot, then, it appears that nightmares and sleep-talking are blessings in disguise. "My burden being shifted to other shoulders," Clemens concludes, "my terrors soon faded away" (*LM*, 552–53).

But was the relief as unqualified and permanent as Clemens would have us believe? In fact, the price of relief is acquiescence in Henry's transparent dissimulation. Given Clemens's intense feelings of guilt, it is perhaps plausible that he should accept his younger brother's absurd verdict. But what of Henry's strategy of hesitation and subtle suggestion, which works insidiously on his brother's fears, drawing him closer and closer to complete self-exposure? The strategy works perfectly, but its employment betrays both the fact, and the nature, of Henry's suspicions. Our misgivings about Henry's motives are confirmed when we reflect that he withholds what he *claims* his sleep-talking brother said until late in the dialogue. We must conclude that he does this in order to further exploit what he perceives to be his strategic advantage. But how can all of this have escaped the notice of one as sensitive to incriminating suggestions as his guilt-ridden brother? And how can he fail to see that the utterly improbable indictment of Ben Coontz is Henry's final, most perfidious stroke? After all, had Henry acted in earnest on his very evident knowledge, he would have accused his brother of murder. But in doing this he would have risked abridgment of his very considerable psychological power. The question of his legal judgment might have been raised, and this would have led to the exposure of the murder charge. At the least, his brother would have been relieved of the anxiety issuing from uncertainty as to Henry's knowledge and intentions. As it is, the narrator's avowed sense of relief must appear the feeblest subterfuge; and the yoke of subjection must grow heavier because Henry's knowledge is at once evident to both of them and acknowledged by neither. The potential here for psychological tyranny is no greater than the answering, murderous resentment it must surely inspire.

My analysis to this point may tend to suggest that I believe the dialogue with Henry actually occurred. In fact, I doubt that it did, at least as it is represented in this text. Judging from internal evidence, which is all we have to go on, the story's conclusion is sufficiently improbable to cast a shadow of doubt over the entire episode. Yet the literal truth of the tale is of slender concern to us. What matters is the fact that the narrative dramatizes Clemens's perception of a relationship in which his own gullible innocence succumbs to his brother's heartless guile. The characterization is perhaps too extreme to be credible, yet we cannot doubt that it is an accurate representation of Clemens's sense of things with his brother. For all of his outward rectitude, Henry is quite clearly perceived to be a malignant and ruthless psychological manipulator. Equally clearly, the narrator is cast as the innocent, and therefore quite justly outraged, victim of his brother's machinations.

Once seen in this light, the story's concluding sense of relief begins to make more sense. For despite surface appearances, the subtext of the narrative works to vindicate the accused and to condemn the righteous judge, and thus to complete the transformation from guilty survivor to oppressed victim that had its tentative first expression in Clemens's 1858 letter home. The cross-bearing posture in that letter, it will be recalled, led me to speculate that Clemens's guilt over his brother's death had an impulse toward self-vindication as its complement. I am the victim of unwarranted self-reproach, protests the survivor; my feelings of guilt, though inevitable in the wake of Henry's death, are as objectively baseless as my resentment of my brother was objectively just. Quite predictably, this shift in the psychological balance is much more pronounced in *Tom Sawyer*, Clemens's major fictional treatment of his relationship with Henry.

In the novel, where the censors restraining autobiographical self-disclosure are characteristically relaxed, Sid, who was modeled on Henry, appears as a jealous killjoy who never misses a chance to betray his half-brother's guilty secrets. On several occasions in the novel he is to be found feigning sleep as Tom steals in from his late-night adventures. The threat of exposure is especially acute for Tom after he and Huck witness the murder of Dr. Robinson in the local graveyard. In desperate fear of Injun Joe, who commits the murder and then turns the blame on feckless Muff Potter, the boys take a blood-oath to "keep mum" about what they have seen. This guilty knowledge makes Tom vulnerable to Sid in precisely the same way that Clemens's guilty knowledge about the incinerated tramp makes him vulnerable to Henry in *Life on the Mississippi*. Indeed, the texts are companion dramatizations of the same, unresolved fraternal ambivalence. In *Tom Sawyer*, Sid is there at his half-brother's bedside, on the alert for damaging revelations. Nor is he disappointed, for

> Tom's fearful secret and gnawing conscience disturbed his sleep for as much as a week after this; and at breakfast one morning Sid said: "Tom, you pitch around and talk in your sleep so much that you keep me awake about half the time."
>
> Tom blanched and dropped his eyes.
>
> "It's a bad sign," said Aunt Polly, gravely. "What you got on your mind, Tom?"
>
> "Nothing. Nothing't I know of." But the boy's hand shook so that he spilled his coffee.
>
> "And you do talk such stuff," Sid said. "Last night you said 'it's blood, it's blood, that's what it is!' You said that over and over. And you said, 'Don't torment me so—I'll tell!' Tell *what*? What is it you'll tell?" (*TS*, 105)

Once again, Henry—now cast as Sid—is a figure of guileful malevolence bent on exposing his wayward brother's guilty secrets. But the fictionalized Henry in *Tom Sawyer* is a much more developed, and for that a much more hateful, character than the "real" Henry, the youthful manipulator and judge who turns up, seven years later, in *Life on the Mississippi*. Sid is a diminutive Satan—alienated, predatory, ruthlessly vindictive, but finally hopeless and pathetic and darkly comical. We are brought to despise him because he takes arms against the all-American idyll of boyhood embodied in the character and setting and action of *Tom Sawyer*. He does not succeed, of course; as Henry Nash Smith long ago observed, the majority of Sid's carefully hoarded secrets are never revealed.[28] But he is despicable nonetheless, simply because he is witness to, and threatens to reveal, the guilt that haunts and harries his half-brother. Like the shriveled, shabby, two-foot dwarf in "The Recent Carnival of Crime in Connecticut," Sid knows what his victim is made of; and that, in the novel at least, gives rise to perfectly open and seemingly justified expressions of anger. Such is the mood in the concluding encounter between the two, when "Tom cuffed Sid's ears and helped him to the door with several kicks. 'Now go and tell auntie if you dare—and tomorrow you'll catch it!' " (*TS*, 265).

But, again, because it was not "true," fiction served Clemens as a relatively "free" space for the expression of charged memories and emotions ordinarily held in check by the censors that presided over his more consciously autobiographical writing. In his letter of 1858, as in the childhood memories recorded in *Life on the Mississippi*, his self-accusing guilt and defensive retreat to the role of long-suffering victim fill the foreground. Only in *Tom Sawyer* is his punitive rage against Henry opened fully to view. Here, clearly on display, is evidence of the murderous childhood wish that seemed fatally to materialize in the *Pennsylvania* explosion, and that fuelled the pathological mourning that followed. *Tom Sawyer* may be said to give unconscious fictional justification and release to feelings admissible to consciousness only as a conspicuous excess of guilt redolent of some nameless offense. Just as clearly, the hostility toward Henry played out in the relatively "free" space of *Tom Sawyer* did little to lay Clemens's guilt-laden ambivalence to rest. He bared his repressed feelings in the novel, but without the resolution that might have come with a more conscious address to vexed undercurrents of feeling. As the result, the emotionally fraught memory of the *Pennsylvania* explosion continued at intervals to oppress him for the rest of his life.

We have already looked at several such troubled memories—in the 1882 notebook, in *Life on the Mississippi*, and in autobiographical reminiscences of Henry walking into the fire, receiving an overdose of morphine, and as a corpse in a metallic coffin. There were many other, often tellingly conflicted and contradictory, recollections over the years after 1858. By reminding Clemens of a joke he once played on his innocent, trusting younger brother, and of Henry's "gentle, reproachful look," his conscience—in "the Recent Carnival of Crime in Connecticut"—maliciously enflames an old, unhealed wound. "Beast," Clemens shoots back, "I have seen [that look] a million times, and shall see it a million more! and may you rot away piecemeal, and suffer till doomsday what I suffer now, for bringing it back to me again!" (*CTSSE*, 1:648–49). Clemens adopted an entirely different tone in reporting to his prospective father-in-law, Jervis Langdon, that among those people who had known him well enough to reliably assess his character, only two had his complete sympathy: his brother Henry, who was dead; and Langdon's admiring daughter, Olivia, whom he aimed to marry (*MCMT*, 90–91). Predictably, Clemens the novelist was much less guarded in the fictional fragment, *Tom Sawyer's Conspiracy*, composed at intervals during the late 1890s. Here Henry, once again cast as Sid, is a loathsome killjoy, "one of them kind," Huck complains, "that don't commit no sin themselves, but ain't satisfied with that, but won't let anybody else have a good time if they can help it. . . . Tom said he was too good for this world, and ought to be translated" (*HH&T*, 182). Such outright aggression could only surface in a novel, and in an unfinished novel at that.

Clemens's sharply polarized feelings about Henry expressed themselves most characteristically in mingled shades of ambivalence and denial. In an undated letter of the mid-1890s to Henry Huttleston Rogers, for example, he exults in recent evidence that he is indeed a person "Born lucky, *always* lucky." But his mood dips perceptibly as he reflects that "when the 'Pennsylvania' blew up and the telegraph reported my brother as fatally injured (with 60 others) but made no mention of me, my uncle said to my mother 'It means that Sam was somewhere else, after being on that boat a year and a half—he was born lucky.' Yes," Clemens concedes, quite enigmatically, "I *was* somewhere else" (*MTL*, 2:621). If we recall that in his 1858 letter home, the stricken survivor asks God to forgive those who call him "lucky," we cannot fail to catch the drift of this kindred, mordantly ironic disclaimer, written nearly 40 years later.

Ambiguity of a rather different stripe turns up in a 1906 autobiographical dictation in which Clemens recalls that as a six-year-old he once intentionally inflicted pain on Henry, who was just four, by tearing loose skin from his heel. "Henry was hurt by this operation," Clemens reports, "and he cried—cried much louder than was necessary, as it seemed to me . . . but I was mainly troubled because it attracted attention and brought rebuke for me and punishment" (*MTE*, 387). Here as elsewhere, an admission of guilty hostility is immediately followed by a retreat to the role of victim. The bad faith denial is further compounded by the frame in which the anecdote is set, a discussion of determinism tracing responsibility for all human events back to God. "I positively believe," Clemens declares, "that the first circumstance that ever happened in this world was the parent of every other circumstance that has happened in this world since; that God ordered that first circumstance and has never ordered another from that day to this" (*MTE*, 386). By such reasoning, which became a prominent fixture of the aging humorist's moral thought, the blame for Henry's suffering lay not with his older brother, but with the irreversible chain of events set in motion by God at the creation. Henry is similarly featured in Albert Bigelow Paine's account of yet another autobiographical session in which guilt is no sooner acknowledged than denied. Clemens "had been dictating that morning his story of the clairvoyant dream which preceded his brother's death," Paine writes, and the talk of foreknowledge had continued. I said that one might logically conclude from such a circumstance that the future was a fixed quantity. "As absolutely fixed as the past," he said. . . . "Even the Almighty Himself cannot check or change that sequence of events once it is started. It is a fixed quantity, and a part of the scheme is a mental condition during certain moments—usually of sleep—when the mind may reach out and grasp some of the acts which are still to come." (*MTB* 4:1270–71)

The dream of Henry's death, so construed, affords the dreamer a window on inevitable catastrophe and at the same time exempts him, the possessor of fatal foreknowledge, from any suggestion of guilty complicity. Like the tragedy it anticipates, the dream is part and parcel of a divine scheme remote from human influence, and therefore from human responsibility.

It bears repeating that such guilty maneuvering did as little to ease Clemens's conscience as it did to stem the flow of memories about Henry's death. Had the denial of guilt been successful, the memories would have ceased. But of course they did not. Clemens's complete innocence in the matter notwithstanding, his remorseless conscience continued to oppress him for the rest of his life. As Justin Kaplan has astutely observed, the survivor's moral fatigue registered clearly in 1876, when his brother's body was moved to a new cemetery. "My darling, my pride, my glory, my *all*," Clemens had mourned in 1858, praying eloquently to change places with the deceased. Now, eighteen years later, the emotional fatigue brought on by the relentless guilt put an end to such sentiment. "Henry Clemens," he wrote wearily to a friend: "Born June 13, 1838—Died June 19, 1858—the above is sufficient for Henry's grave" (*MCMT*, 196).

In addition to constant, quite literal memories of the *Pennsylvania* disaster, Clemens was prey to less direct, at times less fully conscious reminders of the fatal explosion. As Edgar Branch has observed, Henry's terrible fate was surely in the back of Clemens's mind when he reported for the San Francisco *Daily Morning Call* on the destruction of the steamboat *Washoe* near Rio Vista in September 1864. The same may be said for the fictional *Amaranth*, which explodes, with terrible loss of life, in Chapter 4 of *The Gilded Age*. Branch goes on to speculate that the description of the Battle of the Sand-Belt, Hank Morgan's massacre of English knighthood at the end of *A Connecticut Yankee in King Arthur's Court*, "draws heavily on the image, indelible in Mark Twain's imagination, of the skyward thrust of the shattered *Pennsylvania* and its victims."[29] While Branch is surely correct to link such fictional images of fiery combustion to the real-life tragedy of 1858, it is the guilt ignited by the flames that cinches the connection. In the midst of the

Battle of the Sand-Belt, Hank observes that "the stillness was death-like. True, there were the usual night-sounds of the country—the whirr of night-birds, the buzzing of insects, the barking of distant dogs, the mellow lowing of far-off kine—but these didn't seem to break the stillness, they only intensified it, and added a grewsome melancholy to it into the bargain" (*CYA*, 560).

Oppressive stillness of exactly this kind is everywhere in Clemens's writing associated with what I have elsewhere defined as "proleptic guilt"— ominous intimations of guilt that emerge in advance of the circumstances which properly gives it rise.[30] Huck experiences ghostly premonitions of the guilt that subsequently attaches to his troubled relationship with Jim; and Theodor Fischer, in *The Mysterious Stranger*, is similarly afflicted in advance of the death of his friend Nikolaus. Clemens prefaces the cruel burning of an innocent old woman in "No. 44, The Mysterious Stranger" with "a hush [that] spread everywhere: there was no movement, there was not a sound" (*MS*, 327). Just so, as the final preparations for the execution of Joan of Arc are completed, "all noise and movement gradually ceased, and a waiting stillness followed which was solemn and impressive" (*JA*, 454).

As a rule, then, images of fiery combustion in Clemens's writing are most closely reminiscent of the *Pennsylvania* disaster when they are accompanied by evidence of guilt. These are the elements that combine in the persistent memory of the tramp who set himself on fire in the Hannibal jail with matches given to him by young Sam Clemens. In a letter of 1870, Clemens reminds his friend Will Bowen of the time "we accidentally burned up that poor fellow in the calaboose."[31] As we have seen, such regret becomes unbearable guilt in *Life on the Mississippi*, where Henry solemnly declares that the boy who supplied the matches is responsible for the drunkard's horrible death. Kindred sentiments doubtless fuel the flames that consume the poor tramp in the *Autobiography*, the most guilt-ridden account of all. Fire and guilt are horrifically merged in "The United States of Lyncherdom," where we are made witness to "twenty-four miles of blood-and-flesh bonfires unbroken," and to "the shrieks and the agonies" of the hundreds of victims (*CTSSE*, 2:485). Nor, finally, can we doubt that Clemens's hopeless remorse finds a voice in *The Prince and the Pauper*, when Prince Edward cries out in horror as two innocent women are burned at the stake. "That which I have seen, in that one little moment," he protests, "will never go out from my memory, but will abide there; and I shall see it all the days, and dream of it all the nights, till I die. Would God I had been blind!" (*P&P*, 327).[32]

The pervasive imaginative link between fiery combustion and guilt, especially in its gravitation to comparatively unguarded fictional settings, is potent evidence of Clemens's conflicting impulses to reveal and to conceal what he remembered of the *Pennsylvania* disaster. A cognate tension is everywhere on display in his numerous accounts of his experiences in the Civil War. "The Private History of a Campaign that Failed," published in 1885, is the best firsthand evidence on Clemens's decision, after a few weeks of service in a volunteer unit, to abandon the war for the safer adventures that awaited him on the remote mining frontier. It was a difficult decision, we can be sure. Clemens was a romantic who, like Tom Sawyer, aspired to a hero's part in the great struggle that engulfed the nation in 1861. But another, apparently stronger part of him drew back from the conflict. Was his retreat the act of a coward? Doubtless Clemens felt in retrospect that facing that vexed question for the rest of his life was far worse than facing the Union army in battle. The fear—at times the certainty—that others judged him a coward must have seemed a terrible penalty to pay for a perfectly human—arguably perfectly rational—decision. Most of all, we may plausibly surmise, he craved relief from the burden of guilt and shame and injured pride that the memory of the episode imposed. In 1863, in composing a detailed outline of his life, Clemens made no reference to the events that he would later describe in "The Private History." It was as though he had gone from piloting on the Mississippi to prospecting in Nevada without pausing en route to serve, however briefly, in the Civil War.

As a title, "The Private History of a Campaign That Failed" refers both to the failure of Clemens's attempt to become a soldier, which is treated humorously, and to the pointless killing of an anonymous stranger, which is set forth with great gravity as justification for withdrawing for the war. Such extremes of tone bespeak an ambivalence which is just as clearly evident when the title is taken to refer reflexively to the text itself. In this third reading, what fails is the attempt to construct a narrative coherent and believable and forgiving enough to permit emotional closure with the past. Clemens's irreducible uncertainty on this score surfaces in his representation of himself as younger and more naive—and therefore more readily forgiven—than he actually was in 1861. And if, as most scholars agree, the climactic killing is also a fiction, then there is a related species of moral hedging at large in Clemens's implied condemnation of war, and in its correlative justification for running away from it. It is perfectly revealing in this regard that in a later rendering of "The Private History" the killing is treated as dark comedy. Just so, Clemens once toyed with the idea of making Huck and Tom and Jim the protagonists in a broadly humorous treatment of his wartime experiences.[33] "I read your piece about the unsuccessful campaign with the greatest delight," wrote Howells. "It was immensely amusing, with such a bloody bit of heartache in it, too" (*MTHL*, 2:541).

It was not until more than a decade after the end of the war, at a safe remove in time, that Clemens began to construct his narrative of the campaign that failed. In 1877, in a dinner speech for the Ancient and Honorable Artillery Company of Massachusetts, he recalled in broadly humorous terms—and, notably, without mention of bloodshed—that this callow brigade played at soldiering for a while, and then "disbanded itself and tramped off home, with me at the tail of it" (*CTSSE*, 1:681). The success of the speech must have influenced his decision, eight years later, to cast "The Private History" in a similarly humorous mold. Clemens took this step in response to a request from Robert Underwood Johnson, who invited him to submit an account of his military experiences to the very popular Battles and Leaders of the Civil War series in *Century Magazine*. The piece was several months in the making, and seems to have provoked second thoughts about the wisdom of appearing in print alongside legitimate heroes of campaigns that actually succeeded. But Johnson was reassuring: "We shall be glad to see the Missouri sketch," he wrote, "as soon as your timidity as a tyro will admit of your sending it."[34] Months later, when the manuscript finally arrived at the *Century* office, Johnson's faith was amply rewarded. "The 'Private History' is excellent—'roarious,'"[35] he rejoiced, no doubt to its author's relief.

Clearly enough, Clemens was not at ease with what he remembered of his Civil War campaign. His moral unease gave rise to competing impulses to reveal and to conceal the damaging truth of that pivotal episode. "The Private History" expresses that division of feeling by admitting, on one side, that its author was indeed a wartime deserter, but, on the other, by offering that admission in terms that argue for the essential innocence of the deed. We are meant to laugh in sympathy at the bumbling tenderfoot, and to recoil with him in horror at the pointless carnage of war. James M. Cox shrewdly observes that until 1885 the Civil War stood out as a conspicuously neglected chapter in Clemens's published reconstruction of his personal history. He had written copiously about his boyhood, his years as a pilot on the Mississippi, his travels both east and west, and his adult experience of the Gilded Age. Indeed, the more he patched the pieces of the past together, the more the gap in the record stood out. But the war "had been not simply forgotten," Cox insists; rather it had been "evaded—and evaded from the very beginning." Samuel Langhorne Clemens adopted the name "Mark Twain" in the Nevada Territory less than two years after his arrival from the humiliating failure that lay behind him in wartime Missouri. In effect, Cox argues, "the humorous identity and personality of 'Mark Twain' was a grand evasion of the Civil War."[36]

However much it has earned the assent of generations of readers, the evasion attempted in "The Private History" failed utterly to satisfy its author. The guilt repressed in that text returned constantly, to be told and untold in various ways, and with equal futility, for the rest of Clemens's life. Signs of his unease surfaced almost immediately after his departure for the mining regions. For example, we can hardly fail to glimpse the implied self-vindication in a letter home from Carson City written in early February, 1862, in which Clemens advises his sister Pamela to foster aggressiveness in her male offspring. "Teach Sammy to fight," he counsels, "with the same care that you teach him to pray. If he don't learn it when he is a boy, he'll never learn it afterwards, and it will gain him more respect than any other accomplishment he can acquire." As if to acknowledge that he speaks from painful personal experience, Clemens prefaces his advice with the admission that when he was a boy, "Pa wouldn't allow us to fight."[37] A similarly oblique gesture surfaces in a letter to his friend, Billy Claggett, written just a few weeks later. Lamenting reports that rebel troops from Missouri have been defeated by their northern adversaries, Clemens nonetheless takes comfort from the knowledge that "they didn't do it on the Sacred Soil, my boy. They had to chase 'em clear down into Arkansas before they could whip them. There's consolation in *that*. . . . Take a Missourian on his own soil, and he is invincible. Now, when I was on the soil, I used to be as terrible as an army with banners; but out here on this quartz foundation, you see, I don't amount to a Damn. That's what's the matter with *me*."[38]

Quite characteristically, in both letters the impulses to acknowledge and to argue away the craven flight from conflict appear in tandem with one another. I failed to meet the challenge of war, Clemens concedes; but it wasn't my fault. Yet he knows that he was hardly "as terrible as" the Biblical "army with banners" before he left Missouri. While the soil of his home state was still under foot, he was inspired by it not so much to dig in as to light out. That painful self-knowledge, and its corollary—that he doesn't "amount to a Damn" in his own eyes—is "what's the matter with" him. Half-concealed anguish of the same stripe forms an undercurrent in one of Clemens's earliest articles for the Virginia City *Territorial Enterprise*. Published on October 1, 1862, the story recounts a furious Indian attack in which several members of a wagon party were killed, in good part because their friends failed to come to their aid. "Thirty bigger cowards and meaner men than those above mentioned never crossed the plains," Clemens observes, adding—with what must have been rueful irony—"we are certain that every man of them left the States for fear of being drafted into the army."[39]

But even as he condemned himself at one remove for desertion, Clemens gravitated to narratives that illustrated the futility of war and, by implication, the justice of taking all necessary steps to avoid it. Such is the upshot of "Lucretia Smith's Soldier," a story that first appeared in the *Californian* in 1864, to be reprinted three years later in *The Celebrated Jumping Frog of Calaveras County*. A young union soldier goes off to war in order to earn the respect of a girl who is so foolishly selfish that she feels sorry only for herself when the boy goes missing in action. So fixed is the narrative on the hopeless futility of the young man's mission, in love as in war, that Clemens neglects to reveal what finally became of him. "Such is life," he concludes wearily, "and the trail of the serpent is over us all" (*CTSSE*, 1:112). Stories of similar purport—emphasizing the moral confusion of war, and thereby offering oblique justification for Clemens's 1861 departure from Missouri— appear in *Merry Tales*, the volume in which "The Private History" was published in 1892. The aptly entitled "Luck" explores the character of a celebrated British military hero whose exploits in the Crimean War are not, as most people suppose, the products of his sterling personal qualities. In fact, he is "an absolute fool" who succeeds in war only because fate deals him an unbroken string of winning hands.[40] Meanwhile, in the Civil War story, "A Curious Experience," a resourceful but deceitful boy sets off a false alarm that brings the operations of a union fort to complete confusion. Grown men, we are shown, can be stirred to suspicion, fear, anger, and violent action by a groundless fiction hatched in the overheated imagination of a child. So construed, war is a tragedy arising from quixotic illusions and misapprehensions. The pronounced subversion of putative military glory in "Lucretia Smith's Story," "Luck," and "A Curious Experience" is of course reminiscent of the similarly deflationary thrust of "The Private History." In the stories, as in the more conventionally autobiographical narrative, Clemens labors to diminish the heroic luster of military endeavors that he, by his own admission, shrank from attempting.

It is testimony to Clemens's uneasiness with his Civil War record that he was unable to put its memory behind him, and that his treatment of it was invariably defensive. Over and over again, he was driven to retell the story, but never succeeded in shaping it to his own moral satisfaction, and thus setting his conscience to rest. The defensive strain is often quite unmistakable. In an autobiographical dictation of 1906, for example, he recalls that in 1845 he was overtaken by "the consuming desire" to fight in the Mexican War. "But they had no use for boys of twelve and thirteen," he adds, "and before I had a chance in another war the desire to kill people to whom I had not been introduced had passed away" (*MTA*, 2:216).[41] War, then, is for children; mature adults abandon such childish folly and adopt a wise pacifism.

On occasion, Clemens attempted to reduce the moral burden of his flight from combat by treating it as a species of humor. In "The Secret History of Eddypus," an unfinished work written in 1901–2, he visits a pair of crank phrenologists for an assessment of his "disposition and character." They find that on a scale in which 7 is highest, he scores "Combativeness 7, Destructiveness 7, Cautiousness 7, Calculation 7, Firmness 0." Thus, they conclude, "he has stupendous courage and destructiveness, and at first glance would seem to be the most daring and formidable fighter of modern times; but at second glance we perceive that these desperate qualities are kept from breaking loose by those two guardians which hold them in their iron grip day and night,—Cautiousness and Calculation" (*MTFM*, 350–51). Taking a more direct approach, Clemens recalls in the autobiography that he "resigned" from the Civil War "after two weeks' service in the field" on the grounds that he was " 'incapacitated by fatigue' through persistent retreating" (*AMT*, 102). More frequently, however, he approaches the vexed subject in earnest, with oblique pleas for the justice of his behavior. In *What Is Man?*, for example, we are instructed that "a brave man does not *create* his bravery. He is entitled to no personal credit for possessing it. It is born to him" (*WIM*, 131). Clemens follows a similarly deterministic line in a dictation of 1906, arguing that the circumstances, or "accidents," which form turning points in our lives are in fact part of a much larger scheme over which we have no control. Thus, when the outbreak of war in 1861 abruptly ended his piloting career, the time was ripe for a life-determining accident to occur. "Of course," he reports, "the accident happened. My elder bother was appointed Secretary of the new Territory of Nevada, and as I had to pay his passage across the continent I went along with him to see if I could find something to do out there on the frontier" (*MTE*, 389–90). In this version of the past, Clemens's abortive military experience is conspicuously missing. Evidently enough, and for reasons quite beyond his control, it was not meant to happen.

Their differences in directness and tone notwithstanding, all of Clemens's exercises in self-acquittal arise out of an impulse—I am tempted to call it a compulsion—to acknowledge his humiliating failure as a soldier. Cox is surely right to highlight the evasiveness on display here, yet it is no less remarkable that the retreat from the guilty past invariably commences in its reluctant recollection. Successful evasion of the kind Cox has in mind would involve the retreat into complete amnesia. For Clemens, however, conscience is tireless in stirring surges of painful recall that in turn trigger evasive countermaneuvers. The guilty episode is never set aside for good; rather, it is remembered and then evaded, over and over again. Or, to put the matter another way, the impulses to confess and to deny alternate in a repeating, reciprocal cycle. The pattern is nowhere clearer than in the two versions of "The Turning Point of My Life." Because "I came to be occupationless when the war broke out and the boats stopped running," Clemens explains in the first draft, I entered "the military service and [did] what I could to avoid danger during two fearful weeks. Then I resigned." But having told the guilty truth, he took pains to untell it. In the published version, which appeared in *Harper's Bazar* in February, 1910, he takes us directly from the Mississippi River to the mining frontier without pausing to mention the campaign that failed (*WIM*, 528).[42]

Quite clearly, then, Clemens's regret at having fled the Civil War was both profound and enduring. The guilt and shame that attached to the episode were permanent features of his emotional and expressive lives. But there is much more to this complicated story. The evidence assembled so far is comprised of mere skirmishes in a much broader struggle with conscience that had its principal focus in the figure of Ulysses S. Grant. "One of the highest satisfactions of Clemens's often supremely satisfactory life," observes Howells, "was his relation to Grant." Howells notes "the delicate deference Clemens paid our plain hero, and the manly respect with which he listened" when the celebrated leader spoke. Clemens was especially proud to have been the promoter and publisher of Grant's *Personal Memoirs*, a triumphant business venture that spared the dying general's family an ignominious plunge into poverty. It was his friend's "princely pleasure," Howells emphasizes, to present the Grant family with the largest royalty check that "had ever been paid to an author before. He valued even more than this splendid opportunity the sacred moments in which their business brought him into the presence of the slowly dying, heroically living man whom he was so befriending."[43]

For all of his perspicacity, Howells failed to recognize that Clemens's fascination with Grant, which expressed itself outwardly in admiration for the great hero's valor, was inwardly complicated by an antipathy rooted in feelings of personal failure and inadequacy. Having fled from the advancing union army in 1861, Clemens was self-condemned to a lifetime of symbolic combat with that army's most famous leader. Grant in war was all that Clemens was not; esteem for the fabled warrior was thus freighted for the deserter with secret self-contempt. As a result, the campaign that failed did so over and over again, every time Clemens tried once more in vain to redeem himself by outflanking his virtually unassailable hero.

Such is the thrust of Justin Kaplan's searching analysis of the relationship between two of the preeminent figures of their time. Emphasizing the "intensity and complexity of [Clemens's] feelings toward Grant," Kaplan highlights three "levels of relationship" between the admirer and the object of his esteem. At one level, Clemens is the errant "Rebel son" pitted against paternal Grant, who is cast as a "punishing figure of authority." At a second level, there are "the parallel and ironic relationships of anti-hero . . . to hero" ("I knew more about retreating than the man who invented retreating," Clemens jested edgily), "and humorist to victim." In the latter, humorist's role, Clemens gave a speech in 1879 at an Army of the Tennessee banquet for Grant in Chicago in which he invited the assembled dignitaries to imagine their hero, the guest of honor, as an infant "trying to find some way of getting his toe in his mouth." The humor of the image veered so precariously toward irreverence that the audience drew back into "a sort of shuddering silence" that turned to laughter only when Clemens continued: "And if the child is but a prophecy of the man, there are mighty few who will doubt that he succeeded." Kaplan quite properly highlights the aggression on display in the humorist's bold performance. In long letters home an exultant Clemens imagined himself a hero who had "vanquished Grant" with his humor. "By making this iron man laugh and cheer with all the others he had, in a sense, destroyed him," Kaplan observes. " 'I broke him up utterly!' Clemens wrote to Livy. 'The audience *saw* that for once in his life he had been knocked out of his iron serenity.' 'I knew I could lick him,' he told Howells. 'I shook him up like dynamite . . . my truths had wracked all the bones of his body apart.' " Finally, at the third level, which reverses the relationships in the first two, "the former Rebel son, now reconstructed," becomes as publisher "the strong and benevolent figure who rescues the Grant family from poverty" (*MCMT*, 226–27, 275). Subordinated and humiliated, the child rises up in anger to vanquish the father, who is in turn subordinated even as he is saved by his heroic son. In fantasy, then, the deserter changes places with the greatest hero of them all.

Thus even as he proudly pursued an "intimate friendship" with Grant, Clemens was secretly in symbolic combat with the great warrior, and gave signs, Kaplan shows, of wanting "to destroy him" (*MCMT*, 225). Further evidence on this score is not far to seek. Clemens on several occasions speculates that, had he held on a bit longer in wartime Missouri, he might have crossed paths with his hero-antagonist. In the autobiography, for example, he is pleased to report that he once "came near having the distinction of being captured by Colonel Ulysses S. Grant" (*AMT*, 102). In other versions of the same memory, he imagines himself attacking his adversary, and, alternatively, being killed by him. Clemens also worked briefly on a novel in which Tom Sawyer, Huck Finn, and the slave Jim encounter Grant while pursuing the Missouri campaign that the writer himself thought better of in 1861 (*MCMT*, 275). The ambivalent swing between respect and aggressiveness is elsewhere equally in evidence. At a celebration of Lincoln's birthday at Carnegie Hall in 1901, Clemens jested that as a rebel soldier it was his "intention to drive Gen. Grant into the Pacific Ocean."[44] A few years later, he was pleased to discover that his autograph letters were commanding higher prices at auction than the former president's.[45] Clemens once compared his chambermaid to Grant;[46] on another it was Mary Baker Eddy, whom he loathed, that brought the great general to mind (*WIM*, 347). In the first draft of "The Turning Point of My Life," Grant's military prowess is traced back to origins in temperament and circumstance. "Given the circumstances of the battle of the Wilderness," Clemens observes, "General Grant's temperament required him to say 'I will fight it out on this line if it takes all summer.'" Grant had no choice in the matter of his heroism, we are assured; his temperament "made him *do* that desperate work." But, as Clemens is quick to point out, such logic cuts both ways. "My temperament would not have required me to say it, and sixteen temperaments like mine couldn't have made me *do* it. They would have made me go away and get behind something" (*WIM*, 526).[47] It is the nice economy of this deterministic approach to valor that its possession is no more the occasion for praise than its want is the occasion for blame.

A more fully developed illustration of Clemens's desperate attempt to absolve himself by achieving a kind of moral parity with Grant appears in the fragmentary "Which Was the Dream?", which he planned in 1895, and composed two years later, on the anniversary of Susy's death. A young, successful Senator lives with his wife and children in a mansion in Washington, D.C. His heroic military exploits, subsequent political success, and disastrous financial dealings are all reminiscent of Grant, while the details of his courtship, married life, children, love of wealth and display, fragile self-esteem, and decline into bankruptcy are clearly modeled on Clemens himself. The great union general's presence is also felt in the brief appearance of "a young man named Grant"—a graduate of West Point and a veteran of the Mexican War—who takes over and saves lives at a moment of crisis (*WWD*, 51). It is of course a good question what prompted Clemens to so completely merge his own life story with Grant's. The fantasy of rising to fame and glory as a military hero—and, indeed, as *the* military hero whose example so dwarfed and humiliated him in real life—must have been a salve to his wounded ego. Just so, the clear parallel between Grant's catastrophic business failures and his own contained a seed of consolation for Clemens. After all, the great military hero was absolved of his financial sins—all agree in "Which Was the Dream?" that "even the best soldier could botch a trade which he was not fitted for" (*WWD*, 73)—while Clemens never forgave himself for the hardship and humiliation that bankruptcy brought down on his family. Living the bad dream of Grant's life, which in reality he had helped to ameliorate, was for Clemens evidently preferable to enduring the nightmare of his own, which he was powerless to remedy.

If you can't beat them, the saying goes, then join them. But when it came to Grant, Clemens could do neither. For obvious reasons, beating Grant was out of the question, except in fantasy or jest. Joining him, though clearly an attractive alternative, was almost equally out of reach. True, they had catastrophic business failures in common; indeed, bankruptcy is the shared experience that most closely binds their identities in "Which Was the Dream?" But their lives diverged decisively in 1861, and Clemens was never able to bridge the chasm that opened between them when he took flight from the war in which Grant went on to triumph. All of the evidence tends to confirm that Clemens craved the moral acquittal that closing ranks with Grant symbolized; but the same evidence—including his inability to bring "Which Was the Dream?" to completion and the light of day—confirms that satisfaction on that score eluded him. As Kaplan shows, Clemens was so taken with the fantasy of having faced the great union general in battle that he at one time considered the title "My Campaign against Grant" for the autobiographical essay that became "The Private History of a Campaign That Failed." The saving fiction of actual combat with his heroic adversary had obvious appeal, but it placed too great a strain on credulity. As a more plausible, if rather less heroic, alternative, Clemens supplemented "The Private History" with the fictional account of his participation in the killing of a stranger who is mistaken for the enemy. Horrified by what he has done— "I was a murderer . . . I had killed a man—a man who had never done me any harm"—he decides "to retire from this avocation of sham soldiership while I could save some remnant of my self-respect."[48]

But in truth there was no such fatal encounter, no moment of moral revulsion and pacifist resolve, just as there was no meeting on the battlefield with Ulysses S. Grant. Though Clemens certainly had his reasons for abandoning the war effort in 1861, he was never able to settle on a version of the episode that set his uneasiness to rest. Grant at once attracted and eluded Clemens because he succeeded brilliantly where his admirer utterly failed. Even as he attempts in "Which Was the Dream?" to merge his own life story with the greater glory of Grant's, Clemens is brought back again and again to prominent flaws in his own nature: dissimulation ("Secrecy," he confesses, "is the natural refuge of people who are doubtful about their conduct"); vain love of material display ("I was a kind of beggar on horseback, and had no sense of financial proportion, no just notion of values, and—but you know the kind of man I was"); and irrational cruelty ("I could not help it, for deep down in the very web and woof of my nature I was ignoble and ungenerous") (*WWD*, 54, 60, 56). Indeed, the victorious union leader was not merely his hero-adversary in war, he was also a kind of beau ideal of male virtue. Though Clemens wrote copiously about the general's wartime exploits, he was equally drawn to Grant as a moral paragon, a man who is esteemed, it is clearly implied, because he possesses in abundance an array of human qualities that the writer finds wanting in his own makeup. Clemens's admiration for Grant, we are again reminded, is the reflex of diminished self-regard.

To be sure, Clemens is attentive to Grant's distinction as a warrior, and most especially to the great man's stoicism: he is a "statue of iron" in the midst of weaker mortals, able to endure extraordinary suffering without giving any outward sign (*MTHL*, 1:289, 2:571). "Grant," he insists, "was no namby-pamby fool, he was a *man*—all over—rounded and complete" (*MTL*, 2:460). But Clemens refers much more frequently to Grant's selfless and unfailing generosity. The general, he observes in an 1885 dictation, is always "ready and also determined to do a great deal more for you than you could possibly have the effrontery to ask him to do" (*MTA*, 1:24–25).[49] Grant is a man of complete integrity (*MTA*, 1:21, 40); he is a man of his word (*MTA*, 1:25, 49); he is humble, gentle, trusting, indifferent to material possessions, and a writer of "thoroughly trustworthy" books! (*MTA*, 1:26, 29, 44, 45, 48)[50] Clemens's reverence for his hero is nowhere more evident than in a letter to Henry Ward Beecher, written not long after Grant's death in 1885. Among the leading "points of Gen. Grant's character," he emphasizes "his patience; his indestructible equability of temper; his exceeding gentleness, kindness, forbearance, lovingness, charity; his *loyalty*: to friends, to convictions, to promises . . . his aggravatingly trustful nature; his genuineness, simplicity, modesty, diffidence, self-depreciation, poverty in the quality of vanity . . . his toughness as a bargainer when doing business for other people or for his country . . . and his trusting, easy, unexacting fashion when doing business for himself . . . and his fortitude!" (*MTL*, 2:460–61).

In the midst of such comprehensive virtue, it is his hero's essential simplicity that Clemens comes back to most often. This is the bedrock of Grant's character, the foundation for his honesty and sincerity and directness of manner. Grant is "the most simple-hearted of all men" (*MTA*, 1:38), we are assured. His truthfulness, even when the truth is hard, expresses itself "with a frankness and a child-like naivety, indeed, which is enchanting—and stupefying" (*MTL*, 2:459).

Clemens is at once enchanted and stupefied because in the very act of celebrating Grant's triumph as a man and warrior he feels the sting of an inward self-accusation. It may come as something of a surprise to learn that he brought virtually identical feelings to Joan of Arc, another legendary warrior, whose character, like Grant's, was, in Clemens's estimation, grounded in an all-informing simplicity. Both figures are moral paragons whose child-like innocence has a key corollary in extraordinary military prowess. The link between virtue and valor in their characters contrasts sharply, of course, with the conspicuous lack of those same qualities in their admirer's self-reckoning—a lack most shamefully on display in his craven retreat from the Civil War. Clemens was drawn to Joan of Arc, as he was to Grant, both because of what he esteemed in her and what, correspondingly, he could not abide in himself.

Joan was hardly the first female to figure prominently in the sinful life of Samuel Clemens. Livy Langdon Clemens was preeminent in the part, though she had important precursors in her husband's mother, Jane Clemens, and in Mary Mason ("Mother") Fairbanks, who took charge of the irreverent correspondent when they met on the *Quaker City* in 1867. But Joan's closest real-life counterpart was undoubtedly Susy Clemens, the beloved daughter who died in 1896, and who served as the model for the Maid of Orleans as her father labored over the *Personal Recollections of Joan of Arc* in the early 1890s. In the writer's eyes, Susy was sublimely pure. Her sexual innocence and intellectual precocity combined to make her a "wise child" possessed of extraordinary moral authority over her doting and self-doubting parent. Susy "knew her father was a great man," observes Justin Kaplan, "but she was not at all sure a humorist was any better than a clown, and she wanted him to be a great man in some other way, while he in turn had a guilty sense that he had failed her just by being Mark Twain."[51] Susy was critical of Clemens's impatience, his temper, and his rough language. She regarded *Huckleberry Finn* as a coarse book, and much preferred *The Prince and the Pauper* and *Joan of Arc*. Improbable as it may seem, Clemens acquiesced in his daughter's right-minded view. "I like the *Joan of Arc* best of all my books," he wrote in 1908, "& it *is* the best" (*MTB*, 3:1034).

James M. Cox rightly emphasizes that Joan is the "embodiment of all the utterly conventional, utterly somber, utterly reverent attitudes and language upon which Mark Twain's humor had played through all the years of his career." What Cox cannot quite fathom, however, is how the great humorist could have capitulated so completely to the camp of the enemy. "The whole performance is so dismal," he complains, "as to make one wish it were a parody, yet clearly it is no parody. Mark Twain is obviously serious—so serious that he cannot be Mark Twain." The humorist's "identity was threatened," Cox continues, "in direct proportion to the autonomy [Joan of Arc] preempted."[52] Just though it may seem, this view of the matter arises out of a decidedly narrow conception of both the writer and the object of his esteem. If we look past the sentimental in *Joan of Arc*, and focus instead on the maiden warrior comparable in stature to Ulysses S. Grant, and if we expand our conception of the humorist's "identity" to include the side of him that looked back with enduring regret on his failure of valor in 1861, then we are well placed to appreciate the solemnity of Clemens's fascination with Joan. In his reverence for her, as in his reverence for Grant, he paid homage to an ideal of valor that had utterly eluded him in his own campaign that failed.

In his Introduction to *The Oxford Mark Twain* edition of *Personal Recollections of Joan of Arc*, Justin Kaplan touches briefly on some of the elements that linked Joan and Grant in Clemens's imagination. "Like Joan, Grant came from humble and obscure origins, had been elected by history and the Holy Spirit, and was endowed with charisma, military genius, the gift of command, a natural eloquence, and an equally natural reserve that made him seem expressionless, an iron visage of determination and authority"

(*JA*, xli). Had he chosen to, Kaplan might have elaborated much more fully on the close kinship between the two figures, for when it is carefully studied, Clemens's treatment of the maiden warrior appears to have been modeled in detail upon his portrait of the union general. Consider, for example, the overview of her character with which *Personal Recollections of Joan of Arc* commences. It is an admiring portrait closely reminiscent in tone and detail of the tribute to Grant in Clemens's letter to Henry Ward Beecher. Joan of Arc, we read,

> was truthful when lying was the common speech of men; she was honest when honesty was become a lost virtue; she was a keeper of promises when the keeping of a promise was expected of no one; . . . she was steadfast when stability was unknown, and honorable in an age which had forgotten what honor was; she was a rock of convictions in a time when men believed in nothing and scoffed at all things; she was unfailingly true in an age that was false to the core; . . . she was of dauntless courage when hope and courage had perished in the hearts of her nation; she was spotlessly pure in mind and body when society in the highest places was foul in both. . . . She was perhaps the only entirely unselfish person whose name has a place in profane history. No vestige or suggestion of self-seeking can be found in any word or deed of hers. (*JA* vii–viii)

Above all else, Joan compares with Grant in the essential, child-like simplicity of her character. She is young, virginal, unblemished; she is "that wonderful child, that sublime personality, that spirit which in one regard has had no peer and will have none—this: its purity from all alloy of self-seeking, self-interest, personal ambition" (*JA*, 461). In her we are witness to "the most noble life that was ever born into this world save only One" (*JA*, 2).

So numerous and close are the similarities between the paired portraits that, to an informed eye, *Personal Recollections* has the quality of a palimpsest in which Grant's life is everywhere discernible beneath Joan's. Like Grant, Joan is a natural military genius. "*I* think these vast powers and capacities were born in her," observes Sieur Louis de Conte, Joan's friend and the narrator of her life, who goes on to add that "she applied them by an intuition which could not err" (*JA*, 235).[53] Grant was famous for his decisiveness in battle, and for the relentlessness of his attack. "He has the *grit* of a bulldog," said an admiring Lincoln. "Once let him get his 'teeth' *in*, and nothing can shake him off."[54] Joan is equally disinclined to adopt a strategy of "sitting down and starving out." With her, to the contrary, "it is storm! storm! storm! and still storm! storm! storm! and forever storm! storm! storm!

hunt the enemy to his hole, then turn her French hurricanes loose and carry him by storm!" (*JA*, 230) Both, it goes without saying, are utterly fearless soldiers; both display great confidence in command; and yet both are generous with their enemies and share a deep hatred for war (*JA*, 37, 59, 233, 284).[55] Like Grant, Joan is taciturn ("she was reserved, and kept things to herself, as the truly great always do") and retreats from public acclaim ("it was not in her delicate nature to like being conspicuous"). Like him again, she is indifferent to rank and possesses a natural aptitude for statesmanship (*JA*, 103, 128, 217–18, 244).[56] Both, finally, are celebrated national symbols: "Joan," we read, "was France, the spirit of France made flesh," while Grant, according to Theodore Lyman, is "the concentration of all that is American" (*JA*, 174).[57]

The maiden and the general are so nearly identical in their perfection as to appear not so much distinct personalities as projections of the same ideal. Both, that is, have their origin in the moral imagination of a man who revered virtuous warriors in the same degree that he despised himself for having failed to rise to their high standard. Clemens the deserter is always present by implication in the glowing portraits of his paired heroes. Their valor is the reflex of his felt cowardice, their virtue of his felt degradation. How else explain the virtually perfect pattern of opposition between the expansive, volatile, capricious, attention-seeking, self-indulgent, avaricious hoaxer, humorist and fainthearted noncombatant, on one side, and the resolute, self-abnegating, warlike paragons on the other? In their triumph we can begin to measure the depth of his inward self-doubt.

In his shrewd and very helpful book, *Acting Naturally: Mark Twain and the Culture of Performance*, Randall Knoper opens another avenue of approach to Clemens's oblique self-assessment in *Joan of Arc*. Framing his discussion in "a late-nineteenth-century moment that looked more and more pessimistically on the possibilities of realistic representation," Knoper argues that *Joan of Arc* "strives to resecure reliable representation, and plentitude and purity in the expressive sign, in a way crucial for the novel's author." Toward this end, the book undertakes what he describes as "a series of obscurings and melodramatic unveilings of the clarity and purity of Joan's meaning and identity."[58] If Joan's transparency seems to point the way toward a resolution of the crisis, then her friend Paladin, a vain, boasting liar, is one of its leading symptoms. Because he is blessed with "the narrative gift—that great and rare endowment," Paladin always draws an enthusiastic crowd when he launches into one of his vastly inflated stories (*JA*, 116). As James Cox has observed, at such moments he is a figure for "the liar Mark Twain who must exaggerate all experience into a tall tale."[59] Cox's observation is the more apt for the fact that Paladin is a coward whose stories are invariably accounts of his entirely fabricated military exploits. Though his audiences are not deceived, they enjoy the performance both because of the "interest which attaches to lying," and because of the speaker's apparent sincerity. "Nobody believed his narrative," we are assured, "but all believed that he believed it" (*JA*, 119).

Paladin is forgiven his lies, and by implication his lack of courage, because of his apparent sincerity. But of course, as any close observer of Tom Sawyer, or the King and the Duke, will agree, Clemens was well aware that the winning appearance of sincerity was itself readily simulated. Indeed, we may suppose that if Clemens actually believed in Paladin's sincerity, then his belief was mingled with traces of envy. For by contrast with his fictional counterpart, Clemens did not believe in his own accounts of his wartime failure of nerve. Despite its apparent sincerity, "The Private History of a Campaign That Failed" is a lie artfully designed to win amused and sympathetic assent. And the ruse seems to have worked—except with the artist himself, who knew too well that his innocence and sincerity were part of a performance. Clemens was his own best laboratory when it came to the contemporary crisis of representation. By profession, and by inward inclination, he was, he must have recognized, part of the problem. He made his living, just as he construed his identity, by manipulating appearances for an audience willing and even anxious to be deceived. But he was "on" to the game, and so enjoyed few of the consolations reserved for true believers.

Joan's virtuous transparency is variously manifest, not least of all in her use of language—her style. "Joan's talk was fresh and free, sincere and honest, and unmarred by timorous self-watching and constraint. She said the very thing that was in her mind, and said it in a plain, straightforward way." Joan is "perfectly frank and childlike" in her responses; there is nothing of design or self-consciousness in her speech. "How simple it is, and how beautiful," observes Sieur Louis. "And how it beggars the studied eloquence of the masters of oratory. Eloquence was a native gift of Joan of Arc; it came from her lips without effort and without preparation" (*JA*, 123, 382). Grant was for Clemens equally pure and natural in style. "This was the simple soldier," he proclaims, "who, all untaught of the silken phrasemakers, linked words together with an art surpassing the art of the schools," and whose *Memoirs*, as the result, are "thoroughly trustworthy."[60]

By direct and arguably intentional contrast, the style of the fainthearted warrior, Paladin, is decidedly theatrical. In the presentation of his inflated tales he is careful to incorporate "his enlargements without flourish, without emphasis, and so casually that often one failed to notice that a change had been made." Indeed, "he did not seem to know that he was making these extraordinary changes; they dropped from his lips in a quite natural and effortless way" (*JA*, 119). Paladin, it seems clear, is also "on" to the game. His fully self-conscious technique is reminiscent of Clemens's own, as it is set forth in "How to Tell a Story." The successful storyteller, the humorist insists, must "conceal the fact that he even dimly suspects that there is anything funny about" what he has to say. He achieves this goal by so perfectly simulating "simplicity and innocence and sincerity and unconsciousness" as to dispel all suspicion of his genuineness (*CTSSE*, 2:201, 203). But of course it is precisely this pose of guileless innocence that Clemens adopts in "The Private History of a Campaign That Failed," where humor gives way to a catastrophe that is as carefully fabricated as it is all-forgiving of his subsequent retreat from conflict. In the figure of Paladin, then, Clemens discovers his shame, obliquely acknowledging that even as he revered Joan of Arc and General Grant for the fidelity that graced their valor, he numbered himself among those showmen whose simulated transparency had a key correlative in a wartime failure of nerve.

Consider, finally, the episode toward the beginning of *Personal Recollections* in which Joan of Arc faces down a murderous madman while her neighbors flee in terror. When the grateful villagers return and commence "hugging and kissing" their savior, Joan is forced "to tear herself away and go and hide, this glory was so trying to her diffidence." When asked, "Didn't you feel afraid?" she replies, "No—at least not much—very little," though she is unable to explain why. Meanwhile, it is clear to everyone that Joan has been "entirely forgetful of herself and her own danger, and had thought and wrought for the preservation of other people alone." But it is equally clear, observes Sieur Louis de Conte, who speaks for his neighbors, "what a poor figure we had cut in that adventure as contrasted with Joan's performance." Accepting that truth, Sieur Louis admits, is not easy. "I tried to think up some good way of explaining why I had run away and left a little girl at the mercy of a maniac armed with an axe." Others do the same. For example, "Noel Rainguesson fidgeted a while, then broke out with a remark which showed what his mind had been running on: 'The fact is, I was taken by surprise. That is the reason. . . . Pooh! the idea of being afraid of that poor thing! I only wish he would come along now—I'd show you!'" Noel's rationalizations succeed quite well, as do those of his friends, with the result that "they all got back their self-respect; yes, and even added somewhat to it; indeed, when the sitting broke up they had a finer opinion of themselves than they had ever had before." All, that is, save Sieur Louis, who concedes wearily: "all of the explanations that offered themselves to me seemed so cheap and shabby that I gave the matter up and remained still" (*JA*, 36–38).

In his veneration for Joan's selflessness and unhesitating courage; in the radical diminishment he endures when he contrasts her qualities and behavior with his own; in his reflex retreat into rationalization; in the almost envious admission that he is not one of the many whose self-esteem is buoyed up by excuses and braggadocio; and in his secret resignation to his own shameful inadequacy—in all of these linked perspectives, Sieur Louis gives voice to sentiments that Clemens experienced inwardly but could hardly address in an open and systematic way. Here the competing impulses to tell and to untell the same shameful story achieve a kind of equipoise. This is a revelation so guarded and oblique—which is to say, so apparently fictional—that it escaped the vigilant author-cat's notice and found its way, the only way it could, into print.

3   *My List of Permanencies*

"Unconsciously we all have a standard by which we measure other men," Clemens declared in a 1909 autobiographical dictation. "We admire them, we envy them, for great qualities which we ourselves lack. Hero worship consists in just that. Our heroes are men who do the things which we recognize, with regret, and sometimes with a secret shame, that we cannot do. We find not much in ourselves to admire, we are always privately wanting to be like somebody else. If everybody was satisfied with himself, there would be no heroes."[1]

What a perfectly apt—and poignant—commentary on Clemens's overflowing esteem for Grant that it was the precise measure of his own "regret" and "secret shame" at finding so little in himself "to admire." Closely geared as it was to his self-contempt, Clemens's hero-worship was driven by conflicting urges to acknowledge and to evade what he could not morally abide in his memories of 1861. As I have shown, "The Private History of a Campaign That Failed" and *Personal Recollections of Joan of Arc* cannot be properly understood unless this undercurrent of unresolved guilt is drawn fully into focus. "My private and concealed opinion of myself is not of a complimentary sort," Clemens reiterated yet once more in a late-life dictation (*AMT,* 133); his veneration of the general and the maid were the reflex of that harsh and enduring self-estimate.

A kindred dynamic is manifest in Clemens's protracted attempt to resolve his powerfully conflicted feelings about the infamous 1877 birthday dinner for John Greenleaf Whittier. Hosted by the *Atlantic Monthly* at a fashionable Boston hotel, and attended by several dozen of the literary elite, the evening's festivities included what promised to be a characteristically entertaining speech by America's favorite young humorist. What the audience got instead was a rather crude burlesque of Emerson, Holmes, and Longfellow, all in attendance, cast by Clemens as bibulous ruffians who impose themselves on the generosity of a friendly miner. Though reaction to the speech was generally rather favorable—none of subjects of the burlesque seems to have taken permanent offense—Clemens was at once baffled and mortified at what he had wrought, and promptly delivered a profuse apology to his august victims in which he accepted blame for his trespass and yet insisted that it was unpremeditated and therefore essentially innocent. His apology, as Henry Nash Smith has observed, testifies to a "divorce between [the humorist's] conscious and unconscious motives." On one side, Clemens "was not consciously prepared to repudiate the conception of literature represented by Emerson and Longfellow and Holmes"; on the other, "he had a half-suppressed awareness that the role assigned to them by the official culture was false and sterile." When traces of that antagonism surfaced in his burlesque, Clemens became "obscurely aware of his own guilt" (just as he had at the time of Henry's death) and fell prey yet once more to painful, unremitting, and apparently arbitrary assaults of conscience.[2] As he wrote to Howells a few days after the dinner, "My sense of disgrace does not abate. It grows. I see that it is going to add itself to my list of permanencies—a list of humiliations that extends back to when I was seven years old, & which keep on persecuting me regardless of my repentancies" (*MTHL*, 1:212).

Clemens's perennial craving for an end to guilt was accompanied by the virtual certainty that there would be no relief from his "list of permanencies." "The whole matter" of the Whittier debacle "is a dreadful subject," he concluded with Howells; "let me drop it here—at least on paper" (*MTHL*, 1:212).[3] But the time soon came, Howells recalled, "and not so very long afterward, when some mention was made of the incident as a mistake, and he said, with all his fierceness, 'But I don't admit that it *was* a mistake.'"[4] On February 5, 1878, Clemens wrote to his friend Mary Fairbanks that while the speech was undoubtedly "in ill taste," it was "a good one," nonetheless.[5] Clearly, the imagined offense continued to weigh heavily on his mind. It was probably a factor in his decision to remove his family to Europe just a few months later; and it played darkly across his feelings about a breakfast for Holmes that he attended in 1879 (*MTHL*, 1:171, 282–84). On learning of Longfellow's death in 1882, Clemens confessed to Howells that the news brought back memories of the Whittier dinner, "and made me feel," he wrote abjectly, "like an unforgiven criminal" (*MTHL*, 1:398).

Doubtless the event was with him at numerous other intervals during the remaining years of his life, most notably perhaps in January 1906, when he received a request from Laura K. Hudson for a detailed account of the Whittier dinner speech, which she had read about in the newspaper nearly 30 years earlier, and remembered as "the best and funniest thing our great favorite had ever written." Evidently gratified, Clemens nonetheless concedes in his reply that "during the first year or two after it happened, I could not bear to think of it. My pain and shame were so intense, and my sense of having been a fool so settled, established and confirmed, that I drove the episode entirely from my mind." The evasive strategy seems to have failed, however, for he goes on to admit that during "all these twenty-eight or twenty-nine years I have lived in the conviction that my performance of that time was coarse, vulgar, and wholly destitute of humor."[6]

Clemens responded to his admirer's inquiry not to confess, however, but rather to exult in his release from the burden of memory. Indeed, his feelings on the matter ran so high that he devoted an entire autobiographical dictation to its rehearsal. Acknowledging a debt of gratitude to Hudson, he reports that a rereading of the burlesque has left him feeling lighter than air. "If there is any vulgarity about it," he confides, "I am not able to discover it. If it isn't innocently and ridiculously funny, I am no judge. I will see to it that you get a copy." The transcription of the letter to Hudson is followed in the dictation by a transcription of the speech itself. In the immediate sequel, Clemens recalls discussing the episode at length with Mr. and Mrs. A. P. Chamberlaine of Concord, Massachusetts, a friendly couple he and Livy met in Italy in 1888, who stoutly defended the propriety of his performance. This is a reminder, of course, that his guilty suffering persisted, and evidence as well of its great weight. For although "the Chamberlaines comforted me," Clemens reflects, "they did not persuade me to continue to think about that unhappy episode. I resisted that. I tried to get it out of my mind, and let it die, and I succeeded."[7]

But now, prompted by the heartening letter from Hudson, Clemens is emboldened to run the tape of the Whittier dinner all over again. And with perfectly predictable results, for the nightmare of the evening's events comes back in full force. "I shall never be as dead again as I was then," he recalls; "I shall never be as miserable again as I was then." Howells's heavy judgment—"that there was no help for this calamity, this shipwreck, this cataclysm; that this was the most disastrous thing that had ever happened in anybody's history"—scorches his memory. True, having descended once more to the slough of despond, Clemens is buoyed up by the thought that, upon review, his speech is in fact "just as good as good can be. It is smart; it is saturated with humor. There isn't a suggestion of coarseness or vulgarity in it anywhere." This said, however, he slips back into uncertainty, and therefore vows to resolve once and for all the vexed question "whether it was Boston or whether it was myself that was in fault" at that dinner in 1877.[8]

The "test" he settles on—to read the speech before the members of a sophisticated men's club—is conceived in a tone of seriousness and optimism, but his expressed sense of their likely response is rather more sober. "If they do not laugh and admire I shall commit suicide there," he concludes. "I would just as soon do it there as any place; and one time is as good as another to me."[9] But Clemens shrank from applying the test in earnest. In a dictation conducted less than two weeks later, on January 23, he admits that he has abandoned the idea of a public rerun. Having gone over the speech "a couple of times," he now finds it "gross, coarse. . . . I didn't like any part of it, from the beginning to the end"—whereupon his attention turns from the speech itself to the abrupt shift in his assessment of it. "How do I account for this change of view?" he asks. "I don't know. I can't account for it. . . . I am merely moved by instinct. My instinct said, formerly, that it was an innocent speech, and funny. The same instinct, sitting cold and judicial, as a court of last resort, has reversed the verdict. I expect this latest verdict to remain."[10] Quite predictably, his confident conclusion was entirely premature. Four months later, in a handwritten note, he added: "It did remain—until day before yesterday; then I gave it a final & vigorous reading—*aloud*—& dropped straight back to my former admiration of it."[11] This version of things is confirmed by an entry in the Daily Reminder book of Clemens's secretary, Isabel Lyon, dated May 22, 1906: "Mr. Clemens is sitting downstairs in the hall revising the auto-ms. and chuckling with delight over the account of the speech he made 20 years ago at the Whittier dinner. 'Oh, it will do to go into print before I die.'—and the couch shakes with him and his laughter and he calls out that he must begin at once to read it aloud to me."[12]

We can no more doubt the sincerity than we can the impermanence of Clemens's pleasure in his speech. Despite his desperate efforts over three decades to banish the memory of the Whittier dinner from consciousness, the event had a resistless life of its own and would not be gainsaid. The numerous and dramatic affective shifts in 1906 alone are dramatic testimony to the persistence of the unresolved ambivalence that shaped the speech right from the start. Thus even as we find him relishing the old joke as he prepares the autobiographical dictation for print in the *North American Review*, we are reminded that his editorial exertions would include the excision of the paragraph featuring his decision to "test" the speech in public, and to commit suicide if it failed to provoke great laughter.[13] Quite evidently, he glimpsed the dark drift of his earlier reflections, and decided to go public on a more positive note. But he may have noticed, as we do, that he was engaged in telling and untelling of a perfectly familiar species, and that his optimism notwithstanding, the guilty memory of the Whittier dinner was not yet finished with him.

Though guilt was a fixed feature of Clemens's interior life, his suffering became more chronic and more intense as he grew older. With the passage of time, there were more errors and misdeeds and tragedies to regret, and a concomitant deepening of his sense of himself as hopelessly flawed. "If I were going to construct a God," he confided to his notebook in 1896, "I would furnish him with some ways & qualities & characteristics which the present One lacks." For such an ideal deity, he insists, "repentance in a man's heart for a wrong done would cancel & annul that sin." Indeed, God would go further still and "recognize in Himself the Author & Inventor of Sin . . . & would place the whole responsibility where it would of right belong: upon Himself, the only Sinner."[14] There was so little of the *Agnus Dei* in Clemens's Christianity, and so much of the wrathful Jehovah, that repentance led for him not to absolution and newness of life, but to a redoubled burden of guilt. When personal and financial calamities engulfed him in the mid-1890s, that burden became nearly intolerable, as the writing for the period makes clear.

By contrast, because he was young and independent when he wrote it, and because it reports on a journey to faraway places, remote from the scenes and associations of a troubled childhood, Clemens's first travel book, *The Innocents Abroad*, is about as buoyant as anything he ever published. It was only later, when he opened himself in his writing to experiences closer to home, that the deeper shadows began to gather. This is not to suggest that *The Innocents Abroad* is a testament to unmingled serenity. On the contrary, the consciousness presiding over the European travel narrative is irremediably at odds with itself, moving rapidly between polarized perspectives and struggling quite in vain to arrive at a stable point of vantage on experience. "In the glare of day, there is little poetry about Venice," the narrator observes, "but under the charitable moon her stained palaces are white again . . . and the old city seems crowned once more with the grandeur that was hers five hundred years ago" (*IA*, 221). Naples up close is a broadside of "disagreeable sights and smells"; but to survey it "in the early dawn from far up on the side of Vesuvius, is to see a picture of wonderful beauty" (*IA*, 315–16). The departure by rail from Milan commences with views of the grand cathedral behind, and "vast, dreamy, blueish snow-clad mountains twenty miles" ahead. While remote vistas are sublime, however, the scenery closer to hand includes "a monster-headed dwarf and a moustached woman." The narrator's eye recoils as if by reflex from the spectacle of human deformity, and settles on a remote, romantic "range of wild, picturesque hills . . . and ruinous castles perched away up toward the drifting clouds." But almost immediately the tourists fall into the hands of the Italian police, who force them into a dark, airless fumigation chamber. This sudden, jarring shift precipitates a furious execration of "these fumigating, maccaroni-stuffing organ grinders"—an outburst followed, just as abruptly, by an account of a twilight stroll along the placid shores of Lake Como. Such careening between opposed mental states persists until bedtime, when the onset of sleep brings relief—but only temporarily, for the turbulence and inconstancy of waking consciousness has its nocturnal double. "Then a melting away of familiar faces, of cities and of tossing waves, into a great calm of forgetfulness and peace. After which, the nightmare" (*IA*, 199–201).

Quite evidently, the leading characteristic of the mind presiding over these passages, and over many others throughout *The Innocents Abroad*, is its utter instability.[15] Changes in point of view and tone are frequent and extreme, and they occur without warning. Consciousness does not move, it pitches and plummets; it is frantic, exhausting, and there is no good reason to anticipate relief. Quite as notably, however, in the midst of such pervasive instability, Clemens's moral equilibrium holds firm. His feelings about people and places shift constantly, depending on such variables as setting and proximity in time and space, but his inward self-assurance is rarely shaken. Though he is witness to endless imperfections, they are for the most part all "out there" in the various and changeable world through which he passes. True, memory at least once betrays him. The Milan Duomo contains the sculptured figure of a man without skin, "a hideous thing" whose "corded arms" and "dead eyes" remind Clemens of the night during his boyhood when, in guilty flight from parental wrath, he hid in his father's law office, only to find himself at close quarters with a corpse. "That man had been stabbed near the office that afternoon," he recalls, "and they carried him in there to doctor him, but he only lived an hour. I have slept in the same room with him often, since then—in my dreams" (*IA*, 175–77).

But this is an isolated shudder in a consciousness otherwise remarkable for the steadiness of its moral equilibrium in the midst of a veritable storm of mental movement. Clemens's confidence in his New World innocence contrasts sharply with his rapidly shifting perspectives on the mingled grandeur and decadence of the Old World through which he travels. Disenchantment with fabled biblical sights prompts him to reflect that "the magic of the moonlight is a vanity and a fraud"; and the acknowledged sublimity of the Sphinx does not blind him to the profound pathos of ancient history (*IA*, 524, 629). The strained push-pull of his ambivalence about Europe and the Holy Land produces a mental fatigue manifest in his increasing impatience with the long journey. The vexed awareness, not of himself, but of the baffling not-self, grows so wearisome as to produce a recurrent longing for surrender to deep and dreamless sleep. This craving for oblivion—"nothing less," in the words of Roger Salomon, "than severance of the direct relationship between the mind and the world"[16]—would persist with Clemens, though in his later writing it was a longing for relief not so much from the world as from himself that moved him. "The grand pilgrimage is over," he declares at the end of *The Innocents Abroad*. "Good-bye to it, and a pleasant memory to it, I am able to say in all kindness. . . . Things I did not like at all yesterday I like very well to-day, now that I am at home" (*IA*, 647). This assessment is a just one, amply borne out by the long narrative that precedes it. Precisely because critical self-scrutiny has so little place in them, his memories of the journey, even the most unpleasant of them, are readily transformed by the passage of time into sources of pleasure.

The same cannot be said of the memories recorded in *Roughing It*. In 1905, when he was almost seventy, Clemens was invited to attend a pioneer's reunion in Reno, Nevada. "If I were a few years younger," he wrote, "I would accept it, and promptly. I would go. . . . I would renew my youth; and talk—and talk—and talk—and have the time of my life! . . . Those were the days!—those old ones. . . . They were so full to the brim with the wine of life; there have been no others like them" (*MTL*, 2:773). *Roughing It* is of course our most detailed record of those good old days; and while it is certainly an exuberant and often hilarious autobiographical narrative, there is much about it that does not accord with the humorist's smiling recollections of 1905. *Roughing It* is a darker personal narrative than *The Innocents Abroad*, both because of the personal challenges that Clemens faced at the time of the book's composition, and because his experiences in the Far West often undermined the moral equilibrium that had held so firm in *The Innocents Abroad*.

With his marriage to Olivia Langdon in February 1870, Clemens traded a footloose bachelorhood for the emotional and financial responsibilities that went with the life of a prosperous journalist and family man. Because his love for his bride and for money were equally boundless, his new life afforded him much genuine satisfaction; at the same time, however, domesticity and making good were perilous ground for a man of volatile temperament, impatient of schedules and details, and strongly inclined to blame himself for the suffering of those closest to him.

Nor were the moral liabilities of his new estate slow to manifest themselves. At about the time of the wedding, Jervis Langdon, Livy's wealthy and generous father, began to show the symptoms of stomach cancer. Jervis died in August, just as Clemens was getting started on his new, western travel book, which he hoped to finish by the end of the year. But circumstances conspired to frustrate his plans. As Justin Kaplan has shown, the wrenching death in the family, which left Clemens suffering unforgettable guilt over his imagined failings as a son-in-law, was but the first of several domestic crises that obstructed the timely completion of *Roughing It*.[17] Overcome with grief and fatigue, Livy, who was well along in her first pregnancy, suffered a nervous collapse. Her care placed heavy demands on her husband's time and emotional reserves. Nor was it an unmixed blessing that Jervis' grieving widow came to help out. Another visitor, Livy's girlhood friend, Emma Nye, also arrived to lend support, but promptly came down with typhoid fever, and after a month of decline, died in her hosts' bed at the end of September. Following a near-miscarriage in October, Livy had her baby at least a month ahead of schedule, on November 7. It was a boy, named Langdon in memory of his grandfather. He was underweight, frail, and the source of concern to his father, who was already overburdened with worries about his wife and bank account. "Livy is very sick," Clemens wrote to his brother, Orion, "& I do not believe the baby will live five days."[18] Langdon survived for nearly two years, but finally succumbed on June 2, 1872, just a few months after *Roughing It* was published.

Clemens never forgot the emotional turmoil from which his book emerged. More than 30 years later, he recalled that the days before Emma Nye's death were "among the blackest, the gloomiest, the most wretched of my long life. The resulting periodical and sudden changes of mood in me, from deep melancholy to half-insane tempests and cyclones of humor, are among the curiosities of my life" (*MTE*, 251). Such frequent and abrupt shifts between extremes of melancholy and manic hilarity left their mark on the hectic pace, alternating moods, and complex moral fabric of *Roughing It*. This is most readily observed in the sharply polarized point of view that presides over the long narrative. As Henry Nash Smith long ago observed, the "voice" of the tenderfoot narrator in *Roughing* is from the very outset mingled with that of "the veteran," who looks back with contempt on his callow youth. The contrast between the two voices, Smith argues, which implies a "judgment upon the tenderfoot's innocence and a corresponding claim for the superior maturity and sophistication of the old-timer, is the consequence of precisely that journey which the book will describe."[19]

Because he is driven by the certainty that he will soon be rich, the tenderfoot's experience illustrates in bold relief the play of deceit and self-deception on the mining frontier. The characteristic humor of *Roughing It* turns on the sudden, often painful deflation of the wildly exaggerated expectations that Clemens shared with many others in California and Nevada at the time. His letters home clearly illustrate that he was infected with what historian Gilman M. Ostrander describes as "the Comstock fever," a "vision of a whole mountain of gold and silver [which] overwhelmed the senses of thousands of investors and brought them to financial ruin."[20] The letters are by turns optimistic and deflated, buoyant and irascible, and form in the aggregate the portrait of an easily deceived and self-deceived innocent at large in a setting that combines with his personality to launch him on a ride toward an inevitable fall.[21]

The traveler is not far along toward Eldorado before he encounters a famous desperado named Slade—a man at once gentle and savage, heroic and degraded, fearless and craven, whose example illustrates that appearances cannot be trusted and that human behavior "is a conundrum worth investigating" (*RI*, 96). The morally enigmatic Slade was so central to Clemens's understanding of his western experiences that he twice sought additional information about him. In September 1870, when he was just getting under way with *Roughing It*, he wrote to Hezekiah L. Hosmer, a postmaster in the Montana Territory, asking for newspaper accounts of the bad man's capture and execution. In March 1871, when composition was much further along, he asked Orion to "sit down right away & torture your memory & write down in minute detail every fact & exploit in the desperado Slade's life that we heard on the Overland—& also describe his appearance & conversation as we saw him at Rocky Ridge station at breakfast. I want to make up a telling chapter from it for the book."[22] As the Slade chapters appear early in *Roughing It*, it seems likely that the letter to Orion signals Clemens's belated decision to feature the outlaw, and the moral "conundrum" he embodied, at a prominent place in his narrative.

There can be no doubt that Slade's example is a "telling" prologue to the events that follow, in which the narrator comes face to face with a world literally formed out of misleading illusions. Politics, he learns, is a front for corrupt self-interest. The legal system, rife with half-concealed ignorance

and venality, is an obstacle to justice. The police, though ostensibly the ser-
vants of law and order, are in his eyes "the dust-licking pimps and slaves of
the scum" (*RI*, 397). A crooked assayer is forced out of business not because
he is dishonest, but because his success stirs the envy of his equally dishonest
competitors. And American missionaries are pious hypocrites, though they
are no more subject to Clemens's ridicule than their victims, the Hawaiians
(*RI*, 257–58, 463–64).

More crucially, in discovering that the world is throughout deceptive the
narrator also learns, to his deep chagrin, that he is himself quite easily taken
in. Indeed, there is a neat but devastating symmetry to the situation: the
world is replete with deceivers, but the deceivers are also pitifully self-deceived. This is brought home to the narrator most painfully when his determination to strike it rich leads him to gloat over his discovery of an
imagined bonanza. Striding boldly into camp, he assures his companions
that he has "enough to make you all rich in twenty-four hours!" When it
is demonstrated to him that he is rich in the gold of fools, he is appropriately
humiliated and disillusioned.

> Moralizing, I observed, then, that "all that glitters is not gold." Mr. Ballou
> said I could go further than that, and lay it up among my treasures of knowl-
> edge, that *nothing* that glitters is gold. So I learned then, once for all, that
> gold in its native state is but dull, unornamental stuff, and that only low-born
> metals excite the admiration of the ignorant with an ostentatious glitter.
> However, like the rest of the world, I still go on under-rating men of gold
> and glorifying men of mica. Commonplace human nature cannot rise above
> that. (*RI*, 207–8)

To be sure, the mica is deceptive. The narrator sees this, yet promptly
concedes that the lesson of his experience is lost on him, and that he will
continue to mistake falsehood for the truth. His "commonplace human nature" makes that inevitable.

Roughing It is of course noted for its youthful ebullience and outrageous
humor, qualities that contrast sharply with the more somber elements that I
have drawn into the foreground. The result is a narrative pattern of flow
and reflux, of rapidly alternating emotional currents closely akin to those in
The Innocents Abroad. As we have seen, this radical swing between opposed
states, a leading symptom of the mining frontier "boom pathology," is conspicuous in the mingled voice of the narrator. Yet even as it forms a comic
counterpoint to the crumbling moral fabric that the tenderfoot perceives
and reacts to, the humor of *Roughing It* takes its rise from the discovery of

hollowness, pointlessness, collapsed illusions, willful deception, hapless self-deception, and defeat. This is increasingly the case in the later sections of the book, when the comedy forms a kind of epicycle to a progressively more dominant downward curve into disillusionment. Rooted in the perception of shifting surfaces and unreliable appearances, and registering formally in the narrator's distinctive tone, this evolving pattern binds the parts of *Roughing It*, scattered as they are, into a tentative but discernible unity.

It must be clear by now that I do not share Henry Nash Smith's view that the tenderfoot's experience on the mining frontier transforms him into a veteran possessed of "superior maturity and sophistication." I cannot agree that such estimable qualities are manifest in the narrator's declaration that he will "go about of an afternoon . . . and pick up two or three pailfuls of shining slugs, and nuggets of gold and silver on the hillside" (*RI*, 19). The irony that cuts through the simulated innocence is not mature and sophisticated; rather, it is freighted with bitter self-contempt. The same sentiment is much more dramatically evident in a familiar episode involving a coyote—"a long, slim, sick and sorry-looking skeleton, with a gray wolf-skin stretched over it, a tolerably bushy tail that forever sags down with a despairing expression of forsakenness and misery, a furtive and evil eye, and a long, sharp face, with slightly lifted lip and exposed teeth." For all of his apparent destitution, the despicable coyote has a way of asserting himself. When pursued by an ambitious and overconfident dog, he contrives to prolong the chase until the frustrated pursuer is far from his wagon. Only then does the coyote exercise his real speed, leaving his victim "solitary and alone in the midst of a vast solitude!" The humiliated dog "jogs along back to his train, and takes up a humble position under the hindmost wagon, and feels unspeakably mean, and looks ashamed, and hangs his tail at half-mast for a week" (*RI*, 48–51).

By Smith's calculus, the net psychological result of the dog's experience should be reflected in the maturity and sophistication of the voice that presides over the incident. But in fact the narrator admires the coyote's gratuitous cruelty only slightly less than he relishes the shattering humiliation of the dog. "If you start a swift-footed dog after" the coyote, he gloats, "you will enjoy it ever so much—especially if it is a dog that has a good opinion of himself" (*RI*, 50). Quite true, the speaker here is an insider and an old-timer; just as certainly, this is a voice that bespeaks an experience in the Far West not at all unlike the dog's. But it is emphatically not a wise voice, or a mature voice. That the narrator is familiar with crushing humiliation is no less evident than the fact that he takes positive delight in seeing it inflicted on others. This, then, is the voice of a cynic whose head once swam when, without warning, he was made to feel as "unspeakably mean" as that innocent fool, the dog.

Indeed, we are well justified in believing Clemens's narrator when he assures us that the coyote "was not a pretty creature or respectable either, for I got well acquainted with his race afterward, and can speak with confidence." Many chapters later, indigent, solitary and forlorn in San Francisco, he describes himself in terms strikingly reminiscent of the coyote's unwary victim.

> For two months my sole occupation was avoiding acquaintances; for during that time I did not earn a penny, or buy an article of any kind, or pay my board. I became a very adept at "slinking." I slunk from back street to back street, I slunk away from approaching faces that looked familiar, I slunk to my meals, ate them humbly and with a mute apology for every mouthful I robbed my generous landlady of, and at midnight, after wanderings that were but slinkings away from cheerfulness and light, I slunk to my bed. I felt meaner, and lowlier and more despicable than the worms. (*RI*, 428)

To be sure, the tenderfoot's gullibility and overconfidence are essential elements in his undoing. Indeed, the consciousness that he has himself to thank for his condition intensifies the sting of his humiliation. That same consciousness helps to account for the fact that cynicism—and not wisdom and a host of other virtues—is the tenderfoot's portion as he emerges from innocence into far western varieties of experience. His inadvertent but self-propelled entry into this harsh rite of passage has self-contempt as its issue; and self-contempt, in its turn, fosters in the tenderfoot precisely the kind of ruthlessness that inspires the solitary, iconoclastic coyote. In short, as the result of his initiation the innocent becomes, with the narrator and the coyote, a compulsive and extremely accomplished practical joker.

The evidence bearing on Clemens's experience with practical joking is abundant and remarkably consistent. William R. Gillis's observation that "Sam did like fun, but not when the fun was at his expense,"[23] is a neat summary of the situation. We know that young Sam Clemens was an avid and accomplished practical joker, and we can be equally certain that he was not pleased with the bloody nose that one of his youthful exploits cost him.[24] By his own account in *Roughing It*, he did not cease to regret the fact that he once ruined a childhood friendship with "a boyish prank" (*RI*, 102–3). Later, as a young man on the frontier, Clemens was an adept practitioner of the practical joke. C. C. Goodwin recalled that Clemens "would lead his victim up to the shambles he had in waiting for him, and the unconscious creature would never suspect what was going to happen until the ax fell."[25] True to form, however, the joker was temperamentally indisposed to find anything even remotely funny in the role—which he unwitting assumed on dozens of occasions—of victim. His deep annoyance at being exposed in his folly comes out most clearly in Gillis's *Gold Rush Days with Mark Twain*. For the most part a tribute to the Washoe humorist, the volume recounts episode after episode in which Clemens took the bait and then responded angrily, often "lighting out" in a fit of rage and humiliation.[26] Others have confirmed Gillis's account.[27] And Clemens's rather extensive commentary on practical joking in his autobiographical dictations is evidence that the sting of numerous exposures was very much alive in his memory. "During three-fourths of my life," he recalls, "I have held the practical joker in limitless contempt and detestation; I have despised him as I have despised no other criminal, and when I am delivering my opinion about him the reflection that I have been a practical joker myself seems to increase my bitterness rather than to modify it" (*AMT*, 48).[28]

But of course the joker was not alone: "there were many practical jokers in the new Territory" (*AMT*, 103), Clemens recalled, a generalization amply borne out in "'Early Days' in Nevada—Silverland Nabobs," which he wrote for the *Buffalo Express* in 1870. In a series of brief portraits, he recounts the misadventures of would-be millionaires, concluding with apparent satisfaction: "I am sincerely glad that my supernatural stupidity lost me my great windfall before I had a chance to make a more inspired ass of me than I was before."[29] Dan DeQuille's account of the early years is equally replete with anecdotes and stories which feature inflated illusions, collapsed expectations, and their gamesome social expression, the ubiquitous practical joke.[30] The patterned ruse, from bait to the bland, final revelation, was as much a staple of the Washoe experience as it was of the tradition of Southwestern humor so familiar to young Sam Clemens. In view of this personal, social, and cultural background, it is hardly surprising that the humor of *Roughing It* should be rooted in the dynamics of practical joking. From the coyote and the dog, through the masterful deflating of that newcomer and windbag, General Buncombe, to Clemens's humiliating and bitterly remembered exposure on Gold Hill, *Roughing It* recounts episode after episode in which guileless, sometimes foolish innocence succumbs to ruthless, often cynical experience.

Contrary to one variety of popular opinion, practical jokes are not funny. Nor are they meant to be. They are intended to hurt, to expose, to humiliate. Paradoxically, while we must deplore the malice of the practical joker, we must also pity him, for his joke will succeed only if he is capable of putting himself, at least imaginatively, in the place of his intended victim. Indeed, it is probably fair to assume that most practical jokers have in fact experienced the hurt and humiliating exposure which they inflict upon others, for the hurt and humiliation explain what is otherwise inexplicable: the malicious impulse which prompts the contriving and the execution of the joke. In short, the joker has been where he puts his victim, just as the coyote and the narrator have been where they put the dog. By extension, it is difficult to conceive of a successful practical joke born, as it were, *ab ovo*. Rather, one practical joke is the child of an earlier practical joke, and that earlier practical joke is in its turn the child of an even earlier practical joke; and suddenly we see that a practical joke, however trivial in itself, is the manifestation of a sustained, rapidly repeating, and possibly accelerating historical cycle. Being hurt, and hurting; being humiliated, and humiliating; being exposed, and exposing—where the joking started is a conundrum worth investigating; where it ends is too. In *Roughing It*, the joke starts in the first paragraph and goes on for hundreds of pages. The victims, numerous and scattered as they are, form an aggregate from which the narrator never recovered, and through myriad repetitions to a kind of ur-practical joke which has deeply penetrated the culture of the mining frontier.

This is to say that the form of *Roughing It*—its narrative voice, its disconnected anecdotal rhythm, and its characteristic humor—amply reinforces the sense of pervasive moral confusion in the world it describes. William Dean Howells's observation, that Clemens's exaggerations and ironies were ideal rhetorical devices for describing the far west, is particularly astute. "All existence there," Howells writes, "must have looked like an extravagant joke, the humor of which was only deepened by its nether-side of tragedy."[31]

As Clemens represents it, the headlong acquisitiveness everywhere at large in the mining frontier gives rise to a culture of deceit and self-deception in which nothing is what it seems to be. Innocence is easy prey for predatory guile; radical deflation, humiliation, and defeat foster widespread cynicism and self-loathing. Constitutionally both sanguine and emotionally changeable, Clemens was hardly exempt from the moral debasement which his narrative opens to view. Like the dog in the story, his experience in the

Far West reduced him to slinking; and like the coyote, he looked upon his former innocence with contempt, and grew adept at exposing in others what he despised in himself. That he attempted suicide in 1866, not long before his departure for the east, is startling testimony to the "nether-side of tragedy" which Howells caught sight of in *Roughing It*.

The mining frontier, often described as a toxic environment infected with delirium and disease, was a setting in which the image of a bland but covertly malicious old-timer preying on a self-deceived innocent was perceived almost universally as the occasion for a good joke. In the midst of the prevailing ruthlessness and cynical disregard for fair play, the figure of Adolph Sutro emerges as a conspicuous exception. In the view of Gilman M. Ostrander, "all but Sutro played the game according to a generally accepted set of rules. The object was to accumulate as much money as possible, preferably at the expense of rivals. The rules allowed any devious and deceitful means conceivable to attain this goal, including the swindling of one's own partners."[32] Sutro went so far as to attempt, unsuccessfully as it turned out, to reform the rules of the Comstock game. He was joined in this crusade by one Conrad Wiegand, a naive and eccentric, but genuinely idealist, newspaperman. Together they challenged the exploitative hegemony of William Chapman Ralston and the Bank of California. For his efforts, Wiegand was threatened, harassed, and finally brutally assaulted, all with the apparent consent of the local authorities. Wiegand's example is of moment here because Clemens used his pathetic case as the concluding episode in his book. Appendix C, the final chapter in the American edition, is a fitting last hearing of the narrative voice of *Roughing It*.

> If ever there was a harmless man, it is Conrad Wiegand, of Gold Hill,
> Nevada. If ever there was a gentle spirit that thought itself unfired gunpow-
> der and latent ruin, it is Conrad Wiegand. If ever there was an oyster that
> fancied itself a whale; or a jack-o'lantern, confined to a swamp, that fancied
> itself a planet with a billion-mile orbit; or a summer zephyr that deemed
> itself a hurricane, it is Conrad Wiegand. Therefore, what wonder is it that
> when he says a thing, he thinks the world listens; that when he does a thing
> the world stands still to look; and that when he suffers, there is a convulsion
> of nature? . . . Something less than two years ago, Conrad assailed several
> people mercilessly in his little 'People's Tribune,' and got himself into trou-
> ble. Straightway he airs the affair in the 'Territorial Enterprise,' in a commu-
> nication over his own signature, and I propose to reproduce it here, in all its
> native simplicity and more than human candor. (*RI,* 580)

And so it goes: Wiegand is mocked and abused by the seasoned veteran, the cynical old-timer, whose tone exudes sidesplitting delight in the spectacle of innocence under heavy assault. What was it, we may wonder, that prompted Clemens to this final and extreme display of cruelty? What was it in the example of poor Wiegand that so angered him?

The trouble began for Conrad Wiegand when he published an article that strongly suggested that local Bank of California officials were engaging in underhanded business dealings. After being twice assaulted and beaten in the streets of Virginia City, Wiegand was lured into the office of his antagonists and threatened with violence if he failed to retract his allegations. He refused on two grounds. He argued, first, that he had not made charges, but merely indicated areas in which investigation seemed appropriate. In effect, there was nothing to retract. Second, he insisted that authorship of the article in question could not be established, and that he was bound by honor and professional scruple not to make such information public without the consent of the writer. "Of its *authorship*," he said, "I can say nothing whatever, but for its *publication* I assume full, sole and personal responsibility" (*RI*, 589). After being beaten again, and threatened with even worse punishment, Wiegand was released to tell his tale of woe. Clemens's closing remarks on the episode hint with broad irony that as the reward for his cowardice Wiegand had earned the fuller exposure of total, public humiliation.

In its essentials, Clemens's assault on Wiegand has three key elements. First, in his zeal for reform, the would be crusader is inflated in his estimate of his own rectitude and clout, and blind to the realities of the world he seeks to change. In short, he is an innocent, and for that he earns Clemens's scorching contempt. Second, in spite of his own at least plausible protests to the contrary, Wiegand is condemned for slander, and for failing to accept the consequences of his editorial irresponsibility. Finally, his pacifism is ridiculed as a transparent cover for whimpering cowardice. "I do not desire to strain the reader's fancy, hurtfully," Clemens writes, "and yet it would be a favor to me if he would try to fancy this lamb in battle, or the duelling ground or at the head of a vigilance committee" (*RI*, 583).[33]

In attempting to explain the extremity of Clemens's response to Wiegand, we may begin by noting that the humorist was personally familiar with the painful consequences of journalistic impropriety. His most famous hoax, "The Empire City Massacre," was very successful in gaining the credence of its readers. Once revealed, however, the joke backfired completely. Duped editors and citizens responded by threatening to sever all ties with the *Enterprise*. "The joker," according to Paine, "was in despair" (*MTB*, 1:230). Less embarrassingly, perhaps, the threat of reprisals for his attacks on the bigotry and corruption of the San Francisco police seems to have figured in Clemens's decision to flee the city late in 1864. Is there a hint, then, that in pillorying Wiegand for his reforming zeal and subsequent cowardice Clemens was unconsciously judging himself?

We are on much firmer ground when we turn to the abortive duel that occasioned Clemens's abrupt departure from Virginia City in late May, 1864, for here the parallels with Conrad Wiegand are quite striking. The story, as reconstructed by Henry Nash Smith in *Mark Twain of the Enterprise*, may be summarized fairly briefly. On May 17, 1864, in an editorial published in the *Enterprise*, Clemens suggested that the proceeds from a local fancy-dress ball were being sent to a "miscegenation society" in the east, and not, as the organizers claimed, to the Sanitary Fund (the Civil War equivalent of the Red Cross). On May 18, four local women, patronesses of the ball, wrote to the *Enterprise* protesting the falsehood of the suggestion. Two days later, in a letter to his sister-in-law, Clemens accepted responsibility for the editorial, but added by way of explanation that he was drunk when he wrote it, and that it was published by mistake. Public apology, he insisted, was out of the question. On the twenty-first, James L. Laird and J. W. Wilmington of a rival newspaper, the *Daily Union*, went on the attack in print. Clemens replied by challenging Laird, a novice at gunplay, to a duel; Laird in turn responded that Wilmington, a seasoned fighter, was the author of the article and therefore the appropriate recipient of the challenge. As Laird put the situation: "For all editorials appearing in the *Union*, the proprietors are personally responsible; for communications, they hold themselves ready, when properly called upon, either to give the name and address of the author, or failing that, to be themselves responsible."[34] As a counter to Laird's evasive strategy, Steve Gillis, Clemens's feisty second, tried unsuccessfully to lure Wilmington into a duel. Meanwhile, Clemens continued to ridicule Laird for refusing to fight. Finally, on May 29, leaving threats and counterthreats all unresolved, Clemens abruptly departed with Gillis for San Francisco. At the very least, argues Henry Nash Smith, he ran from "the danger of being ridiculous and ridiculed."[35] More likely, he ran for his life. "Mark Twain's beard is full of dirt, and his face is black before the people of Washoe," declared the editorial in the Gold Hill *Evening News* the next day. "He has *vamosed*, cut stick, absquatulated."[36]

James M. Cox has observed that Clemens's "somewhat 'confederate' reference to a miscegenation society is evidence of "a native if not a partisan

Southern cast" to his humor. Cox goes on that the abrupt "departure from Nevada reflects the same evasive action which characterized the resignation from the Confederacy" just three years earlier.[37] In the duel, as in the war before it, Clemens failed to rise to the standards of honor and courage that were paramount in Southern culture, and to which he inwardly subscribed. Once again, that failure triggered competing impulses to confess the truth of his humiliation, and to argue it away. The duel was to become another of his "permanencies," a guilty memory that set in motion a repeating cycle of revelation and concealment that would persist for the rest of his life.

By far the most thorough and penetrating analysis of the Virginia City debacle appears in Leland Krauth's essay "Mark Twain Fights Sam Clemens's Duel." Indeed, Krauth's argument anticipates, both in its general trajectory and in several key details, my own view. Krauth emphasizes that Clemens was unable to lay the memory of the shameful episode to rest, and that dueling became an "obsessive" topic that he returned to in *Roughing It*, *A Tramp Abroad*, *Life on the Mississippi*, *Simon Wheeler, Detective*, and *Pudd'n-head Wilson*, as well as in stories, essays, correspondence, and autobiographical dictations.[38] Invariably, his treatment of the duel betrays a strong impulse to mitigate the sting of shameful humiliation; just as clearly, the regular recurrence of the painful memory is testimony that relief eluded him.

Krauth looks carefully at three of the most substantial and highly fictionalized of Clemens's reconstructions of the conflict with Laird: his "Roughing It" lecture of 1871–72; the tale "How I Escaped Being Killed in a Duel," published in 1873; and the fully elaborated account set forth in an autobiographical dictation in 1906. Though the versions of the story vary somewhat in details, they are at one in portraying Clemens as much less the fool and the coward than he was in fact. For example, not once is there mention of his editorial reference to the "miscegenation society," and of the offense taken by the local ladies; rather, the besotted, bad-tempered culprit contrives to assuage his guilty conscience by imaging himself a victim. In all three versions the antagonists actually meet on the field of combat; and though the duel is finally averted, it is the craven Laird who backs down in fear. Krauth generalizes from these and several other omissions and distortions that "the three accounts of the duel are all designed to exonerate Sam Clemens." More generally, he observes that the differences between the event and the later accounts of it "illuminate the processes whereby Mark Twain characteristically purged through his art that which was painful and humiliating in Sam Clemens's past." "Mark Twain," he concludes, "knew more about evasion than the man who invented it."[39]

It is the measure of Clemens's need to tell the story of the duel that he included it among the "Chapters from My Autobiography" selected for publication in the *North American Review* in 1906–7; it is the measure of his answering need to conceal the truth of the same story that the version he released to the public is fiction of a decidedly self-exculpatory variety. But even as Clemens prepared yet again to make light of the episode, something of the true moral weight of the memory surfaced briefly to view. "I was ashamed of myself," he recalled, more than 40 years on; "the rest of the staff were ashamed of me—but I got along well enough. I had always been accustomed to feeling ashamed of myself, for one thing or another, so there was no novelty for me in the situation."[40] How very poignant and revealing this is, especially in light of what we know about poor Clemens's tyrannical conscience, and his virtual incapacity to forgive himself for any of the real and imagined wrongs that lurked, undying, in his memory.

The parallels between the conflict with Laird and the contemptuous treatment of Conrad Wiegand are too numerous and too close to be entirely coincidental. Indeed, the conspicuous affective surplus driving the Wiegand story invites interpretation as the residue of powerful emotions which attached to the buried memory of the humiliating "duel." The parallels are also rather complex. On one side, they betray Clemens's impulse to avenge himself; on the other, they amount to an admission of defeat and of profound self-contempt.

In its narrative context, Clemens's scorn for Wiegand's pacifism seems extreme. The anger, to our eye, should have given place to pity for the poor man's helpless predicament. However, if we recall that Laird based his refusal to fight on grounds identical to Wiegand's, then the immoderate wrath begins to make sense. In effect, frustration with Laird's evasive maneuvering resurfaces as angry ridicule for an equivalent strategy by Wiegand. Clemens abused Laird as "a fool," insisting that "a publisher is bound to stand responsible for any and all articles printed by him, whether he wants to do it or not."[41] But he got no satisfaction. In observing Wiegand, however, Clemens has the pleasure of seeing the hated strategy fail. And the punishment he once wished on James L. Laird is finally administered, unconsciously, and at a considerable remove in time, on the hapless Wiegand. So much for revenge.

But what of himself did Clemens see in Wiegand? He saw a man who has incurred public humiliation and the wrath of enemies as the result of foolish editorial decisions. Wiegand's rather lame justification for refusing to retract his allegations may have reminded Clemens of his own refusal to apologize for an admitted blunder, and his equally lame insistence that "the affair was a silly joke, and that I and all concerned were drunk."[42] Most damningly, in Wiegand he saw a man who resorted to subterfuge rather than face the consequences of his own actions. He saw a coward. True, Wiegand did not run away. But Clemens expresses the wish that he had. In the final paragraph of *Roughing It*, he imagines for his victim that final, shattering and unforgettable humiliation which, in effect, completes his own unconscious self-portrait:

> The merited castigation of this weak, half-witted child was a thing that ought to have been done in the street, where the poor thing could have a chance to run. When a journalist maligns a citizen, or attacks his good name on hearsay evidence, he deserves to be thrashed for it, even if he *is* a 'non-combatant' weakling; but a generous adversary would at least allow such a lamb the use of his legs at such a time. (*RI*, 591)

The otherwise baffling cruelty on display here makes sense only if we recognize it for what it is: an indirect expression of the guilt and self-inflicted pain that poor Clemens inwardly endured as punishment for what he glimpsed of Conrad Wiegand in himself. It was an anguish that needed telling but that was too shameful for direct expression; and so, like so many of Clemens's most revealing autobiographical disclosures, it surfaces obliquely, undetected by the watchful author-cat.

Ishmael, you will recall, "takes the whole universe for a vast practical joke," with the result that he comes to experience with a "free and easy sort of genial, desperado philosophy."[43] Clemens had the same insight, but he did not take the joke nearly so well. His habit, in later years, was to revive that old, innocent self, to pick him up, steady him, and then, with a ferocity borne of guilty self-contempt, to knock him down again. He does it, for example, in a letter of 1876 in which he looks back on the unforgivable innocence of this youth.

> I can picture myself as I was, 22 years ago. . . . You think I have grown some; upon my word there was room for it. You have described a callow fool, a self-sufficient ass, a mere human tumblebug, stern in air, heaving at his bit of dung & imagining he is remodeling the world & is entirely capable of doing it right. Ignorance, intolerance, egotism, self-assertion, opaque perception, dense & pitiful chuckle-headedness—& an almost pathetic unconsciousness of it all.[44]

The affective extremes of *Roughing It*, geared as they are to tensions between innocence and experience in the narrator and his world, contrast sharply with the steadiness of tone and humorously temperate demeanor of *A Tramp Abroad* (1880). The books are similarly episodic and anecdotal, but where the play of associations in the western narrative often sparks telling personal revelations, it seldom disturbs the narrator's composure as he recounts his European experiences. Pervasive practical joking is increasingly an irritant to the consciousness of *Roughing It*; by contrast, the narrator in *A Tramp Abroad* is quietly gratified by the example of Nicodemus Dodge, an innocent hick from Hannibal who effortlessly thwarts the schemes of "the village smarties" to use him as "a butt to play jokes on" (*TA*, 226). A remote and desolate setting in *Roughing It* makes the narrator feel "like the Last Man, neglected of the judgment, and left pinnacled in mid-heaven, a forgotten relic of a vanished world" (*RI*, 550). At an equally forbidding locale in *A Tramp Abroad*, far "from any suggestion of cheer or hope," his eye is drawn to "a solitary wee forget-me-not . . . holding its bright blue star up with the prettiest and gallantest air in the world, the only happy spirit, the only smiling thing, in all that grisly world. She seemed to say, 'Cheer up!—as long as we are here, let us make the best of it'" (*TA*, 370–71). Clemens's humiliating "duel" in Virginia City was such a painful memory that he avoided it altogether in *Roughing It*, where its conspicuous absence testifies to a potent aversion. By contrast, dueling is strongly featured in Clemens's account of student life in Heidelberg. He understands why "the world in general looks upon the college duels as very farcical affairs," but comes around to the view that "it is a farce which has quite a grave side to it." Indeed, he concludes that "there is blood and pain and danger enough about the college duel to entitle it to a considerable degree of respect," adding that the students regard it as shameful to decline a challenge (*TA*, 61–63).

So relatively placid is the narrative point of view in *A Tramp Abroad* that this highly sensitive topic, elsewhere invariably an emotional catalyst, passes in full review without the slightest hitch in tone. This said, it is likely evidence of a reflex retreat from painful self-reckoning that Clemens turns immediately from German dueling to the degraded French variety, in which overscrupulous deference to proper form substitutes for authentic honor and courage. But even as it signals a shrinking from an accusing example, this detour into farce triggers an apparently nonchalant, but obliquely compromising, revelation. "I have had a good deal to do with duels on the Pacific coast," the narrator observes with ill-guarded contempt for the French, "but I see now that they were crude affairs" (*TA*, 76). We can hardly doubt that the contemptuous cutting edge in the narrator's tone turned inward when he recalled, as we do, that his most memorable duel out West was the one he ran away from.

In the midst of pervasive calm, the rare moments of personal agitation in *A Tramp Abroad* assume a high profile. The treatment of dueling is of course one such moment; the ostensibly humorous rendering of a boyhood dream about Mississippi steamboat "explosions, and conflagrations, and sudden death" (*TA*, 95), clearly reminiscent of the *Pennsylvania* disaster, is another. And a series of associations involving dentists, doctors, and death leads in turn to skeletons, and thence to Jimmy Finn, the Hannibal drunkard who sold his body to the village sawbones for the price of a terminal binge (*TA*, 223–29). It is altogether noteworthy that such infrequent intervals of moral perturbation take rise in *A Tramp Abroad* when Clemens turns from the events of the journey itself to painful, guilt-ridden memories of his childhood and youth.

Somewhat ironically, the relative moral serenity of *A Tramp Abroad* is not a faithful index to Clemens's feelings about either the experiences or the writing that combined to produce the published narrative. "I have been fighting a life-&-death battle with this infernal book" (*MTHL*, 1:286), he complained to Howells early in 1880.[45] The difficulty was in good part traceable to a basic shift in his attitude toward travel. "Formerly I went Abroad as an Innocent," he observes in an unpublished preface, "but this time, fortified with experience and guile, I went Abroad as a Tramp."[46] Disburdened of inflated expectations, Clemens was no longer prey to wrenching disenchantment, and thus came to the narrative of his journey without the ambivalent mingling of perspectives and of selves that figures so centrally in *The Innocents Abroad* and *Roughing It*. The result, as he glimpsed in a letter to Howells, was the loss of the tension so vital to those earlier books. "I *hate* travel," he fumed to his friend, "& I *hate* hotels, & I *hate* the opera, & I *hate* the Old Masters—in truth I don't ever seem to be in a good enough humor with ANYthing to *satirize* it" (*MTHL*, 1:248–49).

Clemens knew that giving way to such strong, uniformly negative sentiments—"showing temper" (*MTHL*, 1:249), as he put it to Howells—would surely undermine the sale of his book. But he recognized as well that the humor of his earlier travel narratives, grounded in the complex persona of the tenderfoot/veteran, had no foundation in the materials presently available to him. In the upshot, his irritation with all that his new book entailed found its antidote in the commitment to a mood of aimless wandering—"a lazy, delightful, irresponsible high-holiday time on the road," as he describes it.[47] The true charm of travel in this mindless mode, Clemens assures us in

A Tramp Abroad, lies not "in the walking, or in the scenery, but in the talking. . . . It is no matter whether one talks wisdom or nonsense, the case is the same, the bulk of the enjoyment lies in the wagging of the gladsome jaw and the flapping of the sympathetic ear" (*TA*, 221). Such talk, on a course going nowhere—or, more precisely, going anywhere *except* toward discord—has a close physical analogue, and its ideal setting, in the aimless drift of a raft on a broad river. "The motion of a raft is the needful motion," Clemens observes, in a passage previously quoted. "It is gentle, and gliding, and smooth, and noiseless; it calms down all feverish activities, it soothes to sleep all nervous hurry and impatience; under its restful influence all the troubles and vexations and sorrows that harass the mind vanish away, and existence becomes a dream, a charm, a deep and tranquil ecstasy" (*TA*, 126).

Such serene, oblivious drifting, like the easy, aimless talk it so much resembles, speaks obliquely in *A Tramp Abroad* of antipodal states of mind held temporarily at bay on the remote margins of consciousness. To the considerable extent that it gives a wide berth to the unforgotten, unforgiven staples of his lifelong self-indictment—indelibly preserved in memories of Hannibal, the river, the war, and the West—*A Tramp Abroad* maintains its tranquil composure. By contrast, *Life on the Mississippi* is a tormented book because it travels directly through those troubled regions of Clemens's life and mind. As we have seen, the conspicuous exception to this general pattern appears in the initial third of *Life on the Mississippi*, chapters 4 to 17, which were first published in 1875 as a series of sketches in the *Atlantic Monthly*, and later incorporated into the larger narrative. Here Clemens sets forth a warmly nostalgic account of his youthful initiation into the elite fraternity of Mississippi riverboat pilots. Like the tenderfoot in *Roughing It*, the "cub" pilot comes to his new experience with a head full of romantic illusions that make him vulnerable to all manner of falls. Unlike his predecessor, however, the youngster rises rapidly through adversity to the maturity and sophistication expected of him in his high calling. Though his education subjects him to a series of practical jokes which exploit and expose his ignorance and gullibility, he looks back with gratitude upon those veteran pilots who "wisely" trained him "by various strategic tricks to look danger in the face a little more calmly" (*LM*, 159).

Like *Tom Sawyer*, which Clemens completed during the same period, the "Old Times" chapters survey childhood and youth from a remote vantage of nearly two decades, and from the point of view of a good-humored, slightly condescending adult who looks back with loving irony on his days of innocence. The rest of *Life on the Mississippi* is also about the past, much of it the same past, but it is composed of memories more recently formed, or re-formed, during the return journey to the river in 1882. The freshness and relative proximity of the impressions make all the difference in the quality of the narrative. Where "Old Times" is uniformly upbeat and coherent, *Life* is fragmentary, without clear focus, utterly erratic in tone, and a minefield of unconscious eruptions and fretful evasions. The contrast is nowhere more evident than in Clemens's remorseful account of his brother Henry's death in the fiery 1858 destruction of the steamboat *Pennsylvania*, which forms the transition between old and new. This deeply unsettling memory colors much that follows in the narrative. The prolonged agony of the Civil War, invariably a spur to submerged guilt, is everywhere present to mind. A pervasive sense of moral disorder is most nakedly evident in the account of the predatory Murel gang, in the human perversity on display in Karl Ritter's story, in the narrative of wartime events at Vicksburg, and in the widespread fraud and self-deception manifest in the chronicle of Southern history. "Well—well, it is a sad world" (*LM*, 395), Clemens reflects wearily at the conclusion of "The Professor's Yarn."

Characteristically, relief from the perverse play of memory is associated with the grand, untroubled flow of the Mississippi itself. In the immediate sequel to his account of the bloody Darnell-Watson feud, Clemens is drawn to the great river, with its "majestic, unchanging sameness of serenity, repose, tranquility, lethargy, vacancy,—symbol of eternity, realization of the heaven pictured by priest and prophet, and longed for by the good and thoughtless!" (*LM*, 292). The Mississippi is invoked again toward the end of the narrative, where it appears "as tranquil and reposeful as dreamland," with "nothing this-worldly about it—nothing to hang a fret or a worry upon" (*LM*, 568–69). But of course the river's serene indifference is not shared by those envying mortals borne along on its mighty tide. In Clemens's case, the fretful, morally troubled tone of his narrative grows ever darker in the chapters (49–56) that recount the journey upriver from New Orleans to Hannibal. The increased gravity is directly geared to ominous stirrings of memory brought on by the approach to the site of his childhood. At first, the weight of accusation registers obliquely in a series of unsettling screen memories that testify to the humorist's characteristically opposed urges to confront and to evade the evidence of what he regarded as his own moral degradation. In surveying the careers of pilots who were his friends in the old days on the river, he remembers Captain Montgomery, who took heroic action as commander of the Confederate fleet in "the great battle before Memphis" (*LM*, 487). The awkward contrast with Clemens's own wartime failure of nerve is not made explicit, but as the apparent price of the omission he is impelled toward an even more painfully compromising recollection. "One of the pilots whom I had known," he recalls, "had died a very honorable death. His boat caught fire, and he remained at the wheel until he got her safe to land. Then he went out over the breast-board with his clothing in flames, and was the last person to get ashore. He died from his injuries in the course of two or three hours" (*LM*, 488). That Henry's name does not arise in connection with this lamentable story merely sharpens our sense of Clemens's reluctance to follow the curve of memory to its anguished point of origin.

Piloting reminiscences lead in due course to the figure of Captain Isaiah Sellers, a veteran of the steamboat days who oppressed young pilots with his encyclopedic knowledge of the river, and who adopted the nom de plume Mark Twain for his brief columns in the New Orleans *Picayune*. Young Sam Clemens, "cub" pilot, practical joker, and budding journalist wrote a long burlesque of Sellers which his friends "eagerly rushed . . . into print in the 'New Orleans True Delta.'" That they did so, Clemens reflects, "was a great pity; for it did nobody any worthy service, and it sent a pang deep into a good man's heart." Insisting that "there was no malice" in his youthful jest, he acknowledges nonetheless that it caused real pain. "I did not know then," he concludes regretfully, "though I do now, that there is no suffering comparable with that which a private person feels when he is for the first time pilloried in print" (*LM*, 497).

Clemens's memory here fashions an accusing montage in which the Sellers episode is proleptically merged with the 1864 "duel" in Virginia City, an even more painful set of circumstances in which, as we have seen, the denial of responsibility for the publication of an offensive newspaper article, the disavowal of malice in the inadvertent infliction of pain, and exquisite public humiliation were also prominently featured. Indeed, we may reasonably surmise that the shadow of the bitter Nevada debacle is projected backward onto the relatively benign Sellers prank, producing its seemingly inordinate gravity. The episodes are even more clearly linked in Clemens's recollection that he "was on the Pacific Coast" when word reached him that Sellers had died. "I was a fresh new journalist," he recalls, "and needed a *nom de guerre*; so I confiscated the ancient mariner's discarded one, and have done my best to make it remain what it was in his hands—a sign and symbol and warrant that whatever is found in its company may be gambled on as being the petrified truth; how I have succeeded, it would not be modest in me to say" (*LM*, 498). The jocular tone here cannot completely conceal nascent preoccupations with journalistic violence, intolerable guilt, and purposeful deception, all of which have their personal nexus in ignominious memories of Virginia City and the illicit appropriation of a fictitious name. Here once again we are witness to the complex dynamics of a recurrent impulse to tell and to untell the same compromising story.[48]

The gathering momentum of Clemens's self-indictment carries him through a reminder of former humiliations—"with somebody else as victim" (*LM*, 501)—and on to St. Louis, where he revisits in memory yet another of his youthful failures of manhood. The episode is introduced as a humorous anecdote in which "a grizzly-headed man" stops him in the street and asks, "Look here, *have you got that drink yet?*" The conversation quickly turns to "the St. Louis riots of about thirty years ago" in which they were both enlisted and armed as temporary peacekeepers. "It was a very hot night," Clemens recalls,

> and my musket was very heavy. We marched and marched; and the nearer we approached the seat of war, the hotter I grew and the thirstier I got I was behind my friend; so, finally, I asked him to hold my musket while I dropped out and got a drink. Then I branched off and went home. I was not feeling any solicitude about *him* of course, because I knew he was so well armed, now, that he could take care of himself without any trouble. If I had had any doubts about that, I would have borrowed another musket for him. I left the city pretty early the next morning, and if this grizzled man had not happened to encounter my name in the papers the other day in St. Louis, and felt moved to seek me out, I should have carried to my grave a heart-torturing uncertainty as to whether he ever got out of the riots all right or not. I ought to have inquired, thirty years ago; I know that. And I would have inquired, if I had had the muskets, but, in the circumstances, he seemed better fixed to conduct the investigations than I was. (*LM*, 506–7)[49]

The jesting reminder of the drink that took the reluctant warrior out of the action, and the ostensibly humorous mock-rationalizing with which the episode concludes, cannot fully obscure the deeper moral unease at large in the narrative. Quite clearly, Clemens's failure of nerve in St. Louis is linked in the recesses of memory with its subsequent reenactments at the commencement of the Civil War and in Virginia City.[50] The anecdote thus lends tacit confirmation to a familiar and damaging self-assessment.

After a chapter given over to the story of Charlie Williams, son of a clergyman, Harvard graduate, and consummate fraud, Clemens arrives at last in Hannibal, his boyhood home. Here, as I have argued at length in chapter 2, indirectly accusatory self-scrutiny finally gives way to a fully conscious and unremitting survey of guilt-laden childhood memories. The drownings of Lem Hackett and the German prodigy stir spasms of conscience which grow sharper still when attention turns to the horrific death of the burning tramp. Henry, ever redolent of remorse, comes last, with his damning judgment of his errant older brother. The homecoming recorded in *Life on the Mississippi* culminates here, as the efflux of memory, stirred in phases by the upstream journey, arrives at last at overt self-condemnation.

If it is our objective to understand the inner life of its creator, then we can hardly exaggerate the autobiographical significance of *Life on the Mississippi*. Clearly, poor Clemens did not like the old self he happened upon in Hannibal. Just as clearly, less sedulous and fully formed versions of that same self were present to him at many places along the journey that the book describes. For here as elsewhere he set himself the impossible task of squaring his thirst for moral equanimity with the fear that he was in his deepest nature hopelessly corrupt. Taking its cues from a dense web of associations linking steamboat days, his brother, the war, dueling, home, and a host of familiar childhood horrors, his memory is host in *Life on the Mississippi* to myriad reminders of his own degradation. Such is the unifying moral thread running through the dark center of the book, and—as we will see in the next chapter—through virtually all of Clemens's fictional forays into "the matter of Hannibal." By contrast—and precisely because it carried him to places relatively free of reminders of his troubled past—the European journey recorded in *A Tramp Abroad* afforded him as much repose as he was likely to find anywhere. The same might have been expected of the last of his travel books, *Following the Equator* (1897), his report on a journey that circled the entire globe. To the extent that it fails to meet such expectations, the book testifies to Clemens's discovery that the dark realities of western imperialism were strangely reminiscent of what troubled him most about his own past.

The account of a global lecture tour undertaken to repay the enormous debts resulting from Clemens's bankruptcy in 1894, *Following the Equator* arose out of assorted tribulations that culminated at journey's end with the sudden death of his favorite daughter, Susy. Composition was understandably an ordeal, though Clemens emerged confident that he had successfully concealed his true feelings of anguish and fatigue. "This book has not exposed me," he wrote in November, 1897, to his friend and benefactor, Henry Huttleson Rogers. "I would rather be hanged, drawn and quartered than write it again. All the heart I had was in Susy's grave and the Webster debts. And so, behold a miracle!—a book which does not give its writer away."[51]

It is striking confirmation of Clemens's notorious blindness to the deeper personal drift of his writing that he so thoroughly misgauged the actual tone and purport of *Following the Equator*. Its humorous interludes notwithstanding, the book is first and foremost a troubled, often angry report on the misery wrought by European imperialism along the equatorial black belt. Time and again he is brought back to the rapacious greed and heartless cruelty of the Europeans spreading across the world. The heat of his outrage at points achieves a Swiftian intensity. "The reduction of the [native] population by Rhodesian methods," he observes ironically,

> is a return to the old-time slow-misery and lingering-death system of a discredited time and a crude "civilization." We humanely reduce an overplus of dogs by swift chloroform; the Boer humanely reduced an overplus of blacks by swift suffocation; the nameless but right-hearted Australian pioneer humanely reduced his overplus of aboriginal neighbors by a sweetened swift death concealed in a poisoned pudding. All these are admirable, and worthy of praise. (*FE*, 691)

The narrator's response to such widespread inhumanity registers in the dozens of brief, sharply ironic observations on the degraded human lot that appear everywhere in the text, but most frequently in the maxims from Pudd'nhead Wilson's New Calendar that serve as epigraphs to each of the book's seventy chapters. "Pity is for the living," we are assured, "envy is for the dead." "Man is the Only Animal that Blushes. Or needs to." And perhaps most tellingly of all: "Everything human is pathetic. The secret source of Humor itself is not joy but sorrow. There is no humor in heaven" (*FE*, 184, 256, 119).[52]

Clemens's misconstruction of his last travel book is no more striking than the revelation of his desire to conceal his deeper feelings about it. The letter to Rogers on this score is echoed in another to Howells. "I wrote my last travel-book in hell," he admits; "but I let on, the best I could, that it was an excursion through heaven. Some day I will read it, & if its lying cheerfulness fools me, then I shall believe it fooled the reader. How I did loathe that journey around the world!—except the sea-part & India" (*MTHL*, 2:690). The characteristic impulse to submerge painful discordancies is one of several elements common to the travel narratives. Another is Clemens's imperfect success at sustaining his "lying cheerfulness," and the familiar tonal ambivalence—the rapid movement back and forth between opposed emotional states—that results. A third is the characteristic drift—along largely unconscious lines of association—into vexed moral questions that emerge from personal memory and from reflections on the journey itself. In its address to such questions, however, *Following the Equator* displays a much greater gravity of tone—more attention to the world's woe, with less, and less ebullient, humor—than the earlier travel books, and a marked tendency to move from specific and local issues and problems to universal perspectives on the human condition. Life is brief and hard; nature is cruel; human nature is corrupt; the direction and significance of things are obscure; social reality and individual identity, in their variety and mutability, are manifest constructions, fictions rooted in self-interest and the need for order. Most importantly, slavery is in some form or another a global phenomenon.

In recoil from its morally degraded condition, humanity immerses itself in lies ("The principal difference between a cat and a lie," Clemens observes, "is that the cat has only nine lives" [*FE*, 622]), and in all manner of "interested" fictions ("The very ink with which all history is written is merely fluid prejudice" [*FE*, 699]). Deceit has its leading corollary in varieties of self-deception widespread among humans, but most flagrantly and perniciously on display among the Western colonial powers who straddle the global black belt. "There are many humorous things in the world," the traveler observes, "among them the white man's notion that he is less savage than the other savages" (*FE*, 213). So pervasive is Western duplicity that its influence is discernible even in matters of dress. "Yes," he insists, "our clothes are a lie, and have been nothing short of that these hundred years. They are insincere, they are the ugly and appropriate outward exposure of an inward sham and a moral decay" (*FE*, 344).

But even as he condemns Western hypocrisy, Clemens is at intervals moved to acknowledge the blessings of colonialism. India of old was a brutal place; but now, thanks to the British, the country has the benefit of new "factories, schools, hospitals, reforms" (*FE*, 385). Indeed, he affirms their subaltern status as "the best service that was ever done to the Indians themselves, those wretched heirs of a hundred centuries of pitiless oppression and abuse" (*FE*, 506). Clemens's tolerance for colonialism will appear contradictory to those more closely familiar with such later, unequivocally anti-imperialist essays as "To the Person Sitting in Darkness" and "King Leopold's Soliloquy," which he wrote only after the United States had become involved in Cuba and the Philippines. At this earlier stage, his moral outrage was to an extent counterbalanced by the view that territorial aggressiveness is a fixed and universal feature of human history. As he observes toward the end of *Following the Equator,* "All the territorial possessions of all the political establishments in the earth—including America, of course—consist of pilferings from other people's wash. No tribe, howsoever insignificant, and no nation, howsoever mighty, occupies a foot of land that was not stolen." Nor is "land-robbery" always a bad thing. "All the savage lands in the world," Clemens predicts, "are going to be brought under subjection to the Christian governments of Europe. I am not sorry, but glad. . . . The sooner the seizure is consummated, the better for the savages. The dreary and dragging ages of bloodshed and disorder and oppression will give place to peace and order and the reign of law" (*FE,* 623–26).

Clemens's vision of a world at peace was more wish than moral certainty. And no amount of wishful thinking could reconcile him to the pious rationalizations of colonial ideology. Yet he could not escape the conclusion that such lies are part and parcel of human nature. Pretensions to right thinking are self-interested constructions designed—as often as not unconsciously—to conceal departures from accepted norms of truth and justice. "There is a Moral Sense," Clemens observes in another of Pudd'nhead's new maxims, "and there is an Immoral Sense. History shows us that the Moral Sense enables us to perceive morality and how to avoid it, and that the Immoral Sense enables us to perceive immorality and how to enjoy it" (*FE,* 161). Thus it is that "custom makes incongruous things congruous," and that "all human rules are more or less idiotic" (*FE,* 400, 477). It is only in the light of the universal human acquiescence in self-interested illusions that Clemens can account for the otherwise unaccountable, morally intolerable realities—racism and slavery most notable among them—that greet him as he circles the globe. In the aggregate, his scattered reflections on the journey combine to form a kind of radical conservatism. He is a radical, to be sure, in his critique of imperialism and its apologists, but conservative in the belief that fallen human nature, irretrievably mired in evasive lies, can do no better. "Don't part with your illusions," he warns. "When they are gone you may still exist but you have ceased to live" (*FE,* 567).[53]

As I have already suggested, Clemens's uncertainty whether to condemn or to affirm colonialism and its culture of morally evasive illusions would tilt sharply toward the negative side once those problems became firmly linked in his mind with conditions in the United States. While it is certainly true that he was among the first to recognize the continuities between American race-slavery and global imperialism, it is notable as well that his progress toward this enlightened perspective was obstructed by deep personal resistance. The condemnation of American slavery—and the late-century horrors of lynching and Jim Crow—as a species of domestic colonialism was the more painful for Clemens because it revived childhood memories of personal complicity in crimes he had learned to hate. "No man," Howells rightly observes, "more perfectly sensed, and more perfectly abhorred, slavery" than his good friend. And because, as Howells goes on, Clemens "held himself responsible for the wrong that the white race had done the black race in slavery," no man endured greater guilt for the iniquity.[54] We will come back to this topic in due course. For now, it will suffice to observe that Clemens's moral vacillation in *Following the Equator* manifests a reluctance not so much to judge colonialism and its culture of lies as to acknowledge his sense of personal entanglement in those very evils.

The potently personal trajectory of Clemens's ambivalence toward imperialism takes culminating expression in chapter 38 of *Following the Equator*, the fascinating account of his visit to Bombay that I have analyzed in close detail in my own chapter 1, above. Recall that the sight of a German tourist mistreating his Indian servant reminds Clemens that similar abuses were visited on slaves in Missouri when he was a boy. This jarring memory, with its clearly accusing implications, is promptly deflected into much less compromising speculations on "the space-annihilating power of thought." Though the traveler's evasive maneuver yields an interval of repose, his moral disquiet resurfaces obliquely in subsequent, ostensibly humorous reflections on his brother animal, the unregenerate Indian crow. The episode perfectly illustrates both the conjunction of personal and national guilt in Clemens's troubled relationship to American race-slavery, and the interplay of competing impulses to accept and to deny the terms of his emergent case against himself and his country. In this extraordinary episode, as elsewhere in *Following the Equator*, his failure to come fully and clearly to terms with imperialism is the symptomatic reflex of a deeper reluctance to confront squarely his compromising memories of the old days in Hannibal.

Consider Clemens's concluding reflections on the inhumane treatment of blacks in Rhodesia. "This is slavery," he insists, "and several times worse than was the American slavery which used to pain England so much." Where now is his memory, so prominently featured in the Bombay chapter, of the slave murdered in the streets of his boyhood home? What of the poor black orphan whose extravagant whistling and whooping grated so strangely on him, and brought his mother to tears? And what of Aunt Rachel, who in "A True Story" looks on in helpless horror as her children are sold at auction? These images are necessarily held in abeyance as Clemens makes his case for the relative benevolence of American slavery. They recede even further from view as he turns his attention to the much happier, "tamed blacks" that he encounters in the major South African towns—

> tamed and Christianized too, I suppose, for they wore the dowdy clothes of our Christian civilization. But for that, many of them would have been remarkably handsome. These fiendish clothes, together with the proper lounging gait, good-natured face, happy air, and easy laugh, make them precise counterparts of our American blacks. . . . One Sunday in King William's Town a score of colored women came mincing across the great barren square dressed—oh, in the last perfection of fashion, and newness, and expensiveness, and showy mixture of unrelated colors,—all just as I had seen it so often at home; and in their faces and their gait was that languishing, aristocratic, divine delight in their finery which was so familiar to me, and had always been such a satisfaction to my eye and my heart. I seemed among old, old friends; friends of fifty years, and I stopped and cordially greeted them. They broke into a good fellowship laugh, flashing their white teeth upon me, and all answered at once. I did not understand a word they said. I was astonished; I was not dreaming that they would answer in anything but American. (*FE*, 691–93)

How very much is accomplished in this seemingly blithe passage! The horrors of racial violence, Rhodesian and American, are dissipated in images of happy African women, and in their equally happy American counterparts. The morally intolerable excesses of the past are redeemed and effaced, while imperialism and American race-slavery are revisited in their happy fruition. Utterly delighted to find himself in the midst of what he takes to be good old friends, Clemens does not pause to reflect on how fully he has surrendered to the subtle seductions of the Moral Sense, and with it to the pious illusions of colonial ideology. (Better than ever perhaps we recognize the secret inward sources of his confident assertions about the universality of self-deception.) Nor does he glimpse the irony lurking in his "astonished" inability to understand what these women are saying. For the moment at least, he is insulated in bad faith from the shameful realities of imperialism, and from the guilty knowledge about his country and himself that his journey has brought home to him.

Clemens knew from long experience, of course, that his carefree mood would soon give way to its opposite. Such serenity, after all, was ordinarily linked in his mind with the idea of travel on water, where he floated free of the painful sights and associations that invariably greeted him on land. "I myself am wholly indifferent as to when we are going to 'get in,'" he wrote, as his long voyage neared its end. "If I had my way we should never get in at all. This sort of sea life is charged with an indestructible charm. There is no weariness, no fatigue, no worry, no responsibility, no work, no depression of spirits. There is nothing like this serenity, this comfort, this peace, this deep contentment, to be found anywhere on land. If I had my way I would sail on for ever and never go to live on the solid ground again" (*FE*, 616–17).

4   Telling Fictions

I have argued that Clemens's explicitly autobiographical writing arose out of a need to confess the truth about himself, and failed because of a countervailing need to conceal the same thing. He recognized his failure for what it was, but knew at the same time that the dark truth would out, the exertions of the vigilant author-cat notwithstanding. It followed—though Clemens was slow to draw this inference—that guilty self-revelations would surface most readily in his travel books and novels, where license to fictionalize doubled as a sedative to the censors. The guilty truth was thus most likely to appear when its exposure was apparently least at issue; the need to confess came closest to satisfaction when the need to conceal seemed least urgent.

This is not to deny that Clemens was prey—constantly, painfully, and often consciously—to the inward sting of conscience. Virtually any thought or human interaction could be turned to offense, and the perverse play of mental associations led almost invariably to one or another of his "permanencies," to the repertoire of real and imagined "sins" that recycled on a regular basis through his consciousness. Indeed, the resurgence and characteristically evasive management of painful memories—of the measles, of Henry, the war, dueling, the Whittier dinner, the burning tramp and other childhood calamities, and slavery—recapitulates the pervasive pattern of telling and untelling so characteristic of Clemens's work. This pattern is nowhere more in evidence, we have found, than in the travel writing, and most especially in the books—*Roughing It, Life on the Mississippi*, and *Following the Equator*—that feature memories of the early days in Missouri and the Far West. We will find the same pattern in the novels, and most especially in those that take rise from the same reservoir of memories—of childhood, the river, slavery—often referred to as the matter of Hannibal. Here, in the putative garden, the idyllic America as yet unspoiled by the Gold Rush, the Civil War, and the age of the Robber Barons, Clemens's memory and imagination shaped fictions as obliquely revealing of his inner anguish as anything he ever committed to print.

   Clemens's first novel, *The Gilded Age* (1873), which he coauthored with his neighbor, Charles Dudley Warner, is a notable exception to this general pattern. Clearly, collaboration was not conducive to autobiographical self-disclosure. Though members of his family served as models for major characters—most famously, Colonel Sellers is based on his mother's cousin, James Lampton—Clemens was not closely identified with anyone in the book. Nor did the novel's thematic emphasis—on private greed and political corruption in the post–Civil War era of its title—arouse moral misgivings that cut close to home. Justin Kaplan has rightly observed that the rapacious speculative code Clemens "detested was also, in part, the one he lived by. He wanted to get rich, not just get along" (*MCMT*, 96). Yet if we are inclined to view such bald acquisitiveness as a grave defect of character, Clemens was not. His father's insolvency and the grinding poverty of his childhood years produced in him a craving for wealth and security so consuming that it overrode most moral restraints. "Oh, it is a fearful thing to be poor!" exclaims a leading character in *The Gilded Age* (*GA*, 85). Avarice for Clemens was a sin in others, but he was himself somehow exempt. As Gregg Camfield has shrewdly observed, it did not bother the novelist that his book attacking greed was itself undertaken primarily in the hope that it would make him rich.[1]

   Because the focus of *The Gilded Age* is directed outward toward the folly of the larger public world of business and politics, Clemens's very considerable moral energy in the novel is seldom turned inward upon himself. To be sure, there is a shudder of self-reckoning early in the narrative, when the engines on the steamboat *Amaranth* explode, leaving many either dead or seriously wounded. "But these things must not be dwelt upon," Clemens observes, doubtless with poor Henry's death foremost in mind. He goes on in spite of himself to add, with rueful irony, that an inquest into the accident concluded: "NOBODY TO BLAME" (*GA*, 52). The novel is also an oblique index to his ongoing concerns about race and slavery. At the numerous points in the narrative where attention is drawn to the plight of former slaves in the post-Reconstruction South, Clemens's sympathy for the freedmen is as obvious as his outrage that they receive little more than cynical lip service from politicians (*GA*, 405–7). Yet in channeling his anger outward toward others he avoids a personal self-reckoning on the same highly charged issue. To the extent that it afforded him such indirect moral shelter, political satire was thus "safe" for the humorist. Indeed, when Colonel Sellers observes that "we would have to go without the services of some of our ablest men . . . if the country were opposed to—to—bribery" (*GA*,

328), the satirical gusto of the attack is in some degree the reflex of relief at personal guilt deflected and at least temporarily deferred.

The contrast between *The Gilded Age*—social and political satire of a decidedly "adult" cast set in the public world of the urban, post-bellum North—and *The Adventures of Tom Sawyer* (1876)—a rural, highly autobiographical idyll of the antebellum South written for and about children—could hardly be more pronounced. Indeed, the latter novel is one manifestation among many that Clemens gravitated to autobiographical narratives set in his childhood home because they seemed to offer a moral antidote to the fallen world of post-war America. Nostalgia was the symptom of mid-life disenchantment. As he remarked in a letter of 1887, "Tom Sawyer is simply a hymn, put into prose form to give it a worldly air" (*MTL*, 2:477). It was in just such a mood that Clemens wrote in 1870 to his old friend, Will Bowen, about the magic of their childhood years in Hannibal. "The fountains of my great deep are broken up," he declares,

> & I have rained reminiscences for four & twenty hours. The old life has swept before me like a panorama; the old days have trooped by in their old glory, again; the old faces have looked out of the mists of the past; old footsteps have sounded in my listening ears; old hands have clasped mine, old voices have greeted me, & the songs I loved ages & ages ago have come wailing down the centuries![2]

The same mood overtook him thirty years later, when he wrote to Bowen's widow:

> The romance of life is the only part of it that is overwhelmingly valuable, & romance dies with youth. After that, life is a drudge, & indeed a sham. . . . I should greatly like to re-live my youth, & then get drowned. I should like to call back Will Bowen & John Garth & the others, & live the life, & be as we were, & make holiday until 15, then all drown together.[3]

Yet for all that it seemed to promise in the way of moral affirmation, the remembered paradise of childhood was, as we have seen, a troubled region of the mind. So powerfully even desperately—was Clemens drawn to the redemptive ideal of youth that time and again he forgot the snakes that invariably turned up to surprise him when he returned to the garden. The difficulty, of course, had its source in the autobiographical well from which the stories sprang, the deeply vexed childhood that Clemens strained to deny in the very act of its telling. Something of this ambivalence surfaces in his acknowledgment that the egregious Sid Sawyer was modeled on his brother Henry. Reflecting in an autobiographical dictation that he "never knew Henry to do a vicious thing toward me or toward anyone else," Clemens is quick to add that "he frequently did righteous ones that cost me as heavily. It was his duty to report me, when I needed reporting and neglected to do it myself, and he was very faithful in discharging that duty." The broadly ironic intimation that Henry was a punitive, self-righteous killjoy leads directly to the acknowledgment that "He is Sid in *Tom Sawyer.*" But Clemens has no sooner made the direct link between life and literature than he draws back from it, insisting that "Sid was not Henry. Henry was a much finer and better boy than ever Sid was" (*AMT,* 33).

We can be sure that Henry *was* a "finer and better" person than Sid, just as we can be sure that Clemens bitterly resented his brother's virtuous example, secretly wished him harm, and suffered the guilt of the damned when that wish seemed to play itself out on the *Pennsylvania* in 1858. We catch glimpses of that entire range of feeling in this late-life, autobiographical equation of Henry with Sid, an affective sequence which ends quite tellingly with an abrupt retreat from an inadvertent and unsettling revelation. Despite the author-cat's attempt to bury the compromising evidence, however, it is clear that there was bad blood between the youngsters in Hannibal, and that it spilled over into the surviving brother's putative idyll about the good old times. Thus the truth of the matter, dutifully—if belatedly—suppressed in the autobiography, surfaces willy-nilly in the fiction.

Kindred missteps and ambiguities emerge in Clemens's scattered comments on the juvenile hero of his novel. "Most of the adventures recorded in this book really occurred," he declares in his Preface, adding that Tom Sawyer "is a combination of the characteristics of three boys whom I knew, and therefore belongs to the composite order of architecture" (*TS,* ix). In his note on sources and characters in the Mark Twain Library Edition of the novel, John C. Gerber declares confidently—and, in my opinion, quite indisputably—that the real life model for the youthful protagonist "must surely have been young Sam Clemens himself, for Tom very much resembles and acts like the boy Mark Twain recalled himself as being."[4] Clemens goes on in the preface to describe his book as "intended mainly for the entertainment of boys and girls," but designed as well "to pleasantly remind adults of what they once were themselves" (*TS,* ix). Clearly, then, at the time of its publication, the author was inclined to view his autobiographical novel as ideally suited to the delicate sensibilities of children, and, at the same time, as happily reminiscent for adults of their early lives. The novel closes on the same note: "So endeth this chronicle. It being strictly a history of a *boy*, it must stop here; the story could not go much further without becoming the history of a *man*" (*TS*, 275).

In the months just before its completion, however, Clemens was not so certain about the line separating juvenile from adult fiction, nor about the propriety of crossing it. "Since there is no plot to the thing," he wrote to Howells on June 25, 1875, "it is likely to follow its own drift, & so is as likely to drift into manhood as anywhere—I won't interpose." He wrote to Howells again ten days later, on July 5, to announce that he had "finished the story & didn't take the chap beyond boyhood." He goes on, "I perhaps made a mistake in not writing it in the first person"; upon further reflection, however, he shifts ground completely, and concludes that "by & by I shall take a boy of twelve & run him on through life (in the first person) but not Tom Sawyer—he would not be a good character for it" (*MTHL*, 1:87–88, 91–92). Several things surface here. Clemens finally decides to confine the novel to Tom's childhood, not only, it is clearly implied, because the onset of manhood marks the end of innocence, but also because Tom is not destined to distinction in his adult years. "If I went on, now, & took him into manhood," he wrote to Howells, "he would be just like all the one-horse men in literature & the reader would conceive a hearty contempt for him" (*MTHL*, 1:91). This latter point is of a piece with Clemens's sense that his hero would be less attractive to us were his story told in the first person. This approach would work well enough with a self-effacing, good-hearted character like Huckleberry Finn; but the intimate exposure of Tom's interior life, he clearly suggests, would produce an erosion of audience respect for the boy's deeper motives. Tom's character, then, is best viewed from the outside, presumably by the genial, forgiving adult narrator who in fact tells the tale. To carry him on into manhood would expose fully the flaws already perceptible in his character.

What, then, was so wrong with young Tom Sawyer that it could not bear close scrutiny? There is of course the unthinking cruelty revealed in his treatment of Jim in *Huckleberry Finn,* and later more fully developed in the fragmentary "Tom Sawyer's Conspiracy," to which we will turn in due course. But there is no hint of this in the novel of 1876. Closer to the mark, no doubt, is the boy's ingenious maneuvering to satisfy his insatiable craving for personal acclaim, preferably in public spectacles. "Tom Sawyer," Clemens wrote in 1902, is "ostentatiously smart & inventive & always *boss*," and a child of "rattle-brained vivacities."[5] What might such a boy become as an adult? We learn toward the end of the novel that "Judge Thatcher hoped to see Tom a great lawyer or a great soldier some day" (*TS,* 269). Clemens himself had a similar view of his hero's likely future. Reflecting critically on his political nemesis, Theodore Roosevelt, he observes in an autobiographical dictation of 1906 that "the President has only one policy and that is to do insanely spectacular things and get himself talked about." "Mr. Roosevelt," he goes on, "is the Tom Sawyer of the political world of the twentieth century; always showing off; always hunting for a chance to show off; in his frenzied imagination the Great Republic is a vast Barnum circus with him for a clown and the whole world for audience; he would go to Halifax for half a chance to show off, and he would go to hell for a whole one" (*MTE,* 48–49).

There is plenty of showing off in *Tom Sawyer,* of course, and the young protagonist never fails to position himself at the center of attention. In this he is clearly akin to Clemens himself, who was as drawn to spectacle and as much a showoff as the fictional boy and the real president. Few have coveted the limelight as Clemens did; few have filled it so completely in their time. "He was the most consummate public performer I ever saw," Howells observes. "He had always a relish for personal effect, which expressed itself in the white suit of complete serge which he wore in his last years, and in the Oxford gown which he put on for every possible occasion, and said he would like to wear all the time."[6] "I should like to dress in a loose and flowing costume made all of silks and velvets resplendent with stunning dyes," Clemens told Paine. "If I should appear on Fifth Avenue on a Sunday morning clothed as I would like to be clothed the churches would all be vacant and the congregation would come tagging after me" (*MTB,* 4:1342).[7] But it was this same delight in public acclaim that brought the internationally celebrated humorist into conflict with his own children. When he offered to introduce Clara at a New York recital in 1906, she declined, insisting that "You'll get all the welcome, and I none." Unfazed, Clemens took the stage after his daughter's performance to deliver a long speech. The press coverage the next day, which gave him the lion's share of the attention, completed his theft of poor Clara's small thunder.[8] Susy suffered equally at the hands of her famous father. Though he promised that he would not include an especially frightening ghost story in his reading to her classmates at Bryn Mawr in 1891, he never seriously considered compromising his program. When he commenced the story, his stricken daughter fled the room in tears, leaving him appalled at his own unaccountable behavior (*MCMT,* 310).

Clemens stayed away from the first-person in *Tom Sawyer,* and decided against taking his hero into manhood, because he shrank from what he glimpsed of himself in the consuming egotism already fully formed in the boy's character. Years later, he would see much more clearly that the man emergent from the boy was a showoff of boundless conceit, a personal defect much less evident to him when he first set pen to paper on his rural idyll. This was to be a story about and for innocent children living in an innocent time and place. Yet Tom's behavior, carefully studied, betrays precisely those qualities that Clemens would later deplore in Theodore Roosevelt and remorsefully acknowledge in himself. It may well be that an intimation of this disturbing potential in his material prompted the retreat to a "safe" narrative perspective on a boy held back from adulthood. Approached in this way, *Tom Sawyer* may be said to dramatize its author's resistance to his story's clear implication that he was never completely innocent, never free from blame.

In taking this view of the novel as autobiography, I am extending the analysis set forth in my book *In Bad Faith: The Dynamics of Deception in Mark Twain's America*. The citizens of St. Petersburg, I there argue, collaborate with each other in the denial of their departures from public codes of morally correct behavior. Because he is gifted with a unique intuitive grasp of the mechanisms of local bad faith, Tom is an adept manipulator who enjoys enormous social, economic, and political advantages. He will be a great leader some day, provided he is able to avoid a conscious reckoning with the subliminal sources of his authority, for full self awareness would be accompanied by the onset of guilt and the subsequent erosion of confidence. At some submerged level, Tom knows that he cannot afford to know what he knows, with the result that he is obliged to expend large sums of psychic energy in the abridgement of guilty self-knowledge. His relationship to himself and his world thus rather precisely recapitulates Clemens's relationship to himself as he is obliquely figured forth in the complex hero of his novel.

Tom recognizes intuitively that the control of other people is readily achieved through the manipulation of their perception of reality. This cardinal principle is nowhere better illustrated than in the famous whitewashing episode, where he persuades his comrades that the work of painting the fence is actually a form of play. The successful execution of the scam leads in turn to the extraction of "a great law of human action . . . namely, that in order to make a man or a boy covet a thing, it is only necessary to make the thing difficult to attain." Yet lest Tom appear too cynically manipulative, the narrator is careful to add that he makes his discovery "without knowing it." Presumably he is equally "innocent" of his own shrewdness when he converts the take on whitewashing privileges into enough tickets to win a Bible. When Tom's fraudulent scheme is finally exposed in church, the narrator steps in to "draw the curtain of charity over the rest of the scene" (*TS*, 32, 52). Once again, we feel the pressure of Clemens's resistance to awkward, indirectly quite personal implication.

Tom's mentor in the elaborate social game of bad faith is his Aunt Polly, who is modeled closely on the author's mother, Jane Clemens. Aunt Polly manipulates Tom, just as his mother surely manipulated young Sam Clemens, with a relentless regimen of guilt. Awaiting punishment for some misdeed, Tom is hopeful that he is going to be flogged;

> but it was not so. His aunt wept over him and asked him how he could go and break her old heart so; and finally told him to go on, and ruin himself and bring her gray hairs with sorrow to the grave, for it was no use for her to try any more. This was worse than a thousand whippings, and Tom's heart was sorer now than his body. He cried, he pleaded for forgiveness, promised reform over and over again and then received his dismissal, feeling that he had won but an imperfect forgiveness and established but a feeble confidence. (*TS*, 99)

But even as he suffers, the boy sees that his entire community is in thrall to the tyranny of conscience. When Sid threatens to betray Tom's secret that Injun Joe killed Doctor Robinson, Aunt Polly intervenes with an astonishing admission. "Sho! It's that dreadful murder," she exclaims. "I dream about it most every night myself. Sometimes I dream it's me that done it" (*TS*, 105). Tom is witness to more of the same when he returns home from a juvenile adventure on Jackson's Island to assure Aunt Polly that he is all right. As he looks on from hiding, his aunt mourns his "death" and weeps remorsefully over her harsh treatment of him. Tom "began to have a nobler opinion of himself than ever before," and barely restrains an impulse to rush out and overwhelm his aunt with joy. Though "the theatrical gorgeousness of the thing appealed strongly to his nature" (*TS*, 131), an even more spectacular scheme is forming in his mind, one that will enhance his opportunities for showing off even as it reduces his vulnerability to guilt. And so he returns to Jackson's Island, abandoning Aunt Polly to her suffering.

In the sequel, Tom displays a talent for showmanship and self-promotion on a par with the genius of Clemens himself. At his own funeral the following Sunday, the young gamesman waits outside the church with Huck Finn and Joe Harper until the assembled congregation has worked itself into a fever of emotion.

The minister related many a touching incident in the lives of the departed . . . which illustrated their sweet, generous natures, and the people could easily see, now, how noble and beautiful those episodes were, and remembered with grief that at the time they occurred they had seemed rank rascalities, well deserving of the cowhide. . . . At last the whole company broke down and joined the weeping mourners in a chorus of anguished sobs, the preacher himself giving way to his feelings, and crying in the pulpit. (*TS,* 146)

Then, while "the minister raised his streaming eyes above his handkerchief, and stood transfixed," Tom leads his small band into the church. "First one and then another pair of eyes followed the minister's, and then almost with one impulse the congregation rose and stared while the three dead boys came marching up the aisle, Tom in the lead." The community's breathless response has the quality, one imagines, of the stunned amazement that would accompany the glimpse of an avatar. The minister's text, "I am the Resurrection and the Life," is still fresh in the minds of his listeners as the boys enter the room, and the unfolding of the familiar religious mystery in palpable form must seem to verge on the miraculous.

Suddenly the minister shouted at the top of his voice: "Praise God from whom all blessings flow—SING!—and put yours hearts in it!"

And they did. Old Hundred swelled up with a triumphant burst, and while it shook the rafters Tom Sawyer the Pirate looked around upon the envying juveniles about him and confessed in his heart that this was the proudest moment of his life.

As the "sold" congregation trooped out they said they would almost be willing to be made ridiculous again to hear Old Hundred sung like that once more (*TS,* 146–47).

The citizens of St. Petersburg have been "sold," and they know it. Yet they are amiably disposed to be pleased with what amounts to an admission of their immersion in bad faith. No one is finally deceived by the mock-resurrection, but no one fails to be moved by its timely reenactment of an ancient fable of birth and regeneration. It is Tom's genius to recognize intuitively that he can "sell" his neighbors with impunity so long as he rewards their credulity with entertaining affirmations of the common life. His exploit repays him with acclaim sufficient to the demands of his voracious ego; as important, it distracts attention from the selfishness and deceit of its contrivance, and thus facilitates the evasion of guilt. True, Aunt Polly challenges Tom to explain how he "could be so hard-hearted to let [her] suffer so," but he responds by referring to a sycamore scroll that he brought with him on the night of his secret visit, and on which he had inscribed a message designed to ease her grief. Later on, when the old woman finds the scroll in Tom's jacket, she is overcome with tears of gratitude. "I could forgive the boy, now," she weeps, "if he'd committed a million sins!" (*TS*, 148–9, 160).

I have argued that Tom would succumb to crippling guilt were he fully sensitized to the selfish manipulation involved in his spectacular exploits. His enjoyment of the fruits of his intuitive mastery of local bad faith is conditional on his blindness to his profound immersion in it. But of course we can see what Tom cannot, just as Clemens belatedly, and by reluctant fits and starts, caught sight of the shrewd operator nascent in his "innocent" alter ego. He wrote home from Hannibal in 1902 about a pleasant visit "to the old house I lived in when I whitewashed the fence 53 years ago."[9] But an autobiographical note from the same period declaring "I am not Tom"[10] indicates much less enthusiasm for sharing an identity with the hero of his famous novel. Indeed, it may well be that reflections on Tom's example played some part in Clemens's accelerating late-life gravitation to a conception of human nature dominated by the drive for self-approval. "The mainspring of man's nature," he wrote in 1885, is "selfishness" (*WIM*, 64). But selfishness is constrained in its operations by the equally potent human susceptibility to guilt. "Conscience," Clemens declares in *What Is Man?*, "that independent Sovereign, that insolent absolute Monarch inside of a man who is the man's Master" (*WIM*, 140–41). Selfishness and the aversion to guilt combine synergistically in the universal human demand for self-approval. "A man must and will have his own approval first of all" is the leading premise of Clemens's 1901 essay "Corn-Pone Opinions" (*WIM*, 95). In "*What Is Man?*" it reappears as "the Sole Impulse which dictates and compels a man's every act: the imperious necessity of securing his own approval, in every emergency and at all costs. To it we owe all that we are" (*WIM*, 147).

That these qualities merge in such a conspicuous and powerful way in Tom Sawyer may help to account for Clemens's gathering ambivalence toward his hero. Tom's compulsive grandstanding is driven by a craving for acclaim that invariably provides a boost to his self-approval. Recall that his nocturnal return from Jackson's Island rewards him with "a nobler opinion of himself than ever before," and that he regards the mock resurrection as "the proudest moment of his life." Let us observe as well, however, that the enjoyment of such levitating self-approval is contingent on the successful evasion of the risk of guilt incurred by its achievement. The sheer gaudiness of the mock resurrection diverts attention from Tom's scheming and leaves the congregation grateful to have been "sold"; the sycamore scroll, mean-while, suffices to appease the more skeptical Aunt Polly. Here as elsewhere in the novel, Tom's audacious virtuosity as a showoff repays him with a maximum of the self-approval that comes with adoring public acclaim and, as important, shelter from guilty reproach.

Because of the risks entailed in feeding his voracious ego, Tom is peren-nially on the verge of crisis. Catastrophe is barely averted when he "wins" his Bible, and again when Aunt Polly's spasm of guilt puts an end to Sid's snooping into the murder of Dr. Robinson. The sycamore scroll succeeds only because it is planted in advance as a rejoinder to an anticipated accusa-tion. The scroll offers itself as evidence of a generous, loving motive; in fact, it is the shrewdly contrived simulation of such a motive, deployed on pur-pose as a stay against guilty exposure. Once again, Tom's behavior clearly anticipates philosophical arguments developed much later in *What Is Man?* "Men pretend to self sacrifices," Clemens insists, "but this is a thing which, in the ordinary value of the phrase, *does not exist and has not existed.* A man often honestly *thinks* he is sacrificing himself merely and solely for some one else, but he is deceived; his bottom impulse is to content a requirement of his nature and training, and thus acquire peace for his soul" (*WIM,* 140). It is Tom's genius to recognize and exploit opportunities to advance his own grandiose selfishness under the shelter of moral impunity purchased by sim-ulated acts of self-sacrifice. When Becky Thatcher accidentally rips a page in the teacher's anatomy book, Tom contrives to take the blame, and thus earns his elusive sweetheart's undying gratitude and love, not to mention the satisfaction of great notoriety among his peers. "Tom, how *could* you be so noble!" (*TS,* 166), Becky exclaims. She acquiesces in the deception be-cause it so perfectly conforms to her own perceived self-interest. Judge Thatcher, who is similarly motivated, declares "with a fine outburst that it was a noble, a generous, a magnanimous lie—a lie that was worthy to hold up its head and march down through history breast to breast with George Washington's lauded Truth about the hatchet!" (*TS,* 269).

Nor is the risk of guilty exposure and collapsed self-approval the only danger that Tom hazards in his headlong egotism. For as the number and scale of his exploits increase, so does the likelihood that he will come into a crippling awareness of the selfishness and fraudulence that drive them. Kin-dred intimations, we may plausibly surmise, had a part to play in Clemens's decisions about his hero's age and his novel's form. The irony brimming over in the description of the Judge's fatuous celebration of Tom's lie leaves little doubt as to the author's restive impatience with the moral folly at large in his idyll—folly that would appear in bolder relief were the boy older or his point of view more intimately on display. But, then, Clemens was his own laboratory in such matters. Tom's selfishly contrived sacrifice in taking Becky's punishment had a partial source in the humorist's memory of having once saved a pretty girl from similar humiliation. "Once I was a hero," he recalled in 1907, fully alert to the essential vanity of the claim. "I can never forget it. . . . I saw my chance to be a hero, and I rose to the occasion."[11]

Strategies of self-interested simulation came almost naturally to young Sam Clemens. When a traveling mesmerist made a stop in Hannibal in 1850, the boy's ego was immediately engaged. "I was fourteen or fifteen years old, the age at which a boy is willing to endure all things, suffer all things short of death by fire, if thereby he may be conspicuous and show off before the public; and so, when I saw the 'subjects' perform their foolish antics on the platform and make the people laugh and shout and admire, I had a burning desire to be a subject myself." At the first chance, he contrived to display the qualities—entirely simulated—of an ideal subject for the mesmerist's trances. "Cautious at first and watchful" lest the showman discover he is "an impostor" and drive him "from the platform in disgrace," Clemens soon warmed to his task and performed with audacious brilliance, accepting repeated pin prickings without giving any visible sign of pain. As the result, he was called back to the platform on a nightly basis, "a hero," he recalls, "and happier than I have ever been in this world since." Looking back over more than a half-century, the veteran entertainer perfectly grasps the complex moral significance of his youthful masquerade. When a small group of "implacable unbelievers" raised questions about the show's authenticity, "I was as hurt," he reports, "as if I were engaged in some honest occupation. There is nothing surprising about this. Human beings feel dishonor the most, sometimes, when they most deserve it." Nor does the knowledge that it is rigged diminish his pleasure in the game of deception. When the last of the doubters capitulates, he recalls, "I knew I was undisputed master of the field; and now after more than fifty years I acknowledge, with a few dry old tears, that I rejoiced without shame." Finally, he observes "how easy it is to make people believe a lie, and how hard it is to undo that work again!" As evidence, he reports that when, years later, he tried to "confess [his] ancient fault" to his mother, she refused to believe that his trances were completely simulated. He could not have faked his indifference to the pain of the pins, she insists. "Here is my arm," he replies; "drive a pin into it—drive it to the head—I shall not wince." But she declines: "You are a man, now, and could dissemble the hurt; but you were only a child then and could not have done it" (*MTE,* 119–30).[12] She is wrong, of course. Like Tom Sawyer, her young son was a seasoned expert in self-interested simulation.

Tom's mastery of the local culture of bad faith achieves culminating expression in the wake of the murder of Dr. Robinson. My discussion of this episode in chapter 2, above, centers on Tom's secret knowledge that Injun Joe did the killing, and that Muff Potter, who is accused of the crime, is actually innocent. Tom expends enormous sums of energy and ingenuity trying to elude the guilt that attaches to his secret. When nothing else seems to work, he surrenders in desperation to a psychosomatic case of the measles. His affliction renders him "dead to the world and its happenings," and thus serves admirably as a distraction from what most deeply ails him. But with recovery comes reentry into a world of moral consequence. A terrific summer storm, with "awful claps of thunder and blinding sheets of lightning," leaves him "in a horror of suspense for his doom; for he had not the shadow of a doubt that all this hubbub was about him. He believed he had taxed the forbearance of the powers above to the extremity of endurance and that this was the result" (*TS,* 179). Clemens used nearly identical words more than thirty years later to describe the "prodigious storm," with "awful thunder-bursts and the white glare of the lightning," that passed through Hannibal during his childhood on the night that Injun Joe died. "By my teachings," he recalls, "I perfectly well knew what all that wild rumpus was for—Satan had come to get Injun Joe. I had no shadow of doubt about it" (*AMT,* 68). It was a long night of guilty self-reckoning for Clemens, as it is for Tom, who now sees that the truth about Injun Joe and Muff Potter must at last be told.

When the last of his many schemes to evade his conscience has failed, Tom is finally forced to confess. But in doing so, he converts potential humiliation into self-aggrandizing, self-exculpating spectacle by masterfully orchestrating the public disclosure of Muff Potter's innocence. The scheme is set in motion when Tom enlists the help of Potter's young lawyer, who cannot resist an opportunity to indulge an appetite for courtroom theatrics. In seizing upon the occasion to show off, the lawyer in turn calls upon the boy to testify, and thus unknowingly abets Tom's ambition to perform in front of a large, breathlessly attentive audience. "Speak out my boy," the lawyer encourages, "don't be diffident. The truth is always respectable." Tom is way ahead of him, of course, and before long "every eye fixed itself upon him; with parted lips and bated breath the audience hung upon his words, taking no note of time, rapt in the ghastly fascinations of the tale" (*TS*, 187). In due course, Muff Potter is exonerated, Injun Joe takes guilty flight from the courtroom, and the townspeople are once again in grateful debt to Tom for an uplifting and intensely exciting spectacle.

Tom's triumph notwithstanding, the irony of the lawyer's equation of truth with respectability is hardly lost on us. For while Tom's confession is ostensibly "respectable" because it serves justice, it is equally in the service of pervasive bad faith. It arises out of and reinforces—it "plays" to—a culture of lies. Most obviously, perhaps, there is the hypocrisy of the villagers, who are so intimidated by Injun Joe that they shrink from prosecuting him, and rush instead to condemn Muff Potter. There is the broadly comical discrepancy between the forthright veracity the lawyer preaches and the vain theatrics he practices. A kindred contradiction emerges when we apply the lawyer's definition of "truth" to the testimony it describes; for justice has almost nothing to do with Tom's motivation for appearing in court. He is moved first and foremost by the desperate need to pacify his ruthless conscience. Were Tom as guilt-free in the matter as Huck Finn, Potter would go to his grave unmourned. He is moved as well to divert attention from the fact that, in utter disregard for the well-being of the entire community, he has put off revealing the truth for a long time. This objective is substantially met in the trial itself, where the star witness's showing off draws attention away from the awkward delay. It is thus Tom's extraordinary genius in bad faith to convert the necessity of a suspiciously belated confession into a spectacle that at once frees him from all guilt and blame and thrusts him into the center of attention. So viewed, respectability is an ingenious confidence-game presided over by a boy of penetrating social intuition and boundless chutzpah.

Most importantly for present purposes, the deeper moral truth of the situation is not entirely lost on Clemens, who here as elsewhere in the novel gives evidence of gathering impatience with untoward developments in his children's idyll. We feel the oblique pressure of his point of view in the lawyer's fatuous insistence that "the truth is always respectable." We feel it more directly and unambiguously in the narrator's reflections in the aftermath of the courtroom spectacle. Not surprisingly, perhaps, he is impatient to the point of contempt with the adults in the community, whose willingness to overlook their hero's negligence is rewarded with pleasurable confirmation of the upright efficiency of their civic institutions, and tacit permission to ignore their own delinquencies in matters of justice. The irony at their expense is unmistakable in the narrator's observation that, "as usual, the fickle, unreasoning world took Muff Potter to its bosom and fondled him as lavishly as it had abused him before." The townspeople are equally inconsistent in their treatment of Tom, who "was a glittering hero once more—the pet of the old, the envy of the young. His name even went into immortal print, for the village paper magnified him." Most tellingly of all, "there were some that believed he would be President, yet, if he escaped hanging" (*TS*, 189).

Here, briefly but emphatically, the Tom Sawyer of the future is present to the consciousness presiding over this carefully restrained "history of a boy." His emergence is occasioned to some extent by the morally compromised circumstances in which we find him. The boy, after all, will surely mirror the values and behavior of the adults in his community—people habituated to lives of "glaring insincerity," Clemens observes, wryly conceding that this "homely truth is unpalatable" (*TS*, 171). But Tom is no passive reflector of St. Petersburg mores. To the contrary, he is intuitively the master of the dynamics of local bad faith, which he turns to his own advantage with unerring dexterity. It is at once attributable to his mastery that he endures, and that he is adept at evading, great guilt. Doubtless his youth has something do with the fact that he conducts his operations without fully grasping their moral implications. As I have suggested more than once, Tom's "innocence" is precarious, and its loss is as certain and imminent as the onset of adulthood. Self-consciousness will bring both a sharpening of moral focus and a concomitant refinement of evasive strategies, which in a boy of Tom's ambition, egotism, and genius for manipulation must almost inevitably lead to a career in—what else?—politics. The townspeople are surely correct that the only thing that stands between their resourceful hero and the presidency is the possibility that the means of his self-aggrandizement will land him in jail. The aptness and validity of their insight are in turn testimony to Clemens's dawning awareness that his hero was the youthful prototype for the most ambitious, egotistical, and successfully manipulative showoff of them all, Theodore Roosevelt. It was the logical inference—one that Clemens seems to have approached quite gingerly—that the qualities rapidly forming in his hero, and fully developed in his presidential nemesis, were quintessentially his own. It was this troubling truth about himself that flashed across the humorist's consciousness as he labored over *The Adventures of Tom Sawyer*.

The Prince and the Pauper (1881) may be viewed as a variation on Clemens's idealization of childhood as a moral alternative to the intolerable degradation of adult reality. Tom Canty and Prince Edward are worlds apart in their backgrounds, but identical in their ability to draw valuable moral lessons from harsh experience, and at the same time to escape the fall into cynicism and bad faith that is the lot of adults. Tom readily relinquishes royal privilege—which he comes to regard as a form of bondage—in favor of the simplicity of a much humbler station. Edward, meanwhile, because he has learned firsthand what it is to suffer hunger and injustice, rules England with unprecedented generosity and compassion. This is precisely the lesson that Clemens had in mind. "My idea," he wrote to Howells in March 1880, "is to afford a realizing sense of the exceeding severity of the laws of that day by inflicting some of their penalties upon the king himself & allowing him a chance to see the rest of them applied to others—all of which is to account for certain mildnesses which distinguished Edward VI's reign from those that preceded & followed it" (*MTHL,* 1:291–92).

Its thematic coherence notwithstanding, modern scholars have not looked with much critical favor on *The Prince and the Pauper.* James M. Cox surely speaks for many in faulting the book for its rather abject surrender to conventional pieties, and for thus forcing "humor to serve a noble purpose instead of forcing all noble purposes to serve humor."[13] Roger B. Salomon argues that the novel's happy ending, in which goodness and power combine to produce a reign of justice, is the stuff of fairy tales, and had no foundation in Clemens's considered view of the world. "To a figure in time and history," he rightly complains, "he gave values which he was unable to locate in time and history."[14] Though Cox and Salomon approach the novel from different critical angles, they are at one in charging Clemens in *The Prince and the Pauper* with being false to himself—false to "the fate of humor," false to his developing sense of the tragedy of history. It may be asked why the same charge is not brought against *Tom Sawyer,* a novel equally committed to what Salomon describes as "the dream of innate goodness which, during this time, was so integral a part of [Clemens's] image of childhood."[15] The answer, of course, is that the earlier novel fails to follow through on its idyllic designs. This is so because *Tom Sawyer* draws directly on the matter of Hannibal, on childhood memories subversive of the idealizing impulse which gave rise to its telling. Unlike Edward VI, Tom achieves preeminence in society not by learning from experience and making benevolent reforms, but by exploiting the bad faith of the adult society to his own personal advantage. Tom is innocent only to the extent that he fails consciously to recognize that he uses the adults against themselves, and will continue to do so with increasing success, so long as he avoids jail, until the onset of adulthood. He has no interest in changing the world; rather, in return for power and acclaim, he "plays to" the self-interested illusions that reinforce the community *status quo*.

To put the matter another way, the fairy-tale ending of *The Prince and the Pauper* could not have been sustained in a narrative that drew directly on the author's personal experience. The book's distinctive tone is geared directly to the fact that it is an historical novel set in a remote time and place. Nonetheless, Clemens was obliged at numerous points along the way to supplement the received historical record—points at which autobiographical materials achieved access to the realm of the long ago and far away, and thus produced the most conspicuous lapses in the novel's dominant tone. Clemens drew directly on David Hume's *History of England* for his treatment of Henry VIII's planned execution of the Duke of Norfolk as a means of hastening the installation of Edward as Prince of Wales.[16] But Hume has nothing to say about how the threat of Norfolk's death affects the Prince, whose role in the novel is now filled by the pauper, young Tom Canty. Tom's delight in his royal masquerade is utterly shattered by the heavy burden of guilt that attaches to his remote implication in the plan for Norfolk's execution. "Turn where he would, he seemed to see floating in the air the severed head and the remembered face of the great Duke of Norfolk, the eyes fixed on him reproachfully" (*P&P* 69). Such extreme feelings arise into the narrative from the troubled memory and imagination of the author himself. We catch a fleeting glimpse here of the face of the burning tramp, his accusing eyes fixed unforgettably on young Sam Clemens. There is a similar sighting later in the novel, when Prince Edward, in the role of the pauper, looks on in horror as two innocent women are burned at the stake. "That which I have seen, in that one little moment," the Prince laments, "will never go out from my memory, but will abide there; and I shall see it all the days, and dream of it all the nights, till I die. Would God I had been blind" (*P&P* 327). Once again, bitterly accusing autobiographical memories thrust upward into the historical narrative.

Norfolk survived, Hume's *History* reports, because Henry VIII suddenly died, and because his council then decided to reverse the order of execution. Clemens again carefully acknowledges his debt to Hume,[17] though he also supplements his source by having the guilty Tom Canty personally intervene to spare the duke's life. Henry is no sooner dead than his apparent successor decrees that "the duke of Norfolk shall not die!" (*P&P* 129). The stay of execution temporarily restores Tom's moral equanimity, but it hardly diminishes the ongoing authority of guilt in his characterization. He is at times painfully reminded that the rightful king is suffering terribly in exile.

Because they make him "feel guilty and ashamed," he banishes such thoughts from consciousness. He does the same with memories of his poor mother and sisters, for "whenever their mournful and accusing faces" arise in his consciousness, they make "him feel more despicable than the worms that crawl" (*P&P* 350). It is of course Clemens's personal voice and moral vision, and not David Hume's, that we witness in the fictional boy's anguish.

Tom's painful subjection to guilt is no more autobiographically resonant than his reason for suppressing it. He draws back from thoughts of changing places with the rightful King and rejoining his family because to do so would spell the end of the orgy of acclaim that he enjoys as the royal pretender. If only barely and temporarily, the opportunity to show off trumps guilt. Like his maker, lowborn Tom Canty cannot get enough of lavish public spectacle. Clemens goes on for pages in loving descriptions of gorgeous Elizabethan pageantry and display. In the midst of it all, "magnificently habited in a doublet of white satin, with a front-piece of purple cloth-of-tissue, powdered with diamonds, and edged with ermine," is Tom himself, "born in a hovel, bred in the gutters of London, familiar with rags and dirt and misery, what a spectacle is this!" (*P&P* 106). Tom delights especially in taking center stage before an adoring multitude. During a "recognition procession" through the streets of London, he "gazed abroad over the surging sea of eager faces, and his heart swelled with exultation; and he felt that the one thing worth living for in this world was to be a king, and a nation's idol" (*P&P* 353, 355).

We can hardly fail to recognize Clemens's immoderate craving for the spotlight in this extraordinary declaration. Just so, the novelist's bondage to guilt manifests itself in his fictional alter-ego's conscience-stricken renunciation of personal glory. In the course of the same procession, Tom suddenly sees his mother in the crowd. When she rushes to embrace him, a guard rudely pushes her away.

> The words "I do not know you, woman!" were falling from Tom Canty's lips when this piteous thing occurred; but it smote him to the heart to see her treated so; and as she turned for a last glimpse of him, whilst the crowd was swallowing her from his sight, she seemed so wounded, so broken-hearted, that a shame fell upon him which consumed his pride to ashes, and withered his stolen royalty. His grandeurs were stricken valueless: they seemed to fall away from him like rotten rags. . . . Royalty had lost its grace and sweetness; its pomps were become a reproach. (*P&P* 358–59)

Tom's mother, like Aunt Polly and Jane Clemens before her, is the agent through which guilt reasserts its moral authority. Tom is now indifferent to the clamorous throngs, and "the accusing voice that went moaning through his comfortless breast was all the sound he heard" (*P&P* 360). His mood grows darker still on coronation day, as the moral weight of his masquerade bears down on him. "The ancient ceremonies went on, with impressive solemnity, whilst the audience gazed." But Tom, who has lost his appetite for glory, "grew pale, and still paler, and a deep and steadily deepening woe and despondency settled down upon his spirits and upon his remorseful heart" (*P&P* 369). Happily enough, Edward arrives in the nick of time to claim the crown and to save his twin from complete despair. Tom is restored to his family; even better, he is made the King's Ward and authorized to appear in public in a distinctive costume. "Whenever he appeared," Clemens is pleased to observe, "the crowd fell apart, making way for him, and whispering, one to another, 'Doff thy hat, it is the King's Ward!' and so they saluted, and got his kindly smile in return" (*P&P* 401).

Like *Tom Sawyer*, *The Prince and the Pauper* is narrated in the third person, a perspective employed in both novels to selectively screen out much of the selfishness and vanity that motivates the youthful protagonists. This was a conscious choice on Clemens's part, just as his decision to adopt the first person in *Adventures of Huckleberry Finn* (1885) was carefully taken. Recall his 1875 letter to Howells in which he promises in time to "take a boy of twelve & run him on through life (in the first person) but not Tom Sawyer" (*MTHL*, 1:92). That boy was Huck Finn, of course, to whose story Clemens first turned in 1876, but which was many years in the making. Much of his difficulty completing the novel centered on another, equally consequential, change in his fictional world—the addition of Jim. The virtual nonexistence of black people and slavery in *Tom Sawyer*—where they might well be expected to appear—is integral to the novel's generally sunny tone. By contrast, Jim's appearance in *Huckleberry Finn* makes all the difference in the book's much darker mood. His woeful story, as it unfolds in the consciousness of Huckleberry Finn, brings with it all the grief that attached to race-slavery, both for the boy who tells the story, and for the man who wrote it.

Clemens did not identify with Huck in the same way that he did with Tom. There was the barrier of class—no small consideration to a man who took great pride in the imagined eminence of his British forebears. Something of his attitude may be glimpsed in a 1903 letter from his daughter, Clara, to her cousin, Samuel E. Moffett. "There has been so much said in the papers lately of my father's being himself the original of Huckleberry

Finn," she writes, "that my mother has worried at the thought that many might believe him to be one of the poor white of the South."[18] Huck is also "other" in the more positive sense that he possesses estimable human qualities that set him apart from Tom. In a 1902 letter to Charles B. Dillingham, Clemens draws attention to "the deeps & the dignity of Huck's character," which "is sharply differentiated from Tom's, & gains a good deal, with its unconscious depth & long-headedness & sobriety."[19]

Despite the difference in class, then, Clemens was inclined to admire Huck, even as he admired Huck's real-life model, Tom Blankenship. "In 'Huckleberry Finn' I have drawn Tom Blankenship exactly as he was," he declares in a 1906 autobiographical dictation.

> He was ignorant, unwashed, insufficiently fed; but he had as good a heart as ever any boy had. His liberties were totally unrestricted. He was the only really independent person—boy or man—in the community, and by consequence he was tranquilly and continuously happy and was envied by all the rest of us. We liked him; we enjoyed his society. (*ATM,* 68)

For a man who bitterly resented all obstacles to what is free and easy and comfortable in life, here was a memorable model of unencumbered bliss.

Tom Blankenship's attraction was doubtless enhanced for Clemens by the example of his older brother, Benson, who for several weeks during the summer in 1847 secretly assisted a runaway slave hidden along the banks of the Mississippi. Blankenship not only turned his back on the fifty-dollar reward offered for the slave's capture, but risked running afoul of the local fear and hatred of abolitionists. "In those old slave-holding days," Clemens recalled in 1895,

> the whole community was agreed as to one thing—the awful sacredness of slave property. To help steal a horse or a cow was a low crime, but to help a hunted slave, or feed him or shelter him, or hide him, or comfort him, in his trouble, his terrors, his despair, or hesitate to promptly betray him to the slave-catcher when opportunity offered was a much baser crime, & carried with it a stain, a moral smirch which nothing could wipe away.[20]

Blankenship's extraordinary humanity and courage were obviously quite impressive to the author of *Huckleberry Finn,* who remembered them many years later when he conceived the juvenile hero and plot of his greatest work. Indeed, Clemens's reminiscences about "those old slave-holding days" are prefaced by his oft-quoted characterization of the novel as "a book of mine where a sound heart & a deformed conscience come into collision & conscience suffers defeat." He goes on to observe that it was "natural enough to me" in those old times, just as it was "natural enough [in] Huck," that they should have conformed to local attitudes about slaves and abolitionists, even "though it seems now absurd."[21]

Clemens's identification with Huck in this vital matter is interesting for several reasons. They were alike, his memory tells him, in their outward adherence to the leading prejudices of a slaveholding community; but they were alike as well in sharing a deeper, heart-felt uneasiness with those same attitudes, the intense pressure of conscience notwithstanding. Somehow they knew that what local convention held to be right and "natural" was in fact wrong and even "absurd." Clemens's defensiveness is manifest both in his felt need to acknowledge that he once subscribed to morally indefensible beliefs about race-slavery—beliefs that he resisted inwardly—and in the impulse to explain his complicity away as the product of a twisted upbringing. Like Huck's, he insists, his own errant childhood beliefs show "that that strange thing, the conscience—that unerring monitor—can be trained to approve any wild thing you *want* it to approve if you begin its education early & stick to it."[22] Clemens thus condemns the twinned evils of slavery and conscience, and aligns himself closely with Huck's instinctive, good-hearted rejection of both. These potent moral impulses are at the very center of his personal investment in *Huckleberry Finn.*

The novel is clear and emphatic in its implicit judgment of race-slavery, and may be said to mark a major threshold in Clemens's concern with the issue over the last quarter-century of his life. The novel is equally clear about conscience. "If I had a yaller dog that didn't know no more than a person's conscience," Huck complains, "I would pison him. It takes up more room than all the rest of a person's insides, and yet ain't no good, nohow" (*HF*, 290). The author of "The Facts Concerning the Recent Carnival of Crime in Connecticut" was of course perfectly at one with Huck on this score, and speaks directly through him. "As a *guide* or *incentive* to any authoritatively prescribed line of morals or conduct," Clemens observes in *What Is Man?*, "a man's conscience is totally valueless" (*WIM*, 141). But agreement on the evils of race-slavery and conscience is hardly the end of the story. True, Huck overcomes his "deformed conscience" when he resolves to risk going to hell in order to steal Jim out of slavery. But much that both precedes and follows his famous decision points to enduring conflicts in his feelings about his black companion—conflicts that reflect even deeper troubles in the heart and mind of his maker. Like Huck, Clemens triumphed over the voice in his conscience that condemned resistance to race-slavery as a sin. Unlike Huck, however, he was unable to forgive himself for his earlier complicity in that great moral error, and continued long after 1885 to experience terrible remorse over his complex involvement in a civilization that endorsed race-slavery. Howells was absolutely right: his friend took the moral burden entirely upon himself. *Huckleberry Finn* helps to explain why.

Arthur G. Pettit has argued persuasively that Clemens was "haunted by memories of slavery" and "consumed with shame and guilt over [the] treatment of the black race" in the South. Over the course of his life he developed in stages "from conscious bigot to unconscious bigot to one who finally became fully aware of his bigotry, fought it, and largely overcame it."[23] He was gradually brought around to the Union side during his Western years, but was much slower to concede racial equality to blacks and to forgo racial humor. "A True Story," published in the *Atlantic Monthly* in 1874, manifests a genuine sympathy for slaves, but in a genteel context and mood entirely of a piece with *Tom Sawyer* and "Old Times on the Mississippi," versions of the Southern boyhood idyll that soon followed. In the 1880s, Clemens was an active promoter of numerous black causes, including a federal appointment for Frederick Douglass and educational support for black university students. But good deeds were accompanied by increasingly troubled thoughts. "Whenever a colored man commits an unright action," he wrote to Karl Gerhardt in 1883, "upon his head is the guilt of only about one tenth of it, and upon your heads and mine and the rest of the white race lies fairly and justly the other nine tenths of the guilt."[24] Over time, that guilt grew ever heavier with Clemens. "Each time he saw a black face," Pettit observes, "his mind veered off in another direction—away from the 1880s and back toward the 1850s."[25] The acknowledgement that blacks were widely mistreated in the present invariably brought with it upsurges of guilt about his own attitudes and misdeeds in antebellum Missouri. A sense of futility began to surface in his writing on racial subjects, and with it an increasing tendency to lump blacks and whites together in a sweeping indictment of the entire human race.

Pettit emphasizes that in attempting to come to terms with his guilty past, Clemens was inclined to indulge himself in memories that minimized the brutality of slavery in Hannibal.[26] In his very valuable new book, *Searching for Jim: Slavery in Sam Clemens's World*, Terrell Dempsey makes the same point, arguing that the writer often gravitated in memory to comforting lies about the treatment of slaves in his boyhood home. Such was the pressure of guilt that it enforced flight to the happy fictions of *Tom Sawyer* and "Old

Times on the Mississippi." But "Hannibal was never the white town drowsing in the sun of Clemens's childhood idyl," Dempsey argues, "but instead a place of turmoil, which increased as the nation slid into civil war." At the center of the turmoil was race-slavery, which brought with it the nagging fear of slave revolt, the dreadful violence and cruelty involved in the discipline and sale of human chattel, the hatred of abolitionists encroaching from nearby Illinois, and the desperate attempt to justify an institution awash in contradiction. Young Sam Clemens was never far from the eye of the storm. He came from a slave-holding family; his father was a leading actor in the local struggle against abolitionists; and the newspaper to which he was apprenticed in 1848 was vigorously partisan. Despite his horror at the violence in his midst, and his instinctive moral recoil from the spectacle of cruelty and injustice, the youngster was swept along in the swirling tide of fear and anger and paranoia. Little wonder that guilt fell so heavily upon him when he was finally at liberty to see clearly what he had formerly strained to ignore and deny; little wonder that he held himself personally responsible for white crimes against black slaves. "This was no abstract social debt," Dempsey insists. "Clemens was making amends for specific wrongs. Perhaps as he wrote out the checks" for black college students "he thought of the six slaves inherited by his parents and sold, the little nine-year-old slave girl his father had seized and sold, Charley," who was accorded similar treatment, "and the slave Henry, who received the twenty lashes." Or he might have thought of the years that the three Illinois abolitionists—whom his father helped to convict "spent in the Missouri State Penitentiary for doing what his character Huck safely did in a novel two decades after the Civil War." Perhaps he thought of the newspaper advertisements for human beings, or the "degrading stories" that "he set and sold" as a printer's apprentice. "For a man with as big a conscience as Sam Clemens's," Dempsey quite rightly concludes, "it must have been a terrible burden."[27]

Huckleberry Finn is our richest source of insight into how Clemens bore up under that "burden" during the late 1870s and the 1880s. The book's autobiographical value is undoubtedly the greater for the fact that it is a fiction, and that its hero, unlike Tom Sawyer, is not a boy with whom Clemens identified directly. Because he saw comparatively little of himself and of his own remembered experience in Huck, and because his unlettered protagonist is the actual narrator of the tale, the author-cat was much less vigilant than he would have been had he been speaking more nearly *in propria persona*. As the result, the novel indirectly betrays much that Clemens would have refrained from articulating in his own voice. Consider that all of his recorded comments on the novel, and most especially those on its controversial hero, support a clear and straightforward understanding of the book's significance. While Tom Sawyer, the shrewdly self-interested games-man, is Clemens's somewhat ambivalent self-portrait, Huck is a lowborn boy who risks everything to help a runaway slave. True, Huck is "humble, timid, ignorant, uninventive," and Tom's "willing slave and enthusiastic ad-mirer."[28] But he has moral depths and dignity where Tom is all show. Most crucially, his good heart triumphs over his deformed conscience when he decides to steal Jim out of slavery.

In the aggregate, Clemens's scattered comments amount to a reading of the novel anchored in chapter 31, where Huck famously elects to risk perdi-tion on behalf of a slave. The chapter is a powerful dramatization of the boy's inner struggle, at its most moving perhaps when he reflects back on his long journey and finds that he cannot strike any "places to harden" him-self against Jim, "but only the other kind" (*HF*, 270). His decision to go to hell is morally heroic, of course, not least of all because it lends emphatic confirmation to his settled view that he is a hopeless sinner. This is the igno-rant, humble, but good-hearted boy whose instinctive sense of justice and moral courage were as central to Clemens's understanding of his novel as they have been in the response of generations of readers. And yet this is not all that the narrative reveals about Huck, any more than Clemens's under-standing of the novel was the one best supported by the entirety of the long, complicated story that he had written. *Huckleberry Finn* is much more searching and troubled in its presentation of Huck and Jim and race-slavery in America than anything its author ever said about it.

We well understand why Hemingway wanted *Huckleberry Finn* to end with chapter 31. It is morally so much simpler and so much more satisfying if Huck overcomes the evil in himself and his society by vowing to deliver Jim from bondage into freedom. But we need go no further than the next chapter to see that this is simply not the end of the story. Recall that in chapter 32 Huck goes to the Phelps plantation in search of Jim, and is there absolutely delighted when he is mistaken by Aunt Sally and Uncle Silas for Tom Sawyer. "But if they was joyful," Huck reports, "it warn't nothing to what I was; for it was like being born again, I was so glad to find out who I was" (*HF*, 282). Many readers are shocked and dismayed that Huck should surrender so eagerly to this unlikely identity, and to the cruel trials that the real Tom Sawyer's subsequent "evasion" entails for poor Jim. What has be-come of the "real" Huck Finn, the heroic boy of chapter 31, who here, so suddenly and shamelessly, seizes on the opportunity to abandon his commitment to Jim?

In fact, the Huck Finn we come to know over the course of the novel is torn between totally irreconcilable attitudes toward his friend. In chapter 31, as elsewhere, Huck acknowledges Jim's humanity and reaches out to him as a brother. But at many other points he betrays an inclination to think of Jim as an inferior, as chattel. When Aunt Sally asks if anybody was hurt in the steamboat accident, Huck promptly replies: "No'm. Killed a nigger" (*HF,* 279). True, in chapter 31 he answers an impulse to question the Christian civilization that keeps black people in bondage. In the main, however, he concedes the necessity and propriety of the institution, and centers his troubled soul-searching on his own sinfulness in failing to "do the right thing and the clean thing" (*HF,* 269). His decision to go to hell is an unequivocal assertion of the justice of the system that enslaves Jim. Indeed, his psychological equilibrium is more precarious than ever precisely because of his heroic resolve to rescue Jim, for that decision is a conscious and consequential violation of social prohibitions that he has internalized. Thus divided against himself, the real Huck Finn—the marginal, ambivalent, guilt-haunted fugitive—falls prey to the demons that arise from within his troubled mind. In this perspective, it is neither surprising nor inconsistent that he should take refuge in the comparatively unambivalent and supremely socialized identity of Tom Sawyer.

This is not to suggest that Huck somehow loses his good heart in chapter 32; rather, it is to argue that his story bears with it the discouraging message that a good heart alone is woefully inadequate to the moral challenges posed by race-slavery. Clemens as a child was evidently quite good-hearted in his attitude toward slaves. Annual visits to his Uncle John Quarles' farm brought him into close contact with slaves, chief among whom was "Uncle Dan'l," the real-life model for Jim, and "a faithful and affectionate good friend." It was on the farm, Clemens recalls in his autobiography, "that I got my strong liking for his race and my appreciation of certain of its fine qualities." Virtually in the same breath, however, he concedes that "in my schoolboy days I had no aversion to slavery. I was not aware that there was anything wrong about it" (*AMT,* 6). His moral disclaimer notwithstanding, the novelist was deeply troubled by the spectacle of slave suffering, and most especially by the grief brought on when slaves were separated from their families and sold. Huck, who is notably like-minded in all such matters, surely speaks for Clemens at the auction of the Wilkes' slaves: "It most made me down sick to see it," he complains. "The girls said they hadn't ever dreamed of seeing the family separated or sold away from the town. I can't ever get it out of my memory, the sight of them poor miserable girls and niggers hanging around each other's necks and crying" (*HF*, 234).[29]

Though commendable, such good-hearted sentiments do nothing to help the slaves, and little in the short run to influence the bearer's attitudes about the inferiority of black people. Moreover, they betray the fact that at a suppressed level of consciousness both young Sam Clemens and Huck do in fact recognize that there *is* something morally wrong with slavery. For his part, Huck retreats from the psychologically intolerable weight of this knowledge when he embraces the identity of Tom Sawyer. Yet the suppressed truth obliquely manifests itself in the haunted mood that overtakes him as he approaches the Phelps plantation.

> When I got there it was all still and Sunday-like, and hot and sun-shiny—the hands was gone to the fields; and there was them kind of faint dronings of bugs and flies in the air that makes it seem so lonesome and like everybody's dead and gone; and if a breeze fans along and quivers the leaves, it makes you feel mournful, because you feel like it's spirits whispering—spirits that's been dead ever so many years—and you always think they're talking about *you*. As a general thing, it makes a body wish *he* was dead,too, and done with it all. (*HF*, 276)

I have elsewhere written at length about this striking passage, and about many others like it in Clemens's work.[30] The key elements common to such passages are feelings of loneliness, life-weariness, and the wish to die, accompanied by soft, haunting sounds, which seem to be the voices of ghosts seeking compassion and murmuring about death. These recurrent forebodings are almost invariably geared to the workings of conscience—more particularly, to stirrings of guilt emerging *in advance* of the events which properly give them rise. A similarly eerie stillness, pregnant with suppressed moral implication, frames Clemens's admission that as a boy he was among those who refused to acknowledge the truth about slavery. "Argue and plead and pray as they might," he recalls in "My First Lie and How I Got Out of It," the opponents of abolition "could not break the universal stillness that reigned, from pulpit and press all the way down to the bottom of society—the clammy stillness created and maintained by the lie of silent assertion—the silent assertion that there wasn't anything going on in which humane and intelligent people were interested" (*CTSSE*, 2:440). The "universal" and "clammy stillness" betrays the suppressed intentionality of the profoundly consequential moral evasion for which Clemens would endure a lifetime of remorse. Theodor Fischer experiences a related species of proleptic guilt in *The Mysterious Stranger*. When he learns from Young Satan that his friend Nikolaus is fated to die in twelve days, Theodor's consciousness is flooded with memories of his former mistreatment of his doomed companion. "No, I could not sleep," he complains. "These little shabby wrongs upbraided me and tortured me; and with a pain much sharper than one feels when the wrongs have been done to the living. Nikolaus *was* living, but no matter: he was to me as one already dead. The wind was still moaning about the eaves, the rain still pattering upon the panes" (*MS*, 122).

The fretful anxiety, the preoccupation with death, the solitude and the drone of ghostly sounds—the setting and the state of mind closely parallel Huck's at the Phelps plantation. Theodor's foreknowledge of his friend's misfortune prompts feelings of guilt that would ordinarily arise only after the fatal episode has occurred, and that derive much of their disproportionate energy from his awareness that he is powerless to avert the disaster. Even more crucially, in thinking of Nikolaus as "one already dead," Theodor expresses both grief and an unconscious homicidal impulse; his prescience is in fact a murderous wish. Clemens was of course well acquainted with such extreme feelings, and with the baffling predations of conscience and ensuing life weariness that they fostered. His childhood surrender to the "lie of silent assertion" was undoubtedly driven by a sense of helpless complicity in the very crimes from which he inwardly recoiled; and his dream of Henry's death, as we have seen, was itself the expression of an ambivalence that had an unconscious fratricidal wish as one of its poles, and that left him with a guilty longing to change places with his deceased brother.

Similar parallels surface in the comparison of Theodor and Huck. Both boys are alone and depressed and anxious. Both hear ghostly sounds. They are preoccupied with death, and they share dark forebodings about future developments which they feel powerless to control. In the course of their reflections, both decide that life is a burden and that death is a welcome respite from intolerable suffering. For Theodor, these latter sentiments are the conscious reflex of repressed guilt. In Huck's case, the death wish is perfectly manifest, and there are strong suggestions that guilt somehow figures in his dark state of mind. In light of such prominent similarities, it remains to press Theodor's example a step further, and to ask what it is that Huck's mood presages. What ambivalence gives rise to his spectral premonitions of disaster and death? What buried wish feeds his sense of the inevitable and explains both his premature remorse and his expiatory desire to end his own life? In other words, who plays for Huck the role that Nikolaus plays for Theodor, and that his younger brother Henry played for Clemens? Of course, it must be Jim.

When he arrives at the Phelps plantation, Huck is host to an upwelling of guilty anxiety that obliquely forecasts his abandonment of his own identity, and with it his commitment to Jim. It can be argued that in a character as intensely complex and divided as Huck, such feelings do not exceed the bounds of psychological verisimilitude. At the same time, however, we can hardly ignore the fact that variations on Huck's feelings are widely on display in Clemens's writing, and that the author was himself prey to similarly guilt-inflected states of mind. Henry Nash Smith draws on this parallel in venturing that "the most probable explanation" for Huck's mood is that it registers Clemens's admission "that Huck's and Jim's journey down the river could not be imagined as leading to freedom for either of them." The same admission accounts for Huck's retreat into Tom's identity, and the novel's morally evasive conclusion. "We can hardly fail," Smith insists, "to perceive the weight of the author's feeling in Huck's statement. . . : 'it was like being born again, I was so glad to find out who I was.' Mark Twain has found out who he must be in order to end his book: he must be Tom."[31]

While I value and draw upon Smith's views on this matter, I want to highlight some equally important differences in our critical perspectives. First, let me reiterate my sense that the guilt at the heart of Huck's troubled ruminations is quite plausibly his own. To be sure, these are feelings deeply rooted in Clemens's truly profound moral anguish on the score of race-slavery. Indeed, I want to emphasize, in a way that Smith does not, the enormous weight of guilt in the novelist's feelings about slavery—a weight that increased dramatically during the last decades of his career, and that registers powerfully throughout *Huckleberry Finn*, and not just at isolated points in the narrative. Thus while I agree with Smith that Huck's mood as he approaches the Phelps plantation "is derived from sources outside the story"—that is to say, from Clemens himself—I cannot agree that "the emotion is the author's rather than Huck's," and has no foundation in the novel.[32] As I will argue shortly, Huck's guilty forebodings about Jim arise at the very beginning of the novel, and play themselves out to the bitter end. His consistency is the index to his dark intuition that he will fail Jim, a sentiment interfused with Clemens's intimations that the obstacles to racial justice—both in himself and in the world—were substantial, morally intolerable, but very likely insurmountable, and hence the spur to feelings of guilt and life-weariness. It follows, finally, that I do not share Smith's view that Huck and Jim stand to lose equally because their "quest for free-dom must end in failure."[33] Not only will Jim be the greater loser if the story is allowed to run its tragic course, but his terrible loss will be in good part attributable—by the stern logic of the novel—to Huck's failure to meet the challenge of their shared journey down the river.

In Huck, then, we are indirectly witness to Clemens's sense of inevitable failure and personal remorse in the matter of racial injustice. Nor, as I have already suggested, is this a mood that belatedly descends upon the narrative. Quite to the contrary, we are not far into the first chapter of the novel before Huck succumbs to anxious depression. He introduces himself, describes the rigors of civilized life with the Widow Douglas, and, finally weary with Miss Watson's interminable "pecking" at him about "the good place," withdraws to his room.

> Then I set down in a chair by the window and tried to think of something cheerful, but it warn't no use. I felt so lonesome I most wished I was dead. The stars was shining, and the leaves rustled in the woods ever so mournful; and I heard an owl, away off, who-whooing about somebody that was dead, and a whippowill and a dog crying about somebody that was going to die; and the wind was trying to whisper something to me and I couldn't make out what it was, and so it made the cold shivers run over me. Then away out in the woods I heard that kind of a sound that a ghost makes when it wants to tell about something that's on its mind and can't make itself under-stood, and so can't rest easy in its grave and has to go about that way every night, grieving. I got so down-hearted and scared, I did wish I had some company. Pretty soon a spider went crawling up my shoulder, and I flipped it off and it lit in the candle; and before I could budge it was all shriveled up. I didn't need anybody to tell me that that was an awful bad sign and would fetch me some bad luck, so I was scared and most shook the clothes off of me. I got up and turned around in my tracks three times and crossed my breast every time; and then I tied up a little lock of my hair with a thread to keep witches away. But I hadn't no confidence. (*HF*, 4)

Though the similarities between Huck's mood here and at the Phelps plantation are perfectly obvious, the element that binds them most deeply is proleptic guilt—their oblique anticipation of Huck's failure to follow through on his heroic commitment to Jim. This grave foreboding is thus at large in the novel right from the start. As James M. Cox has observed, "the possibility that Huck will abandon or betray Jim is . . . at the very center of the whole journey—and the two fugitives can never believe in each other sufficiently to annihilate it." It is integral to Cox's understanding of the novel that in order to survive in a supremely hostile environment Jim must be "shrewd, as shrewd as Huck," and that the leading expression of his shrewdness is his deft concealment of that very quality behind the mask of the docile, gullible, pliant "darky."[34] Jim operates quite effectively on the altogether realistic assumption that Huck, son of an egregious drunkard and racial bigot, and ward of the Widow Douglas and Miss Watson, cannot be trusted to sympathize with a slave's point of view, much less a slave on the run. For his part, Huck is always in some degree condescending to his companion, though there is evidence that he is influenced by Jim's deft manipulations, and the suggestion, especially at novel's end, that he at least glimpses the reality of the situation. At any rate, the trouble in their world bleeds into the relationship between the fugitives, and registers obliquely in Huck's consciousness, right from the start. This undercurrent of suspicion and discord is in turn an expression of Clemens's deeper misgivings about slavery and the prospects for racial justice in America, a personal, guilt-laden strain running athwart the much more optimistic assessments in chapter 31 and in his extratextual commentary.

Jim's circumstances could hardly be more perilous. He is a runaway slave in slave territory, and he is a leading suspect in what is taken to be Huck's murder. For white people who know him, he is the object of angry pursuit; for those who do not, he is an object of suspicion and heartless grasping after quick profits. As the result, Jim must run by night, hide by day, and through it all endure loneliness, fear verging on panic, and a crippling lack of information. Little wonder, then, that he is always gratified to see Huck. Jim may in time come to love the white boy; but from the beginning he needs him desperately. Huck is the living proof that Jim is not a murderer. And Huck gives him eyes and ears, information, an alibi, and some small leverage in the event of trouble. On those occasions in the novel when Jim welcomes Huck back to the raft, this desperate need, and the sense of breathless relief, provide the warmth in what is usually taken for outbursts of unmingled affection. The boy is Jim's best chance for survival; naturally, he is pleased to have him back.

But Huck shares Jim's feelings, and for good reason. When he discovers the identity of his companion on Jackson's Island, Huck's enthusiasm is immediately manifest: "I bet I was glad to see him," he exults (*HF,* 50). His reaction is often taken to express his respect and friendship for Jim. There may be something of this in his feelings, but in larger part his pleasure has

its foundation in relief, and unlooked relief at that. Huck is at first understandably fearful of the mysterious figure asleep in the makeshift camp. He
is afraid that he will be recognized, and that his desperate scheme to get
away from his father will be revealed, leaving him more perilously vulnerable than ever to Pap's really pathological violence. Thus when it is Jim who
emerges from under the blankets, an enormous weight of doubt and fear is
lifted. Huck seems to think of Jim in a friendly way; and there can be no
doubt that his relief has some foundation in grateful release from the nightmares that always pursue him into solitude. But at bottom Jim is a source of
relief to Huck—in a way that almost no one else could be—because as a
runaway he is as much hostage to Huck as Huck is to him. "I warn't afraid
of *him* telling the people where I was," he assures himself (*HF,* 51). He is
pleased to see Jim, as Jim is pleased to see him, not primarily because of
friendship, or because of incipient promptings toward community or family,
but because they find themselves, quite by surprise, bound together in mutual desperation. They need each other long before they learn to respect or
love one another; and once their needs are satisfied—when Jim is finally
freed from slavery, and Huck is freed from fear of Pap—they separate, immediately. They stay together because it appears that they can use one another in relative safety—a safety to be matched by neither of them with any
other companion. And this is so because there is between them, arising out
of their desperate secrets from a hostile, encroaching world, a balance of
power to betray, an equality in suspicion and fear, and therefore a tenuous
bond of mutual protection.

The tension and uncertainty between the fugitives appear first as ripples
of ambiguity in gestures of ostensible reassurance. "I ain't agoing to tell, and
I ain't agoing back there, anyways," says Huck; "I 'uz powerful sorry you's
killed, Huck," Jim replies, "but I ain't no mo,' now" (*HF,* 53). They are
much more clearly evident in a series of practical jokes that Huck feels compelled to spring on his companion, and in Jim's decision to conceal the
identity of the corpse in the house of death. As several scholars have noted,
Jim's seeming generosity, by veiling the truth about Pap's death, artificially
preserves Huck's principal motive for flight. So long as Jim controls this
information, he maintains the balance of power and thus retains a substantial
measure of control over his companion.[35] This carefully guarded illusion of
bondage of course anticipates Tom's cruel "evasion" at the Phelps plantation. As important, it confirms—what the novel confirms time and again—
that Clemens's understanding of Jim's character significantly transcends the
stereotype of the minstrel "darky." Jim is shrewdly alert to his own interests

and perfectly willing and able to manipulate circumstances—Huck principally among them—to his own ends.

Huck's impulse to play mean tricks on Jim, and his decision in chapter 16 to turn him over to the authorities, arise out of an ambivalence about his companion, and about black people generally, that is in turn rooted in the racist ideology of white society. Huck is free enough of the dominant culture to respond to Jim as a human being; but he is also prone to sudden reversals of feeling that betray his deep immersion in the mentality of the white majority. This dividedness in Huck is conspicuously at work in his cruel joke with the "trash" (after he and Jim have been separated in the fog), his prompt apology, his equally sudden decision to betray Jim, and the brilliant, spontaneous outwitting of the predatory slave hunters that immediately follows. These abrupt, radical reversals are evidence of the boy's wavering marginality, and speak clearly to his restlessness in the ambiguous ties that bind him to Jim.

Jim cannot fail to observe this ambivalence in Huck, and he must recognize it as a leading threat to his survival. His management of the discovery of Pap's corpse is an index to his penetration on this score, and serves to reinforce the impression that his characteristic response to the threat of betrayal is oblique rather than direct, dissimulation and manipulation rather than open confrontation. He knows that principled appeals to justice and good faith will backfire by highlighting the cruel truth that such considerations are irrelevant in dealings with slaves, except as incitements to turn them in. Instead, Jim does what he must to survive: he resorts to all manner of deception. His mastery in this line is first and most vitally manifest in his seeming incapacity to deceive. Without that simulated two-dimensional face, that happy, carefree, gullible fraud that he retreats to more and more as the hostile world closes in, Jim would be helpless to defend himself. Not the least of his resources in this obligatory game of cat and mouse is the deep cultural investment among white people in the conception of slaves as happy children—gullible, harmless, essentially good. It is profoundly to Jim's advantage that in retreating to this preposterous stereotype, he satisfies the urgent need—the offspring of guilt and fear—in the culture of the oppressors. There is safety, he knows, in their readiness to be deceived.

Almost from the moment of Jim's first appearance in the novel we are witness to hints and glancing suggestions that there may be an artful and self-interested deceiver at work behind the gullible mask that he presents to the world. Tom and Huck do not doubt that Jim is completely deceived by their little prank in chapter 2, and so fail utterly to recognize how completely he turns the situation to his own advantage. A cognate irony runs through the hairball episode in chapter 4, in which Jim relieves Huck of a counterfeit quarter in return for advice from the oracle. The irony is compounded by the fact that Huck regards the quarter as worthless, but offers it to Jim anyway, preferring to "say nothing about the dollar I got from the judge." This rather minor moment of selfish deception, which takes rise from assumptions about Jim's gullibility and genial willingness to be exploited, is abruptly reversed when the slave reveals his plan to use a potato to fix the quarter "so anybody in town would take it in a minute, let alone a hair-ball." The irony grows even deeper when Huck refuses to acknowledge that he has been fooled. "Well, I knowed a potato would do that, before," he insists, quite lamely, "but I had forgot it" (*HF,* 21). We suspect that what Jim has to say about potatoes, true or false, is news to Huck. But by insisting that he forgot what in fact he never knew, the boy submerges the awkward revelation that the tables have been turned on him. Such an acknowledgement would so conflict with the racist prepossessions manifest in his attempt to deceive Jim that he cannot rise to it. Instead, as if to seal the slave's triumph, and to invite its repetition, he clings to the flimsy delusion that Jim has been an easy mark, and not the other way around.

These early episodes may be viewed as opening gambits in a very serious game whose leading dynamics are racist self-deception rooted in cruel prejudice but replete with openings for manipulation by the seemingly hapless, in fact shrewdly resourceful, victims. Of course, the cruelest joke is always at the slave's expense; but *Huckleberry Finn* offers us a window on the ways and means employed by the victims in their attempt to retrieve such shreds of power and dignity and laughter as fall within their reach. To this end, there is a premium on the masterful control of appearances, and on the ability to penetrate beneath the shifting surfaces of things to the hidden designs of others. Thus at the same time that the slave contrives to deceive, even to the extent of seeming without guile, he must also be undeceived while appearing incorrigibly gullible. Such is the dual objective of Jim's constant indulgence in what appears to be runaway superstition, an excess that reinforces Huck's assumption that Jim is gullible, naively overconfident, and harmlessly if rather annoyingly voluble in the matter of signs. This, I strongly suspect, is precisely what Jim wants, as it so fixes Huck in his prejudice that he is blinded to the deeper coherence and purpose of his companion's behavior. The recognition of Jim's acuity, even when forthcoming, is accompanied by the inevitable racial qualifier. "Well," Huck reflects, Jim "was right; he was most always right; he had an uncommon level head, for a nigger" (*HF,* 93). This barrier to respect and understanding, which Jim attempts, with mixed results, to exploit, arises from the heart of the slave ideology.

Clearly, then, the trouble between Huck and Jim is deep, and deeply rooted in a synergistic dynamic of insurmountable pride and prejudice on one side, and shrewd, virtually impenetrable strategies of survival on the other. Viewed in this light, it is entirely appropriate that a snake should first lead Huck to Jim, and that their ongoing, highly fraught struggle for supremacy in the reading of signs should come to focus on what to make of snake skins. It is equally appropriate, and mordantly ironic, that the old betrayer should reappear in the narrative immediately in the wake of the house of death. Huck wants "to talk about the dead man and guess out how he come to be killed, but Jim didn't want to" (*HF,* 63). Preferring for obvious reasons to avoid this dangerously compromised subject, Jim retreats to what passes for superstition, but what is—like much of the rest of what he offers up as superstition—a strategic maneuver, in this case an evasion. Such speculation "would fetch bad luck," he insists. But when they find eight dollars hidden in the lining of a coat taken off the wreck, Huck's native relish for reading signs, given an added edge perhaps by Jim's uncharacteristic reluctance to try his hand, prompts a direct assault on the foundation of his companion's position.

> "Now you think it's bad luck; but what did you say when I fetched in the snake-skin that I found on the top of the ridge day before yesterday? You said it was the worst bad luck in the world to touch a snake-skin with my hands. Well, here's your bad luck! We've raked in all this truck and eight dollars besides. I wish we could have some bad luck like this every day, Jim."
>
> "Never you mind, honey, never you mind. Don't you git too peart. It's a-comin.' Mind I tell you, it's a-comin'." (*HF,* 63)

Perhaps Jim's response is no more than sullen retreat; more likely, it records a glimpse of the trouble beginning to emerge, inevitably, irresistibly, from his dissimulation about Pap, and ultimately from the cruelly alienating slave system itself, which makes that concealment necessary, makes escape virtually impossible, and hopelessly undermines the movements of goodness between black people and white. Perhaps he sees that the snake is with them on the raft, hidden, but at large now, and coiled to strike.

The first strike follows almost immediately, when Huck plants a dead rattlesnake at the foot of the bed, "thinking there'd be some fun when Jim found him there" (*HF*, 64). The joke backfires when the snake's mate arrives and nearly kills poor Jim. This "mistake" springs directly from Huck's incapacity to sit comfortably with Jim's accomplishments in the reading of signs. Rather than acknowledge what is obvious, the boy resorts to spiteful jokes designed to betray the gullibility and superstition of a racial inferior. Quite ironically, however, the joke's outcome is testimony to Jim's stunning clairvoyance, and serves to underscore Huck's credulous attachment to empty racial stereotypes. It also exemplifies bad faith, the denial, itself denied, of violations of public ideals of truth and justice. Huck's bad faith is the more complete for his decision, once Jim is through the worst of the danger and the pain, to slip out and throw "the snakes clear away amongst the bushes; for I warn't going to let Jim find out it was all my fault," he says, "not if I could help it" (*HF*, 65). Huck inwardly concedes that he is directly at "fault" for Jim's suffering. Quite as clearly, he is ashamed of himself, for he gets rid of the dead snakes with the intent of permanently removing his moral lapse from sight and mind. As subsequent developments show, however, he is also hiding from himself. Before long, on those numerous occasions when he is reminded of the snakes, Huck notes that they have been the source of much bad luck, but neglects to acknowledge his own agency in the shifts of fortune. This denial is at the dark center of Huck's bad faith, and confirms his acculturation to the twisted logic of race-slavery. He never tells Jim the truth about the snakes; and he appears to succeed in forgetting the painful truth about himself, and about his relationship to Jim, that the episode betrays. Of course, the denial of the deed is more potent for harm than the deed itself; the deed is done, but its denial is the next thing to a guarantee that it will be repeated. And it is repeated, again and again, right through to the novel's end, when Huck runs one more time, quite hopelessly I think, from the bad-faith civilization in himself.

Rather than join Huck in straining to expel this painful episode from memory, Jim clings to it, recognizing perhaps that its timely deployment affords him subtle but significant control over his companion's conscience. Thus a few days after the commission of the nearly fatal "joke," Huck vows that he "wouldn't ever take aholt of a snake-skin again with my hands, now that I see what had come of it. Jim said he reckoned I would believe him, next time. And he said that handling a snake-skin was such awful bad luck that maybe we hadn't got to the end of it yet" (*HF*, 65). At one level, such remarks are persistent reminders of Jim's apparently superstitious investment in the interpretation of signs. But they also serve to remind Huck in a most direct and painful way of his hand in Jim's suffering. In effect, Jim's remarks interpose an obstacle to Huck's bad-faith denial. To what extent, we may ask, is Jim consciously playing along with Huck's moral evasiveness in order that he may, in a self-interested way, manipulate the guilt behind it? The answer to this question hangs on our assessment of Jim's penetration into Huck's responsibility for the snakes. For myself, I suspect that Jim has had intimations of the truth behind his close call with death. He may have been stirred to a vague uneasiness by the coincidence of the snake's advent with Huck's resolute views on bad luck; and the sudden, unexplained disappearance of the dead snakes may not have escaped his notice. In short, there may be a trace of suspicion in Jim's remarks, and even some preliminary testing of the hidden leverage that this dawning insight affords.

Still, there is no short-run evidence that Jim has been provoked into settled, suspicious vigilance. Rather, he is confident, not to say incautious, in the subsequent, shrewdly penetrating analysis of the threat posed by Judith Loftus and her husband, and in aggressively advancing his views on King Solomon, and on the propriety of human beings speaking French. Jim cannot know that Huck reacts to the latter display of confidence by withdrawing to a sullen rehearsal of the familiar, self-indulgent lie about a slave's racial inferiority. "You can't learn a nigger to argue," Huck reflects, "so I quit" (*HF*, 98). Because he is unaware that his argumentative agility has rekindled his companion's resentment, Jim is unprepared for the trick that Huck springs after they have been separated in a fog that carries them past Cairo and the junction with the Ohio River. Ignoring the "leaves and branches and dirt" that have collected on the raft during the long night's passage, Huck persuades Jim that his memory of the fog is no more than a dream—and a dream in need of interpretation. Quite clearly, of course, the trick is yet another designed to expose Jim's putative gullibility and superstition. This time, though, once the cruel joke has been played, Jim recognizes the snake for what it is. You are trash, he tells Huck, a person "dat puts dirt on de head er dey fren's en makes 'em ashamed." Huck is deeply shaken by Jim's response. "It was fifteen minutes," he reports contritely, "before I could work myself up to go and humble myself to a nigger—but I done it, and I warn't ever sorry for it afterwards, neither. I didn't do him no more mean tricks, and I wouldn't done that one if I'd a knowed it would make him feel that way" (*HF*, 105).

Huck's apology, though appropriate, is woefully inadequate as a stay against his ambivalent feelings toward Jim. The trouble is writ large in his sense that he has humbled himself not to his friend, but "to a nigger." And it is transparent bad-faith denial to insist that he would have foregone the trick had he properly anticipated Jim's reaction. Huck knew the trick would humiliate Jim; that was the point in playing it. What he did not anticipate was that Jim would respond to the offense with a sharp, dignified rebuke. Huck was unprepared to hear the truth about his cruel joking. But his bad faith is most graphically evident in his declaration that he "didn't do him no more mean tricks." This characterization of what follows overlooks a multitude of sins, not least the decision, in the very next chapter, to turn Jim over to the authorities.

When Jim calls Huck "trash," he indicates that such earlier suspicions as he may have had about the snakes have been irresistibly confirmed. He now knows that while Huck is at times a great boon, he is equally a part of the terrible trouble shadowing the raft. Not surprisingly, then, Jim is increasingly preoccupied with Cairo, the Ohio River, and the prospect of freedom. No doubt he is energized by his recent moral victory; but his almost frantic animation suggests that a measure of panic, the issue of freshly confirmed fears, also colors his mood. Huck, meanwhile, just as borne down by his recent humiliation, has displaced his misery in spasms of conscience over Jim's behavior, and in a cozy commitment to do right by poor Miss Watson. Buoyed up in turn and feeling "light as a feather" in his evasion of guilt, and in the pious rationalization of his urge to put the uppity slave back in his place, Huck prepares to leave the raft, ostensibly to inquire about Cairo, in fact to betray his companion. Jim senses that something is amiss. Huck's departure, which may remind him of their ill-fated separation in the fog, seems to stir the fears submerged in his rather fervid elation. Suddenly his levitating assertions of independent initiative give way to declarations of absolute dependence on Huck and undying gratitude for his faithful friendship. "Pooty soon I'll be a-shout'n for joy," Jim calls out to the departing boy, "en I'll say, it's all on accounts o' Huck; I's a free man, en I couldn' ever ben free ef it hadn' ben for Huck; Huck done it. Jim won't ever forget you, Huck; you's de bes' fren' Jim's ever had; en you's de *only* fren' ole Jim's got, now" (*HF*, 125).

In light of Jim's foregoing observations on "trash," there is something decidedly false in this outpouring. But the falseness is true in a deeper sense to the features of the mask of the gullible, passive, grateful slave that Jim is obliged to wear. This simulated identity, he knows, is his best defense against white cruelty and infidelity. And, to a point, it works. Huck fails entirely to perceive the inaccuracy of Jim's characterization of their relationship, and he fails because Jim's servile gratitude conforms perfectly to the contours of his bad-faith denial. This fawning man-child so confirms his fond prepossessions that, he says, "it seemed to kind of take the tuck all out of me." His resolution slips even further when Jim continues, "Dah you goes, de ole true Huck; de on'y white genlman dat ever kep' his promise to ole Jim" (*HF,* 125). It is remarkable that Huck is so ready to accept this characterization of himself, so proof in his bad faith against the potent ironies poised in full view on the face of Jim's words. Characteristically, one of the broadest of these ironies turns on the fact that the innocence, the gullibility, the hapless surrender to false but grateful illusions, is hardly Jim's.

It is also remarkable that Jim is willing to range so far from the truth in maneuvering for his safety. Such boldness is a tribute to his acuity in measuring Huck's self-deception, but it is also a mark of desperation. His fear is of course well founded. He can hardly know that his appeal to Huck's bad faith, while shrewdly orchestrated, is finally not enough to stop the boy, who presses forward with his faithless scheme, muttering "I *got* to do it—I can't get *out* of it." Things go from bad to worse with the sudden advent of two slave hunters, who intercept and interrogate Huck. Jim looks on from hiding as Huck pauses, obviously weighing the alternatives, when asked: "Is your man white, or black?" (*HF,* 125)

If we imagine that all the drama here is in Huck's mind, then we miss the even greater tension, the terror verging on blind panic, that Jim must endure as the boy wavers over an answer. He is of course perfectly alive to the brilliance of Huck's subsequent outwitting of the encroaching predators. But his gratitude must pale before the much darker emotions that attach to this spectacle of white cruelty and greed. We must imagine that he is inwardly numb and quivering, a deeply shaken man. He cannot fail to have noticed the ease and skill with which Huck moves in the terribly fallen adult world. Huck knows his way around; indeed, were he not much more adept than the slave hunters at the darkly cynical game, Jim would pay a heavy price. But Jim sees that the obvious correlative to Huck's familiarity with adult degradation is an impulse, here only barely restrained, to join the enemy. Now more clearly than ever Jim perceives that the snakes on Jackson's Island, and the other serpentine tricks that have pursued him down the river, are akin in important ways to the varieties of evil manifest in the slave hunters. As they drift downriver away from this near-disaster, but ever deeper into even greater potential dangers, Jim begins to face the fact that Cairo, and the slender hope that Cairo holds out, are now behind him. "Maybe we went by Cairo in the fog that night," Huck ventures. "Doan' less talk about it," Jim replies.

"Po' niggers can't have no luck. I alwuz 'spected dat rattle-snake skin warn't done wid its work."

"I wish I'd never seen that snake-skin, Jim—I do wish I'd never laid eyes on it."

"It ain't yo' fault, Huck; you didn' know. Don't you blame yo'self 'bout it" (*HF*, 129).

The ironies here are multiple and, quite appropriately, not fully penetrable. Does Huck's regret at having seen the snakeskin bear with it the unspoken acknowledgement of his carefully concealed moral responsibility for the troubles that the snakes brought with them? If so, then he suffers exquisitely as Jim tenders his emphatic absolution. Or, alternatively, has Huck's bad-faith denial advanced to the point that he is no longer conscious of the guilt that the snakes formerly stirred in him? If this is the case, then the irony is just as painfully at his expense, and equally an index to his immersion in bad faith. In either case, there is a quite extraordinary overarching irony to be observed namely, that whether he is conscious of it or not, Huck's bad-faith denial leads him into the adoption of precisely that superstitious view of snakes that his original practical joke was designed to expose and ridicule.

Turning to Jim's role in the dialogue, we come upon another, even sharper edge to the irony. For while Huck retreats to transparent bad-faith credulousness, Jim maneuvers, in full self-consciousness, behind a mask of simulated superstition. He knows and conceals what Huck does not want to know, and conceals. Jim does this because he is aware that anything approaching a full disclosure of Huck's actual role would threaten a break in the slender thread of hope that their troubled friendship holds out. Thus he opts for the appearance of tenacious gullibility because it confirms the white stereotype of the slave mentality, and thus plausibly stands in place of the truth—about Jim's humanity and suffering and rage, and about his young friend's spiteful racist malice—none of which Huck can bear to acknowledge, least of all to Jim, and at Jim's bidding. Huck denies the truth about the snakes because he cannot bear it; Jim is denying it too, because he recognizes that for a slave in the twisted moral world of race-slavery, the truth can only exacerbate the already terrible trouble. Meanwhile, it if gives him some consolation to look on as Huck squirms in bad faith, it is, we must suppose, a slender, bitter reward. For in assuring Huck that "it ain't yo' fault," he is telling the boy exactly what he wants to hear, and to believe.

Huck's subsequent observations on the snakes do not clearly resolve the question of the level of his consciousness in bad faith. But it is telling that the words are not shared with Jim. Rather, they are a silent resolution, advanced in the name of necessity and rooted in superstition, to keep silence on the score of snakeskins. "We both knowed well enough," he reports, when the raft and canoe disappear during the night, that "it was some more work of the rattlesnake skin; so what was the use to talk about it? It would only look like we was finding fault, and that would be bound to fetch more bad luck—and keep on fetching it, too, till we knowed enough to keep still" (*HF,* 129). This ostensible surrender to superstitious necessity imperfectly conceals Huck's craving to be free of the guilt that torments him. But so long as he continues to deny in bad faith the truth about his treatment of Jim, that truth will continue both to haunt him and to elude him. For that long he will continue to violate Jim without fully knowing it, and he will continue to run without getting anywhere. For Jim, meanwhile, bound as he is to a kind of silent complicity in this accelerating cycle, there is no obvious way to avert almost inevitable disaster.

It is over this complex spectacle of errant human suffering that the steamboat sweeps in judgment at the end of chapter 16. Thereafter we see and hear much less of Jim. He is displaced by the likes of the king and the duke, who are more baldly malign than Huck, and by Tom Sawyer, who is meant to be more amusing. It should be stressed that Jim's reduced visibility is entirely in character. He has even less control over his fate once outsiders intrude upon the scene, and so he retreats as completely as he can from the center of the action. But his radically reduced role also spelled relief for Clemens, whose humorous sequel to *Tom Sawyer* had evolved in its first phase of composition into a darkly probing analysis of the grave, twisted, even hopeless moral confusion that descends upon those engaged in race-slavery.

By his own admission, Clemens had other, happier plans for his narrative. Yet something in him balked at the Hannibal idyll of innocent children and happy slaves. He knew better. Tom, whose schemes Huck abruptly dismisses as "lies" bearing "all the marks of a Sunday school" (*HF,* 17), is summarily swept from view in chapter 3, to be displaced by the flight to freedom on the raft. Clemens of course knew at first hand both the horrors of race-slavery, and the diabolical complexity of its social and psychological dynamics—of evasion and concealment, buried guilt and suppressed rage. Furthermore, he felt deeply and painfully his own complicity in the wrongdoing, and labored under the fear that the trouble was beyond cure, and could only get worse with time. It was Clemens, after all, who anatomized "the lie of silent assertion," and who in doing so placed himself first in line among the willfully self-deceived.

It follows, then, that *Huckleberry Finn* shaped itself almost in spite of him, and emerged reluctantly, over a period of nearly a decade, as the yield on an anguished moral imperative. Conscience, we imagine, seized upon Jim's advent in an innocent children's story as the occasion for half-conscious, guilt-inflected ruminations on the sins of slavery. Would a child, and especially an outsider to the slaveholding culture, be immune to the inhumanity of the institution? Would such a child, for example, be able to feel compassion for an escaped slave? How would that slave in turn respond to the apparent good will of the child? In short, would essentially good people be able to overcome the obstacles set in their way by race-slavery and achieve genuine fellow feeling, friendship, and even love? These were questions, we know, of urgent and abiding personal concern to Clemens—questions whose hold on him tightened over the years as hopeful responses grew ever more difficult to sustain. As his sense of his own inward degradation deepened in later life, the country itself surrendered to the fatal lure of wealth and empire, a sweeping moral declension epitomized in the epidemic of racial hatred and lynching that followed at century's end. The moral confusion wrought by race-slavery and its aftermath was as integral to Clemens's disenchantment with himself as it was to his gathering contempt for "the damned human race."

But if conscience prompted the confession obliquely rendered in the breakdown between Huck and Jim, resistance to that bleak self-analysis was equally a motive in the halting formation of the narrative. As we have seen, the steamboat Leviathan in chapter 16 enforces separation, and with it temporary relief from intolerable moral ironies. But as his story swerved irresistibly back again toward reunion between Huck and Jim, and to the inevitable resumption of their troubles, Clemens abruptly set the manuscript aside. His frustration with his new boy's book comes across clearly in a letter of August, 1876, to Howells. "It is Huck Finn's Autobiography," he reports. "I like it only tolerably well, as far as I have got, & may possibly pigeonhole or burn the *MS* when it is done" (*MTHL,* 1:144). He knew that he would have to finish the book, but he knew just as well that he might want to destroy it when it was completed. The paired impulses to tell and untell, to reveal even more about what inwardly tormented him, and to conceal the same thing, achieved a kind of truce that lasted until 1880, when he answered an urge to resume work on his recalcitrant manuscript.

Having witnessed the horrifying bloodbath between the Grangerfords and Shepherdsons—which gives him nightmares and inspires a vague sense of guilt (*HF,* 153)—Huck is quite naturally pleased to be back on the raft with Jim. But as if to concede that the divisions between his principals are too deep to be avoided for long, Clemens almost immediately brings the king and duke on board. We are of course alternately amused and disgusted by these odious frauds, as we are by the colorful parade of characters and events that fill the foreground of the narrative in the chapters that follow. Good and evil are easily identified in these episodes, which may be said to express Clemens's impulse to retreat from entanglement in the much more ambiguous moral issues at large in the relationship between Huck and Jim. The balance shifts briefly in chapter 31, when Huck wrestles heroically with his deformed conscience. As we have seen, however, his resolve, though noble, is inadequate as a stay against the craving for relief from the confusion that his journey with Jim has entailed. Once again, then, Clemens recoils from the dark personal drift of the novel, this time by turning the action over to Tom Sawyer.

Only when the end is safely in sight does Clemens glance one last time at the hopeless human implication of his story. To Tom's suggestion that Huck and Jim join him in the Territory for some "howling adventures amongst the Indians," Huck replies that he can't afford "to buy the outfit" for the trip, as Pap has doubtless taken the money he left with Judge Thatcher. Tom assures his friend that his money is where he left it, and that Pap has not, to his knowledge, been back in St. Petersburg. Jim now enters the conversation, declaring, "kind of solemn,"

> "He ain't a comin' back no mo,' Huck."
> I says:
> "Why, Jim?"
> "Nemmine why, Huck—but he ain't comin' back no mo."
> But I kept at him; so at last he says:
> 'Doan' you 'member de house dat was float'n down de river, en dey wuz a man in dah, kivered up, en I went in en unkivered him en didn' let you come in? Well, den, you k'n git yo' money when you wants it; kase dat wuz him." (*HF,* 361–62)

Jim is reluctant to go into the details about Pap, it is perfectly clear, because he does not want Huck to see through the mask of the docile, loving slave to the self-interested human being on the other side. Nor can there be any doubt that Huck grasps the far-reaching significance of Jim's halting disclosure. He sees now not only why Jim refused to talk about the corpse in the half-sunk house, but also, and even more astonishingly, that Jim is fully capable of recognizing his own interests, and of pursuing those interests with selfishness and guile. This is no simple man, Huck must see, but an intelligent and wily adversary, the depth of whose shrewdness is measured in the audacious brilliance of his disguise. Disenchanted perspectives on Jim's reiterated expressions of love, and on the deeper significance of his treatment of signs—most especially of snakeskins—must surely follow. Huck will also come to see himself in a new, painfully diminished perspective. He will recognize how terribly deceived he has been, first by himself, and in turn by a wily slave. He will wince at the blind complacency of his racist assumptions about black inferiority, and at the price in hapless humiliation, not to mention grave physical danger, to which his folly has exposed him. Perhaps, too, he will supplement the guilt that has plagued his feelings about race-slavery with fear—the fear of what a man as fully human and resourceful as Jim might do were his attention to turn from the escape from bondage to revenge against those who put him there.

It is altogether telling that Huck makes no direct response to Jim's breathtaking disclosure. How, after all, could he possibly shape what he now knows into words? Put another way, how could he possibly convey it more forcefully than with knowing silence? It is over between Huck and Jim. The old, happy illusion has now completely collapsed, and in its place Huck beholds a world more complex, more guilt-ridden, and more potentially dangerous than the one he left behind. How strange he must feel in this moment of morally fraught, speechless communion with Jim, from whom he is now hopelessly alienated; stranger still, perhaps, to find himself in company with the bland, optimistic, morally self deceived white folks who are, after all, his "people." It is a small scene, as subtle and in its way as powerful as anything in *Benito Cereno*.

Immediately on the heels of Jim's speech, Huck closes his narrative in a brief paragraph. How utterly absurd it must now seem to him that Tom proudly displays—on a watch-guard around his neck—the bullet that almost killed him. In light of his friend's delusions, and of all that they obliquely reveal about the even more fantastic and dangerous delusions of the slave culture from which they take rise, it is little wonder that Huck is ready to be done with his story. "There ain't nothing more to write about, and I am rotten glad of it," he grouses, "because if I'd a knowed what a trouble it is to make a book I wouldn't a tackled it and ain't agoing to no more." Rather than dwell further on the unforeseen difficulties that have overtaken his story, however, Huck characteristically takes the path of least resistance. "I reckon I got to light out for the Territory ahead of the rest," he declares, "because aunt Sally she's going to adopt me and sivilize me and I can't stand it. I been there before" (*HF,* 362). Even as he takes flight one last time from the intolerable moral weight of race-slavery, Huck has an intimation of the deeper source of his woe. It is civilization as he knows it, the whole world of smothering piety and prejudice, wound up in pervasive bad faith, that he glimpses at the root of what so troubles his mind. What he cannot see is that there is no escape from the forces that have shaped his life, not even for one so marginal and apparently uncivilized as himself. "The thing in man which makes him cruel to a slave," Clemens reflected not long after *Huckleberry Finn* was published, "is in him permanently and will not be rooted out for a million years" (*MTN,* 198).

Nowhere in the novel does Huck speak more directly for Clemens than in bitterly protesting the "trouble it was to make a book." His words surely give voice to the author's chagrin that something so apparently simple and innocuous as more of Tom Sawyer's adventures should have become so complex and depressing. This was not the way it was supposed to go. But how, then, did the novel actually take shape? What were the potent creative processes that transformed comedy for children into something so grave that most adults have retreated in bad faith from a reckoning with its moral im-plications?[36] It was guilt that performed the alchemy—guilt that drove both Clemens's need to confess and the countervailing need to submerge his sense of unbearable complicity in the sins of race-slavery. Those powerfully conflicting motives ran like alternating currents in the writer's mind, prompting him to reveal his darkest insights and, virtually at the same time, to expel them from consciousness, thereby producing a narrative replete with insights no sooner born than abandoned.

In Huck, Clemens was witness by fits and starts to what he feared was his own inability to transcend the crippling prejudices of his culture. In Jim, he penetrated, again by fits and starts, to the human reality behind the mask of the docile slave, and to a recognition of the entirely incompatible invest-ments of whites and blacks in that masquerade. Because he wrote from depths that his own bad-faith evasions frequently eclipsed from sight and mind, Clemens here plausibly conforms to the "jack-leg" identity that he would later lay claim to in *Puddn'head Wilson.* There is indeed good evi-dence in *Huckleberry Finn* that he had "no clear idea of his story," and that the novel evolved, quite without seeking his approval, from a happy tale for children into something much more complex and somber (*PW,* 119). Kindred intimations of lost control register obliquely in the famous cautionary "Notice" at the front of the novel. "Persons attempting to find a Motive in this narrative will be prosecuted; persons attempting to find a Moral in it will be banished; persons attempting to find a Plot in it will be shot" (*HF* xxxi).[37] To be sure, the tone of the admonition is genially self-effacing: what follows, we are advised, is but a trifle and carries nothing of any weight or significance. Clemens knew better, of course; he knew there was motive and moral and plot aplenty in his book, and that it involved a struggle between Huck's heart and conscience. But the real depths of what he had wrought were cloaked in bad-faith denial, and the evasion left him feeling vulnerable and somehow exposed. The jesting tone of the "Notice" characteristically reveals and conceals this underlying apprehension. Clemens acknowledges as much in "A Little Note to M. Paul Bourget," an essay of 1897 in which he quotes the entire "Notice," ascribes it to *Tom Sawyer,* and characterizes it as a "cunning" way of discouraging readers from taking books too "seriously."[38] It may be that Clemens's memory assigned the genial warning to *Tom Sawyer* because it accorded better with the humorous tone of that novel. In its proper context, however, the jest is in fact an uncertain, equivocal gesture, on a par with Tom Sawyer's "evasion," in which Clemens tries to make light of what has grown unaccountably "serious" in his novel. It is yet another, perfectly characteristic attempt to conceal what he dimly suspects—and fears—that his fiction may reveal about him.[39]

5   *Dreaming Better Dreams*

Clemens's later life was crossed by extremes of adversity and emotional up-heaval. The worst of the trouble began in 1894 when, after years of impru-dent financial speculation, he suffered a humiliating plunge into bankruptcy. He partially righted himself by undertaking an around-the-world lecture tour, but that brief triumph was bitterly overturned by news that his favorite daughter, Susy, had succumbed to spinal meningitis in August 1896. The shock was so great that Clemens wavered between feelings of hatred for life and blank indifference to what it might bring. Death, he decided, was a blessing, and he looked forward to his own, Andrew Hoffman observes, "as a release from the dreadful responsibility he accepted for his daughter's de-mise"[1] Similar feelings overtook him when his beloved wife, Olivia, died in 1904. "I looked for the last time upon that dear face," he confided to his notebook, "and I was full of remorse for things done and said in the 34 years of married life that hurt Livy's heart" (*MTN,* 387). His youngest daughter, Jean, an epileptic, was equally distraught, and suffered her first seizure in more than a year, while her older sister, Clara, collapsed in shock. Clemens himself endured a variety of ailments, most ominously a heart condition di-agnosed late in 1909. Toward the end of that year, on Christmas Eve, Jean suffered her last seizure and drowned in the bathtub. "In her loss," her father wrote, "I am almost bankrupt, and my life is a bitterness, but I am content: for she has been enriched with the most precious of all gifts—that gift which makes all other gifts mean and poor—death" (*AMT,* 375). He was similarly enriched just four months later.

Clemens's late works are centrally preoccupied with forming and articu-lating judgments of God, human nature, national and global politics, and—most urgently and compulsively—himself. Now more than ever before in his long career he was disposed to find a depressing sameness in the spread of human folly over all time and space. "Really," remarked his friend Joseph Twichell in 1901, "you are getting quite orthodox on the doctrine of Total Human Depravity."[2] Granting as we must the broad sweep of Clemens's late-life quarrel with the world, it cannot be too much emphasized that his anger was anchored in a profound and consuming quarrel with himself. The writing of the period, Bernard DeVoto long ago observed, bears witness to "the terrible force of an inner cry: Do not blame me, for it was not my fault."[3]

Unlike DeVoto, who concludes that Clemens finally triumphed over crippling guilt, Hamlin Hill believes that the writer's subjection to conscience was exacerbated by the adversity of his late years. "Much of the last decade of his life," Hill somberly observes, "he lived in hell."[4] I am strongly inclined to accept the main thrust of Hill's argument; and I agree emphatically with DeVoto that Clemens's chronic guilt became more sharply acute toward the end of his life. I hasten to add, however, that these are not uncontroversial positions. Several recent scholars—William R. Macnaughton, Bruce Michelson, and Karen Lystra among them[5]—have objected that Hill gives too little attention to Clemens's resilient relish for life and to the energy and exuberance of his late writing. These are important, often well-argued perspectives. But while I readily concede that Hill is at points too relentlessly dark and unforgiving in his judgments, and that he tends to undervalue the late writing, his portrait of a man engulfed by volatile, often destructive emotions is thoroughly plausible and well-grounded. To deny these realities is to turn a blind eye to a virtual mountain of direct testimony to the aging writer's contempt for human nature, hatred of God, anguished self-loathing, and impatient longing for the oblivion of the grave. True, Clemens was resilient; true as well, he was baffled by his gravitation to the light. "Shall I ever be cheerful again, happy again?" he asked, just after Jean's death. "Yes. And soon. For I know my temperament. And I know that the temperament is *master of the man*, and that he is its fettered and helpless slave" (*MTB*, 4:1552). It is altogether telling that Clemens viewed his emotional levitations as an embarrassment, a constitutional perversity for which he took no personal responsibility, and whose evanescence he surely recognized. "He could wave aside care and grief and remorse," Paine observed at first hand, "but in the end he had only driven them ahead a little way and they waited by his path" (*MTB*, 3:1073–74). Intervals of relief notwithstanding, varieties of grief and rage and remorse were the dire but durable burden of Clemens's later life. Much of the rest of it—the banquets and speeches and fat-cat pleasure cruises, the late-night booze and billiards, and the flirtations with little girls—was distraction, often rather desperate, from what deeply ailed him.

As we have seen, there is evidence of oblique self-reckoning in *Tom Sawyer*, and graver misgivings, most especially on the score of race-slavery,
clearly at large in *Huckleberry Finn*. The trend in the fiction toward ever
sharper—though almost certainly sub-intentional—moral self-scrutiny persists in *A Connecticut Yankee in King Arthur's Court* (1889). Critics are generally in agreement with Howard G. Baetzhold, who observes that as the
writing of the novel progressed over the years between 1884 and 1889,
Hank Morgan became "more and more the spokesman for Clemens's current opinions."[6] Justin Kaplan goes further in this vein and argues that "to
a great extent Hank Morgan *is* Mark Twain. Both are showmen who love
gaudy effects. . . . Both combine idealism and nostalgia with shrewd practi-
cality and devotion to profit. Their revolutionary, humanitarian zeal is tem-
pered and at times defeated by their despairing view of human nature"
(*MCMT,* 297). Louis J. Budd is confident that "Twain intended Hank to
embody a natural-rights democracy for all times and climes,"[7] a view amply
supported by the novelist's late-life declaration that his book contrasted
conditions in medieval England "with the life of modern Christendom and
modern civilization—to the advantage of the latter, of course" (*MTE,* 211).
But there is broad assent as well to Henry Nash Smith's detection of "a
conflict within Mark Twain's mind between a conscious endorsement of
progress and a latent revulsion against the nonhuman imperatives of the machine and all it stood for."[8] Roger B. Salomon is similarly alive to evidence
of "unresolved psychic and intellectual problems" in the "divided artistic
consciousness" that presides over the narrative. He traces the problem to
"the fundamental disparity between Twain's predominantly optimistic theory of history and his personal pessimism. This disparity," he argues, "is reflected in the split personality of the Yankee."[9]

The aggregate view of *A Connecticut Yankee*—that it is a novel whose
contradictory perspectives on history, progress, and human nature are the
issue of unresolved conflicts in its author's psyche—is entirely compatible
with my critical sense of things. In its deep dividedness, its resistance to tidy
closure, and its troubled autobiographical intimations, the book offers itself
as a kind of gateway or prologue to Clemens's late fiction, the stories undertaken—though often neither completed nor published—during the last two
decades of his life. The novel anticipates the late writing in other ways as
well. Experience, as Hank finds, is a terrible dream that comes to seem real,
and from which he cannot awaken. Human nature is corrupt, selfish in all
things, contemptible. Deceit and self-deception, fraud and humbug, are
pervasive realities of life. Moral determinism—the assignment of blame for

the human condition to training, circumstance, or God—does little to leave a gathering bitterness of tone and a tendency toward nihilism. Death, the only consolation, is eagerly anticipated.

Virtually all of these elements have their point of intersection in what Gregg Camfield aptly describes as the novel's "obsession with slavery."[10] Clemens is intensely preoccupied in *A Connecticut Yankee* with varieties of involuntary servitude—to our fallen natures, to the mysterious depths and movements of the mind, to widespread deceit and self-deception, to training, circumstance, God, and, of course, to legalized subjection as it is practiced in medieval England and in the American south. Hank Morgan takes it as his civilizing mission in Camelot to free the multitudes from the lies and delusions to which they are heir as humans, and which are exploited by the state and the religious establishment to produce a nation of slaves, both the kind that "wore the iron collar on their necks," and all the rest as well, who "were slaves in fact, but without the name." Such people, Hank observes with dismay, "imagined themselves men and freemen, and called themselves so" (*CYA*, 98). He is at this stage persuaded that a vast moral gulf separates medieval Camelot, a deluded world of slaves, from late nineteenth-century Hartford, a rational world of free men; and he is confident of his own ability to bridge the gulf by bringing the blessings of civilized progress to benighted antiquity. "If I lived and prospered," Hank resolves, "I would be the death of slavery" (*CYA*, 263).

The hero's optimism, clearly shared at this point by his maker, is in the course of the narrative gradually eroded, as he is made witness both to the intractability of people and institutions, and to answering weaknesses in his own nature. The moral divide separating the two worlds steadily narrows until Hank finally recognizes that medieval slavery and modern slavery are virtually one and the same. He never directly acknowledges the clear implication of what his story has revealed: human beings in the nineteenth century are as blindly enslaved to themselves, to their beliefs and institutions, and to each other, as the English were in the sixth century. In his rather baffled reticence on this score, Hank recoils—as Clemens surely did—from a direct reckoning with the painful revelation emergent from his own narrative, and settled instead for groping, imperfect denial. Bitterly disenchanted with a world irredeemably enslaved, and overtaken yet again by irrepressible reminders of his guilty complicity in it, Clemens moves Hank to detonate what he cannot reform, and then suspends him in a dream between Hartford and Camelot, neither palpably real, and both so morally fraught as to be uninhabitable. Characteristically, Hank, quite in the manner of his maker, retreats to the distracting consolations of showmanship, and is just "getting up his last 'effect'" (*CYA*, 575) when death, the only durable solution, finally overtakes him.

I say "durable solution" somewhat tentatively, for Hank shares with Clemens the fear that death may be no more than another of the dreams to which he flees in vain for relief from the guilt that finds its way into every region, no matter how remote, of his tormented psyche, and that invariably devolves into nightmares of remorse. In dread of a return to the nineteenth century, Hank appeals to his wife for support. "It was awful—awfuler than you can image, Sandy. Ah, watch by me, Sandy—stay by me every moment—*don't* let me go out of my mind again; death is nothing, let it come, but not with those dreams, not with the torture of those hideous dreams—I cannot endure *that* again" (*CYA*, 574). Death is the solution to Hank's tormented psyche only if it is the bearer of complete, utter oblivion, the permanent surcease of all consciousness, dreams above all else included.

Before turning to a closer analysis of the text itself, I want to reflect in a brief, preliminary way on slavery, the nightmare that indeed obsessed the aging humorist—as it obsesses Hank Morgan—and that was preeminent among the spurs to his remorse. In the most fundamental way, Clemens felt guilty about slavery because it deprived others of what he himself valued above all things, freedom, and because it was his lot in life to have been complicit, though quite against his best human instincts, in the subjection of black people to conditions that he came in time to regard as morally indefensible. To have looked the other way in the face of the iniquity of slavery was the unpardonable sin for which Clemens never forgave himself. Scholars assure us that when it came to describing the worst horrors of slavery in *A Connecticut Yankee*, the cruel coffling of entire families in chapters 21 and 34, Clemens drew principally on secondary sources.[11] While there is good reason to believe that the novelist was influenced by what he read, that influence was felt most deeply not in matters of detail, but in its quickening of accusing childhood memories. "It stung me as if I had been hit instead," Hank winces, when the slave driver's lash bites into the shoulder of a helpless woman. Later on he is moved by the horror to admit, "I could not take my eyes away from these worn and wasted wrecks of humanity." Nowhere in the novel is the author's voice more clearly present to us than when Hank acknowledges the grave moral weight of these images burned indelibly into his memory. "Well," he reflects, as a male slave is rudely separated from his wife and child, "the look of him one might not bear at all, and so I turned away; but I knew I should never get this picture out of my mind again, and there it is to this day, to wring my heart-strings whenever I think of it" (*CYA*, 262, 447, 263). Now listen to Clemens, in a passage previously cited, from his biographical profile of his mother:

> I vividly remember seeing a dozen black men and women chained to one another, once, and lying in a group on the pavement, awaiting shipment to the Southern slave market. Those were the saddest faces I have ever seen. Chained slaves could not have been a common sight, or this picture would not have made so strong and lasting an impression upon me. (*MTA*, 1:124)

It is a reliable measure of the moral anguish that interfuses such writing that Clemens was at pains to deny the true extent of his actual involvement in what he describes. This was something he witnessed only "once," he is careful to note; such cruel spectacles "could not have been a common sight" in Hannibal. In fact, Terrell Dempsey observes quite unequivocally, "Clemens tried to minimize the numbers of slaves transported in this fashion," just as he underplayed community acquiescence in the evils of slave trading, and rationalized his family's decision to sell their own slave, Jennie, as something she brought upon herself. "The slave trader was an important and accepted part of slave culture," Dempsey writes, and Clemens's account of poor Jennie's fate has about it "all the trappings of a comforting lie slaveholders told themselves about slavery."[12] His retreat to bad-faith denial is the surest sign that Clemens's memories of slavery so challenged his moral self-regard that he could no more forget them than he could bear to remember them. This double movement in memory was driven not merely by the horror of the things remembered, but also by Clemens's certainty that he was morally entangled in what he so vividly recalled. This certainty in turn gave rise to a range of compensating reconstructions of the past—as a childhood idyll, as a dream indistinguishable from waking reality, or as the unfolding in time of the eternally foreordained—in which guilt has no apparent part to play. But because his guilt would not be permanently gainsaid, the desired condition of complete amnesia was never achieved; the idyll invariably fractured, the dream invariably turned to nightmare, and the retreat to determinism proved an imperfect stay against resurgent self-accusation. It is one among many ironies here that Clemens's attempts to dispel his guilt about slavery were so often grounded in more or less explicit claims of his own enslavement to forces—training, circumstance, God—over which he had no control.

Like Huck, Hank elects to take the side of the enslaved. Like Huck again, however, Hank is from the very beginning subject to intimations of failure.

Upon coming to consciousness in Camelot, he is struck by the "soft, reposeful summer landscape, as lovely as a dream, and as lonesome as Sunday.
The air was full of the smell of flowers, and the buzzing of insects, and the
twittering of birds, and there were no people, no wagons, there was no stir
of life, nothing going on" (*CYA*, 27). The scene is reminiscent in key details
of chapters 1 and 31 of *Huckleberry Finn*, in which Huck is overtaken by
what I have described as "proleptic guilt," ominous indications that he will
fail Jim. In Hank's case, the signs portend a parallel inability to follow
through on a commitment to end slavery—both the sixth-century institution itself, and the broader enslavement of medieval England to feudalism.
Quite appropriately, the ominous silence descends again just as the Battle of
the Sand-Belt—Hank's final and most apocalyptic failure as a liberator—is
about to begin. "As for sounds," he reflects, "there were none. The stillness
was death-like. True, there were the usual night-sounds of the country—
the whir of night-birds, the buzzing of insects, the barking of distant dogs,
the mellow lowing of far-off kine—but these didn't seem to break the stillness, they only intensified it, and added a grewsome melancholy to it into
the bargain" (*CYA*, 559–60).

The Battle of the Sand Belt certainly demonstrates the destructive power
of nineteenth-century technology, but it does nothing to alleviate the suffering of slaves, and thus dramatizes Hank's utter failure to achieve his enlightened humanitarian goals. Indeed, the battle invites interpretation as the
ostensible victor's temper tantrum in the face of profound moral defeat. Like
Clemens, Hank is always already burdened with the guilt of his complicity
in the very thing he hates. The eerie silence that precedes the battle tends
to confirm that, here as elsewhere in the novel, he has advance intimations
of the terrible futility of his idealistic mission. When it dawns upon him that
he has been blind for years to the irrational cruelty of nineteenth-century
slave laws, Hank is strangely unmoved by the evidence of his moral derelic-
tion. "Well," he observes with resignation, "that's the way we are made"
(*CYA*, 449). His human qualities of course contribute substantially to the
failure of his plans for the liberation of England. He readily admits that he
would rather show off than pursue reform, resorts unconscionably to fraud
and humbug, indulges himself in outbursts of cruelty, allows that he is as
irrational as the next man, and lusts quite knowingly after power. "Yes," he
concedes, "there was more or less human nature in me; I found that out"
(*CYA*, 64, 72, 134, 206, 402, 421–22, 514). At the same time, however, he
never fully relinquishes his sense of himself as a free moral agent able to

transcend his many limitations. Hank has it both ways on this score, alternately asserting his moral autonomy and conceding his hopelessly fallen humanity. When he succeeds at bending the world to his ideals, he is a proud, moral free agent; when he fails, he feels guilty and looks—in good bad faith—for excuses.

This pattern of contradiction surfaces clearly in a pivotal episode at the castle of Morgan le Fay, a queen famed for her ruthlessness and cruelty. Hank at first succeeds in restraining his royal hostess from an act of characteristic inhumanity, and seems confident that she can be converted to more enlightened ways. But his optimism wavers when he himself surrenders to the temptations of arbitrary power, and collapses altogether in the face of Morgan's utter intractability. "Oh, it was no use to waste sense on her," he fumes.

> Training—training is everything; training is all there is *to* a person. We speak of nature; it is folly; there is no such thing as nature; what we call by that misleading name is merely heredity and training. We have no thoughts of our own, no opinions of our own; they are transmitted to us, trained into us. All that is original in us, and therefore fairly creditable or discreditable to us, can be covered up and hidden by the point of a cambric needle, all the rest being atoms contributed by, and inherited from, a procession of ancestors that stretches back a billion years to the Adam-clam or grasshopper or monkey from whom our race has been so tediously and ostentatiously and unprofitably developed. And as for me, all that I think about in this plodding sad pilgrimage, this pathetic drift between the eternities, is to look out and humbly live a pure and high and blameless life, and save that one microscopic atom in me that is truly *me*: the rest may land in Sheol and welcome for all I care. (*CYA*, 217)[13]

Clemens is speaking quite directly through Hank Morgan here. The turn to determinism is central, of course, but it cannot be too much emphasized that Clemens is moved philosophically not by an interest in metaphysics, but by a desperate craving for moral self-acquittal. This is all about guilt. The ways and means of causation are of scant concern except as the foreordination of events procures release from responsibility for the intolerable cruelty and injustice of mortal experience. Clemens embraces *moral* determinism for one reason only: it seems to offer shelter from crippling remorse. So anguished is his sense of entanglement and moral complicity in human enslavement, whether ancient or modern, English or American, that he surrenders his free will as the price of relief. True, he promptly contradicts himself by laying claim to a "microscopic atom" of moral agency. But he is no more persuaded than we are of his actual ability to "humbly live a pure and high and blameless life." What impresses us here is not moral self-confidence, but a sense of baffled, hopeless subjection to life's "plodding sad pilgrimage, this pathetic drift between the eternities."

Free will and determinism are both inadequate to Hank's needs because neither doctrine wins the kind of undoubting assent requisite to the achievement of moral repose. Free will falls short because he does not believe that he can rise above his essential human selfishness. Determinism releases him from responsibility, to be sure, but he is both constitutionally disinclined to relinquish precious personal freedom, and prey to the suspicion that his high-sounding philosophical gambit is a moral ruse. Viewed in the light of such nagging doubts, it is little surprise that Hank temporarily abandons the search for a philosophical resolution of his guilt, and turns instead to the imagined extinction of the problem at its very source. "If I had the remaking of man," he reflects,

> he wouldn't have any conscience. It is one of the most disagreeable things connected with a person; and although it certainly does a great deal of good, it cannot be said to pay, in the long run; it would be much better to have less good and more comfort. . . . I have noticed my conscience for many years, and I know it is more trouble and bother to me than anything else I started with. I suppose that in the beginning I prized it, because we prize anything that is ours; and yet how foolish it was to think so. . . . There isn't any way that you can work off a conscience—at least so it will stay worked off; not that I know of, anyway. (*CYA*, 219–20)

Imperfectly reconciled to the moral consolations of philosophy, Clemens, speaking through his hero, effectively capitulates to the tyranny of conscience. He could no more reason his guilt away than he could excise it in an act of radical self-refashioning.

This is not to suggest that Clemens ever gave up trying to gain relief from the accusations that inwardly tormented him. He would come back again and again to the temporary solace of determinism; and he would never give up on the hope that conscience was after all just a bad dream from which he would awaken to blissful moral indifference. Relief came most frequently in the many distractions that his active public life afforded him, and in a resilience of spirit that gave him purchase on intervals of optimism and good humor. But he knew very well that there was no way to work his conscience off, at least so it would stay that way. It was always there, even in the good times, and most especially in the remote hours of the night, poised on the nether side of consciousness. It was there as well in much that he wrote, and in virtually all the stories that arose from his memories of childhood, and that invariably transformed themselves from comedy into tragedy. This of course happens in *A Connecticut Yankee*, which anticipates much that followed in its foundering on the moral reef of slavery, the irresistible theme to which memory and imagination recurred, inciting conscience with reminders that the thing in man which makes him cruel to a slave is indeed forever fixed in his nature. As resistance to the inevitable stiffened, the subtlety of conscience perforce sharpened, with the result that the recoil into bad-faith denial became more desperate and ornate—and futile—than ever.

It is no small measure of Clemens's enduring cultural relevance and value for Americans that he dramatizes for us the burden of a national history at times so unbearable, especially in matters of race and slavery, that we surrender to the temptation of bad faith, the denial, itself denied, of our failures to walk the walk of our highest ideals. It is equally telling that this compelling moral drama is most conspicuously at play in the works that we come back to most often, and that we claim, without quite knowing why, as most distinctively our own. Yet so great was the weight of Clemens's guilt that it left its mark on virtually everything he wrote, especially in his later years. *The American Claimant* (1892), a satire and farce cobbled together in a couple of months and published with quick profits principally in mind, is no exception. Almost certainly the least read of Clemens's completed novels, the book attracted little critical attention until quite recently, when a small handful of scholars began to take notice. There is between them an emergent consensus that *The American Claimant* is deeply flawed, but that it betrays inchoate preoccupations with social and economic problems in late-century American life, with the destabilization of identity, with contemporary developments in "mental science," and with moral relativism. In his thorough and balanced critical overview, Peter Messent gives special emphasis to the novel's movement between genres—science fiction, fantasy, farce, satire, romance, and success narrative—commenting that the confusion expresses the writer's "ongoing attempts to find a form to contain [the] disparate but complex themes" at large in his book.[14]

Useful though it is, none of the recent commentary foregrounds Clemens's ongoing fictional negotiations with guilt, which are woven into several of the novel's apparently disparate thematic strands, and which influenced its final devolution into romance. Consider that we are not many pages along in *The American Claimant* before the morally vexed topic of slavery surfaces in the narrative. Elaborating on her husband's unfailing generosity, Mrs. Sellers refers proudly to his treatment of

> old Dan'l and old Jinny, that the sheriff sold south one of the times that we got bankrupted before the war—they came wandering back after the peace, worn out and used up on the cotton plantations, helpless, and not another lick of work left in their old hides for the rest of this earthly pilgrimage—and we so pinched, *oh* so pinched for the very crumbs to keep life in us, and he just flung the door wide, and the way he received them you'd have thought they had come straight from heaven in answer to prayer. (*AC*, 38–39)

Such is Clemens's fictional redaction of a familiar but much more compromising chapter in his family history. Old Dan'l is a fictitious character, though his name is reminiscent of Uncle Dan'l, the model for Jim in *Huckleberry Finn*, who was freed by Clemens's uncle John Quarles in 1855. The real-life Jinny (or Jennie) was much less fortunate. As I have already noted, she was sold downriver in early 1843 by James Marshall Clemens, who seems to have invented the comforting story that the sale was a reluctant concession to the slave woman's wishes. The utter implausibility of such a claim testifies to a desperate grasping after moral acquittal clearly akin to the bad-faith fictionalizing of the episode in *The American Claimant*, where the abandoned chattel are restored to the loving care of their former "family." The unforgettable truth of the matter was something Clemens felt compelled to reveal, but that he shrank from in the actual telling.[15]

Guilt figures more generally in the Colonel Sellers sections of the novel by its conspicuous absence in places where we are strongly inclined to look for it. In thrall to the fantasy of limitless personal wealth, the old man lays plans to staff the workforce with the cheap and efficient labor of legions of dead people restored to life. He betrays not the slightest moral unease about his bizarre scheme, and blithely contemplates the murder of his black exslaves, with the thought of revivifying them as compliant machines, "adjustable," he exults, "with a screw or something" (*AC*, 82). Nor does he hesitate to falsify the identity of human remains returned to England for burial. His daughter Gwendolen has no doubt about the impropriety of the deed, but refrains from protest, recognizing that "her father's mind was made up and there was a chance for him to appear upon that sad scene down yonder in an authentic and official way" (*AC*, 83). Like Clemens, Colonel Sellers is unable to pass up a chance to show off; unlike Clemens, the old man is seemingly invulnerable to the attacks of conscience that made life miserable for his maker.

In fact, *The American Claimant* is notably attentive to the ways and means of the Colonel's unruffled moral serenity, and to the management of guilt feelings more generally. The novel thus dramatizes in fictional terms the immunity from conscience that Clemens longed for, but that eluded him in real life. Sellers is "a Mind-Cure dabbler" who admonishes sufferers to "banish care." "You'll be the healthier for it every time," he insists, "every time" (*AC*, 28–29). Clemens was similarly persuaded of the benefits of mind cure, so much so that he urged his variously troubled wife and daughters to seek its consolations.[16] Nor did he deny that Christian Science—a religious variation on the mind-cure movement—freed its adherents from subjection to all manner of mental torment. Though he regarded Mary Baker Eddy as a shameless fraud and hypocrite, he believed that her religion was irresistibly seductive to those afflicted with guilt and depression. "The vacuous vulgarity" of Eddy's writings "was a perpetual joy to him," Howells shrewdly observes, "while he bowed with serious respect to the sagacity which built so securely upon the everlasting rock of human credulity and folly."[17]

Years of guilty suffering had taught Clemens that peace of mind was an elusive prize to be valued on virtually any terms, including faith in Mrs. Eddy's preposterous religion. "Personally," he admits with envy, "I have not known a Scientist who did not seem to be serene, contented, unharassed", they are blissfully exempt from the dread "black hours" of self-accusation that the humorist knew so well (*WIM*, 349). The problem, of course, was that Clemens knew too much about "human credulity and folly," his own included, to take the leap of faith requisite to mental healing on the mind-cure plan. Hardened skepticism in matters of religion made him vulnerable to the tyranny of his own worst demons, a predicament that he shrewdly analyzes in *Christian Science*. Allowing that "the power which a man's imagination has over his body to heal it or to make it sick is a force which none of us is born without," he goes on to observe that most people, left to themselves, either succumb to "the mischievous half of the force— the half which invents imaginary ailments"—or "scoff at the beneficent half of the force and deny its existence." Infidels may be saved, Clemens adds, by the ministrations of an "outsider, B," who "must imagine that *his* incantations are the healing-power that is curing A, and A must imagine that this is so." Well and good, if it works, though the obdurate skeptic is quick to add, "I think it is not so, at all" (*WIM*, 257).

It is surely the key to Clemens's grudging regard for Mary Baker Eddy that he joined her in acknowledging the healing potential of faith. It is just as clear that he numbered himself among the solitary minority made prey by their unbelief to a life of mental turmoil. This was precisely his wife Livy's view of the darkness that engulfed her husband and his writing during their last years together. "I am absolutely wretched today on account of your state of mind—your state of intellect," she complained, probably in early 1902.

> Why don't you let the better side of you work? . . . *Do* darling change your mental attitude, *try to change it.* The trouble is you don't want to. When you asked me to try mental science I tried it & I keep trying it.
>
> Where is the mind that wrote the Prince & P. Jeanne d'Arc, The Yankee &c &c &c. Bring it back! You can if you will—if you wish to. Think of the side I know; the sweet dear, tender side—that I love so. Why not show this more to the world? Does it help the world to always rail at it? . . . Why always dwell on the evil until those who live beside you are crushed to the earth & you seem almost like a monomaniac. O I love you so & wish you would listen and take heed.[18]

In Colonel Sellers, the mind-cure enthusiast and credulous optimist, Clemens gave rein to imaginative speculation on what a life given over to the healing power of the imagination might be like. Nagging guilt about slavery, as we have seen, would be replaced by happy illusions of paternalistic racial benevolence. But the Colonel's formidable ameliorative powers are in fact equal to virtually any challenge to his moral equanimity. "No doubt it's a blessed thing to have an imagination that can always make you satisfied, no matter how you are fixed," observes his wife. "Uncle Dave Hopkins used to always say, 'Turn me into John Calvin, and I want to know which place I'm going to; turn me into Mulberry Sellers and I don't care" (*AC,* 56). Burdened as he was with what he referred to more than once as his "trained Presbyterian conscience" (*AMT,* 41),[19] Clemens clearly yearned for the kind of serenity enjoyed by the Colonel. But the prize eluded him because Sellers's brand of self-willed ignorance was not an option for him.[20] Nor was he adept at the kind of mental maneuvering advocated by the rather mysterious Mr. Barrow, who enters the novel in Chapter 11 to offer counsel—all of it entirely of a piece with the hothouse complacency of Colonel Sellers—to the morally troubled Lord Berkeley. As a general thing, Mr. Barrow advises, you must "drag your thoughts away from your troubles—by the ears, by the heels, or any other way, so you manage it; it's the healthiest thing a body can do; dwelling on troubles is deadly, just deadly" (*AC,* 161). This is of course just the sort of retreat from mental conflict that

Clemens urged upon his wife and children, but that either eluded him, or afforded no permanent stay against inner torment.

Barrow contributes to Lord Berkeley's moral education by trying to help him resolve deeply felt questions about political and social justice, especially as they bear on his right-minded ambitions to divest himself of inherited privilege and to pursue life in America on an equal, democratic footing with others. Clemens's endorsement of the young peer's idealistic egalitarianism is no more obvious than his attraction to the pleasures of wealth and status that the English aristocrat feels compelled to put behind him. In the course of Berkeley's earnest deliberations, two things become clear. First, like Clemens, he is guided in his political and social theorizing almost entirely by conscience. The task is not so much to formulate a rational and just position as it is to settle into views that banish guilt. Second, it is ever more obvious that moral closure on these grounds is unattainable, simply because the fictional lord is no more able than the real life novelist to relinquish the material and psychological advantages of morally unjustifiable privilege It is Hank Morgan's dilemma all over again.

When Berkeley's idealism collides—as, inevitably, it must—with the harsh realities of life in competitive American society, he admits to himself that he misses "the respect" and "the deference" that he enjoyed in England, and bends to Barrow's rationalization that "in a republic where all are free and equal, prosperity and position constitute *rank*." But no sooner has Berkeley persuaded himself that it is his duty to himself and his family to return to his former life in England than he hears an American workingman heaping contempt on those who dishonor themselves by clinging to un- earned wealth and social position. "Every word spoken by this stranger seemed to leave a blister on [Berkeley's] conscience, and by the time the speech was finished he felt that he was all conscience and one blister." Bar- row promptly denounces the speaker in terms that "whitewashed" the young lord's "shame." (Adds Clemens: "That is a good service to have when you can't get the best of all verdicts, self-acquittal.") Barrow persists in this rationalizing vein, until Berkeley's "conscience was comfortable once more" (*AC*, 128–29, 146–47, 153).

Howells, you will recall, brilliantly characterizes Clemens as a theoretical socialist and a practical aristocrat (*MTHL*, 2:579).[21] Berkeley perfectly em- bodies this division in the novelist's makeup, as his shuttling between self- indulgent rationalization and painful bouts of conscience clearly demon- strates. It is entirely telling that the novel is no more successful at reconciling these radically divergent tendencies than Clemens was in real life. Instead, and as Lawrence Howe aptly observes, "the narrative cops out, as do the characters," and Lord Berkeley is permitted to return, without further attacks of conscience, to the life of an aristocrat.[22] *The American Claimant* eludes the horns of an accelerating moral dilemma by an abrupt genre shift, from searching social satire to all-forgiving romance. Because Lord Berkeley and the Colonel's daughter, Sally Sellers, are in love, "all anxiety, apprehension, [and] uncertainty vanished out of [their] hearts and left them filled with a great peace." This is not to suggest that romance resolves moral issues. When she surrenders to momentary doubts, Sally endures the "kind of sleep [that] resembles fire," and, as Clemens well knew, that leaves one "with his brain baked and his physical forces fried out of him." Love banishes such discord, in good part by relaxing the demand for moral consistency. Barrow decides that it's healthiest to humor Berkeley's delusions, and the normally scrupulous Sally Sellers insists on being indulged with comforting lies (*AC*, 221, 235, 249–50, 253). Thanks to its generic detour, the novel's sweeping evasion of moral implication has its payoff in a wedding that heals all wounds, levels all uncertainty, and reconciles the protagonists to the carefree enjoyment of their privileged station in life.

To what extent was Clemens aware of the bad faith on display in his management of *The American Claimant*? The novel is quite clearly concerned with the same kinds of personally charged moral issues that surface virtually everywhere in his fiction, but that rarely if ever rise to the level of sustained, fully conscious development. This is so, as we have seen, because the questions that most engaged him were triggered by conscience, and thus by reflex resistance at the same time. An oblique approach to an acknowledgment of precisely this dynamic surfaces toward the beginning of the novel. "I have noticed, in such literary experiences as I have had," declares Colonel Sellers, "that one of the most taking things to do is to conceal your meaning when you are *trying* to conceal it. Whereas, if you go at literature with a free conscience and nothing to conceal, you can turn out a book, every time, that the very elect can't understand" (*AC*, 64). That the sense here is a little garbled is doubtless symptomatic of the fact that Clemens was groping through his character for clarity on an issue that deeply concerned him. The Colonel believes that it is difficult if not impossible in literature to conceal conscious motives. This much is clear. It is less clear why it should matter that "the very elect can't understand" when there is "nothing to conceal," unless, of course, the Colonel is suggesting that so long as the writer is unaware of such meanings, and of his wish to conceal them, he will enjoy the "free conscience" that accompanies the illusion that he has "nothing to conceal."

As applied to Clemens himself, this reading of the Colonel's intentions goes to the very heart of bad-faith denial. As we have seen, the author-cat acknowledged the futility of his attempts to conceal the "remorseless truth" about himself in his writing; for all of his "wily diligences" in the matter, he was aware both that he had something to hide and—his professed commitment to candor notwithstanding—that he was deeply moved to hide it. The Colonel's "free conscience" in the matter of hidden meanings, like his pliant susceptibility to mind cure, was the projection in fiction of an immunity that Clemens craved but never enjoyed in real life. It was not that he was consciously the host to an irrepressible impulse to reveal the worst of himself in his fiction. Rather, he was subject to intimations that shameful personal "revealments," imperceptible to him save in transient monitions of self-betrayal, somehow surfaced "between the lines"—as he put it—of his work. He was thus anxiously aware of guilty "meanings" arising surreptitiously from beneath the level of his consciousness into the fabric of his writing. Such is the contradiction of self-deception and bad faith: that we know and un-know at the same time, and are therefore liable to reveal what is concealed, and to tell what may appear to have gone untold.

Writing to Clemens about autobiography in early 1904, Howells draws attention to a key "temperamental difference" between himself and his friend, a difference manifest both in their personalities and in their work. "You are dramatic and unconscious," he observes, while "I am cursed with consciousness to the core" (*MTHL*, 2:780). Clemens offered no resistance to his friend's insight, doubtless because it accorded so well with his own views in the matter, and most especially with his approach to his stories and novels. There is scant evidence that Clemens came to fictional composition with clear plots or themes in mind, and none at all that such planning ever paid off for him. His novels emerged gradually from fragmentary episodes and anecdotes or from vague conceptions of character. "Who can tell what is to become of a character once created?" he asked in 1907:

> I never deliberately sat down and 'created' a character in my life. I begin to write incidents out of real life. One of the persons I write about begins to talk this way and one another, and pretty soon I find that these creatures of the imagination have developed into characters, and have for me a distinct personality. These are not 'made,' they just grow naturally out of the subject. That was the way Tom Sawyer, Huck Finn and other characters came to

exist. I couldn't to save my life deliberately sit down and plan out a character according to a diagram. In fact, every book I ever wrote just wrote itself.[23]

Clemens's inability to conceive plots and characters in advance had its corollary in his refusal to elaborate fictional materials once his narratives were under way. "As long as a book would write itself," he observes in a 1906 *Harper's* article, "I was a faithful and interested amanuensis and my industry did not flag, but the minute that the book tried to shift to *my* head the labor of contriving its situations, inventing its adventures and conducting its conversations, I put it away and dropped it out of my mind" (*MTE,* 196). This characteristic retreat from texts that refused to write themselves was almost invariably a sign that his narrative was leading him, all unawares, to a place—a very personal place—to which he did not want to go. The unconscious impulse to approach such places, as it intersects with the equally unreflecting reflex to draw back from them, conforms exactly to the pattern of telling and untelling, revealing and concealing, that so dominates Clemens's writing about himself.

Such patterns of tension, already prominent in the early fiction, surface in especially bold relief in *The Tragedy of Pudd'nhead Wilson and the Comedy Those Extraordinary Twins* (1894). The latter story, a farce about Siamese twins, was undertaken first, but in the course of composition unaccountably transformed itself into what its baffled creator describes as a "tragedy." As it evolved, the narrative drew Clemens away from a subject he found benignly humorous toward one—race-slavery—that was profoundly troubling for him. Ordinarily under such circumstances, he might have set the project aside. But in this instance, as Frederick Anderson has observed, Clemens was writing under great financial pressure, and so—"absorbed by a demand for returns from his creative investment"—he pressed on with his recalcitrant narrative.[24] The result is a book profoundly divided against itself, and just as profoundly given up to denial about the cruelty and moral cowardice that its treatment of race-slavery lays open to view. As he prepared his ill-matched and entangled stories for publication, Clemens held on to the delusion that he had written a fast-paced murder mystery, and not a penetrating indictment of the peculiar institution. "The whole story is centered on the murder and the trial," he assured his publisher; "everything that is done or said or that happens is a preparation for those events."[25] In effect, Clemens denied to himself the terrible, very personal moral anguish that this errant farce had exacted as the price of its completion. Then he denied that denial.

But no sooner had Clemens denied denial than he affirmed it—or, at least, acknowledged intimations of things unseen in the tangled fabric of his novel. The first American edition, published in 1894, includes both *Pudd'n-head Wilson* and, as a kind of addendum, *Those Extraordinary Twins*, the "suppressed farce," which Clemens insisted on including, at least in part because it brought him an additional $1,500 from his publisher.[26] He recognized that the juxtaposition was strange, not to say bizarre, and acknowledges as much in the interstitial commentary he wrote as a bridge between the two stories. "A man who is not born with the novel-writing gift has a troublesome time of it when he tries to build a novel," he begins.

> I know this from experience. He has no clear idea of his story; in fact he has no story. He merely has some people in his mind, and an incident or two, also a locality. He knows these people, he knows the selected locality, and he trusts that he can plunge those people into those incidents with interesting results. So he goes to work. To write a novel? No—that is a thought which comes later; in the beginning he is only proposing to tell a little tale; a very little tale; a six-page tale. But as it is a tale which he is not acquainted with, and can only find out what it is by listening as it goes along telling itself, it is more than apt to go on and on and on till it spreads itself into a book. I know about this, because it has happened to me so many times.

As the tale grows into a novel, Clemens continues, "another thing" happens: "The original intention (or motif) is apt to get abolished and find itself superseded by a quite different one." It happened with *The Prince and the Pauper*, and again with *Pudd'nhead Wilson*, which "changed itself from a farce to a tragedy while I was going along with it,—a most embarrassing circumstance." Worse yet, the two stories got "tangled together," but in a way that eluded easy detection. After several months of confusion, Clemens finally "saw where the difficulty lay," and so "pulled one of the stories out by the roots, and left the other one," a process he describes as "a kind of literary Caesarean operation" (*PW*, 119).

The tone here is complex. Because Clemens's self-effacement is leavened with irony, the jest is never at risk of becoming an admission of downright incompetence. At the same time, his perplexity with his own enigmatic creativity, and with its freakish productions, is perfectly genuine. This is the way it is with me, he concedes, and, with a kind of genial bewilderment, sets the riddle aside. His subsequent remarks offer the impression that he is satisfied that the artistic problem has been solved. "The defect," he observes, "turned out to be the one already spoken of—two stories in one, a farce and a tragedy. So I pulled out the farce and left the tragedy." But his commentary concludes with a half-turn back toward its initial uncertainty. Because *Pudd'nhead Wilson* no longer featured the Siamese twins—the Italian brothers, Angelo and Luigi—of the original farce, Clemens notes that he took them "apart and made two separate men of them." Finally, and quite tellingly, he adds: "They had no occasion to have foreign names now, but it was too much trouble to remove them all through, so I left them christened as they were and made no explanation" (*PW*, 122).

Admission, denial, oblique acknowledgment—the pattern is of course familiar, as is the implied invitation to look carefully for personal revelations that Clemens senses but cannot see, and that—as if in response to a deep if half-glimpsed moral imperative—he draws obliquely to our attention. We are drawn to the same point if we observe the conspicuous omission in Clemens's interstitial commentary of any attempt to explain *why* his tales expand into novels, and *why* his humorous stories transform themselves into tragedies. He is hesitant, we may be reasonably confident, because of intimations that inquiry into the riddle of his creativity will open a window on the possibility that something important, even "embarrassing," is revealed in the deformity of its unaccountable productions. We are present, in other words, at a sighting of the author-cat.

It is entirely apposite in this regard that Clemens's interstitial commentary is given over almost entirely to a detailed account of the changes his "literary Caesarean operation" has produced in *Those Extraordinary Twins*. He has much less to say about *Pudd'nhead Wilson*, the long, featured narrative in his dual text. He describes the story as a "tragedy," but displays no inclination to elaborate on that key term, or to spell out in any detail the changes that were requisite to its completion. To the contrary, his very brief remarks focus almost entirely on the way the novel's principal characters—Pudd'nhead, Roxy, and Tom Driscoll—"got to intruding themselves" into the midst of his farce. "Before the book was half finished," he complains, "those three were taking things almost entirely into their own hands and working the whole tale as a private venture of their own—a tale which they had nothing at all to do with, by rights" (*PW*, 120). Once again, the arch tone hardly diminishes the importance of Clemens's telling disavowal. His story took an untoward and inexplicable turn toward the "tragic." Why this has happened, and what it means, he does not venture to say. He acknowledges that something is deeply awry in his book, goes on to suggest that the problem has been solved, only to hint in closing that the trouble has persisted.

That unacknowledged trouble, of course, is race-slavery—Clemens's resurgent memories of guilty complicity in the terrible injustice and suffering inflicted on its victims. This is the unmentionable "tragedy" that erupts as if from nowhere into the humorist's benign "little tale," as it does again and again into the presumptive idyll of his childhood. In fact, close attention to the intended "farce" reveals that the arrival of the Italian Siamese twins precipitates an overreaction symptomatic of graver boundary anxieties at large in Dawson's Landing. The twins, whose distinctive personalities occupy a single body, inspire a kind of moral panic because their palpable doubleness is a challenge to the complacent local consensus that distinctions between good and evil, black and white, and one person and another are perfectly clear and easily maintained At their most subversive, the twins are an uncanny reminder of the town's bad-faith denial of the truth about race-slavery—their blindness to the omnipresent evidence of miscegenation in their midst, and to the larger, utterly self-serving fiction of racial difference. Here once again, then, was the permanent racial subtext of the matter of Hannibal, which in this telling arises irresistibly from the seemingly innocuous, but in fact powerfully overdetermined, image of human doubleness. Viewed in this light, Clemens's blindness to the dark transformation of his narrative perfectly recapitulates the blindness of his characters to the lie at the very center of their common life. Their story is his story, his story theirs.

It is symptomatic of Clemens's resistance to the moral trajectory of his restive tale that he continued to elaborate his farce cum mystery materials long after Roxy's advent and the commencement of the "tragic" race-slavery plot. The divergent strands surfaced on page after page of his manuscript, as if they belonged there together. And belong they did, not only in their covert, subversive linkage, but also because their simultaneous emergence served the artist's reflexive impulse to conceal what his refractory narrative seemed bound to reveal. This is to say that in releasing Roxy into his manuscript, Clemens responded to a countering impulse to contain her, to blunt and obscure the morally unsettling thrust of her story. The farce and mystery plots admirably answered this need. They filled narrative space and time, thus diminishing the full force of the unfolding race-slavery plot, and they gave rise to distracting conclusions to both the comic and the tragic stories, which were composed in tandem and then only belatedly separated in the "literary Caesarean operation." Struggling almost literally against her maker's resistance, Roxy forced her way into the center of *Pudd'nhead Wilson*; Clemens capitulated to her, and to the anguished moral reckoning she thrust upon him, but only on condition that her story compete for attention—his *and* ours—with farce and mystery. Such was his truce with conscience.

Roxy supplements the humorous matter of Hannibal with the hard historical realities of race-slavery, of miscegenation, and of the social tensions and simmering racial hatred that inevitably follow. Clemens was imaginatively quite alive to such things, of course, even as he was inwardly tormented by their implications. When Tom Driscoll learns that he is Roxy's son, and therefore technically black, he erupts in volcanic rage. "I am a nigger—a nigger! . . . Yesterday I hated nobody very much, but now I hate the whole human race. . . . If I had the courage, I would kill—somebody—anybody" (*PW*, 191). But Tom's outburst and others like it are to be found only in scattered manuscripts; Clemens shrank from including them in the published version of the novel.

He shrank as well, we may be sure, from the deeper sexual significance of Roxy's disruptive emergence into his narrative. Critics are virtually at one in declaring the proud slave unique among Clemens's fictional women. She alone among them is passionate and manifestly sexual; and, of course, she is black. In all of this, she invites comparison with the "negro wench" who turned up a few years later in a most memorable dream. "She was very vivid to me," Clemens confided to his notebook,

> round black face, shiny black eyes, thick lips, very white regular teeth showing through her smile. She was about 22, and plump—not fleshy, not fat, merely rounded and plump; and good-natured and not at all bad-looking. She had but one garment on—a coarse tow-linen shirt that reached from her neck to her ankles without break. She sold me a pie; a mushy apple pie—hot. She was eating one herself with a tin teaspoon. She made a disgusting proposition to me. Although it was disgusting it did not surprise me—for I was young (I was never old in a dream yet) and it seemed quite natural that it should come from her. It was disgusting, but I did not say so; I merely made a chaffing remark, brushing aside the matter—a little jeeringly—and this embarrassed her and she made an awkward pretence that I had misunderstood her. I made a sarcastic remark about this pretence, and asked for a spoon to eat my pie with. She had but the one, and she took it out of her mouth, in a quite matter-of-course way, and offered it to me. My stomach rose—there everything vanished. (*MTN*, 351–52)

The most remarkable thing about this altogether extraordinary personal record is Clemens's blindness to its brimming sexual significance. The best evidence on this score is the simple existence of the notebook entry itself; for had he been conscious of what his dream revealed, the sexually fastidious Clemens would never have committed it to paper. The contrast between this inadvertently erotic fantasy with a "negro wench" and "My Platonic Sweetheart," the 1898 account of his perfectly chaste dream encounters with a virginal white girl—"I have never known her to shame herself with an impropriety of conduct or utter a speech which I should not be willing that all the world might hear," Clemens declares[27]—is profoundly telling. Roxy is at once irresistible and dangerous for Clemens because she embodies the unspeakable sexual allure of black women for white men in American slave culture. As Justin Kaplan is quick to observe, the novelist grew up in a society that looked the other way when it came to the sexual exploitation of slave girls by young white men (*MCMT*, 341–42).[28] Indeed, Clemens's notorious sexual prudishness was doubtless driven in some degree by reflex recoil from guilty memories and persistent upwellings of errant, interracial desire. No such restiveness disturbs the dreams in "My Platonic Sweetheart," where, he observes rather enigmatically, "everything that happened was natural & right, & was not perplexed with the unexpected, or with any forms of surprise, & so there was no occasion for explanations."[29]

Clemens's record of his erotic dream is a signal example of the unconscious gravitation toward self-betrayal that the author-cat struggles unsuccessfully to contain. The diary entry reveals the guilty thing that the dreamer most fervently wishes to conceal, even from himself. Rather characteristically, the account bears with it the suggestion that the dreamer sensed in some remote way that his dream unwittingly unveiled a shameful secret. This impression is substantially reinforced by the animated discussion of human duality that immediately precedes the stunning advent of the "negro wench." As if in some way to acknowledge and even explain the self-subversive impulse to which he is about to surrender, Clemens ponders "the presence in us of another *person*; not a slave of ours, but free and independent, and with a character distinctly its own." At one time, he recalls— directly invoking "The Facts Concerning the Recent Carnival of Crime in Connecticut"—"I made my conscience that other person and it came before me in the form of a malignant dwarf and told me plain things about myself and shamed me and scoffed at me and derided me." More recently, however, he has been drawn to *The Strange Case of Dr. Jekyll and Mr. Hyde* (1886), in which Robert Louis Stevenson takes the further step of giving each of the dual personalities its own conscience. Clemens in turn insists that Stevenson has erred in supposing that the twinned selves have conscious command over one another. In fact, he concludes, "the two persons in a man do not even *know* each other and are not aware of each other's existence." To the waking and the unconscious selves, Clemens adds what he calls the "dream self"—the "ordinary body and mind freed from clogging flesh"—which is host to the dreams that remain in memory once sleep has passed. It is from this latter, "spiritualized body and mind" that his memorable encounter with the "negro wench" arises. "It was not a dream," he insists; "it all *happened*. I was actually there in person—in my spiritualized condition. My, how vivid it all was!" (*MTN*, 348–52).

Clemens's developing model of the psyche bears very significantly on the inadvertently revealing dream which he offers as its illustration. He recalls the "negro wench" in all her vividness, he says, because of the stellar force and purity of the "dream self." In insisting as he does on the chasteness of his dream, Clemens surely protests too much, and thereby betrays a suppressed intimation that traces of "the clogging flesh" quite alien to the "dream self" may be obliquely manifest in his memory. He bends further toward such an admission by giving place in the psyche to that "other self" buried within us, unknown and incommunicado. "The French," he observes—presumably referring to Jean-Martin Charcot, Pierre Janet, and others—"have lately shown (apparently) that that other person is in command during the somnambulic sleep; that it has a memory of its own and can recall its acts when hypnotized and thrown again into that sleep, but that *you* have no memory of its acts. You are not present at all" (*MTN*, 349). What better explanation for the hints of impurity in Clemens's revealing dream than this autonomous "other self" operating beneath the surface of consciousness? Because it is both independent and in some sense unknown, its errant activities are in theory no challenge to the moral equanimity of its unwitting host; quite to the contrary, in fact, its putatively "secret" operations provide an explanation for intrusions into consciousness of elements otherwise unaccountable in a morally acceptable way.

Like the waking self, the secret "other" is equipped with conscience—"a mere machine," as Clemens describes it, shaped entirely by "whatever one's mother and Bible and comrades and laws and system of government and habitat and heredities have made it" (*MTN*, 348–49)—and is therefore solely accountable for its moral judgments, however defective they may be. It is thus a kind of scapegoat within the psyche, a "place" where the intolerable darkness in the self may be safely—which is to say very discreetly—sequestered. If the "other self" is to succeed as the agent covertly responsible for the effacement of intolerable guilt, however, then it must be posited in such a way that its raison d'être is itself effaced; its unstated but urgent role in the moral scheme of things must be told and untold at the same time. This is of course precisely how Clemens treats the "other self." He asserts its "secret" existence outside of consciousness, equips it with a machine-like conscience of its own, and then moves on without assigning it a role in the exemplary dream that immediately follows. That role is to serve as the "secret" source of the untoward sexual energies, themselves officially a "secret," that find their way into Clemens's complexly "vivid" account of the "negro wench."

In tandem with his denigration of conscience, Clemens's groping embrace of the unconscious "other self" worked in effect to blind him to morally compromising revelations as they surfaced in his thought and writing. Furtive moral evasion thus gave relatively free rein in consciousness to the very images and memories that first compelled the resort to bad-faith denial. Clemens's evidently complacent account of his dream of the fetching "negro wench" is the best possible evidence on this score. The same may be said of his acquiescence in the transformation of the putative comedy of *Those Extraordinary Twins* by Roxy and the "tragic" race-slavery plot that she brings with her into *Pudd'nhead Wilson*. Clemens's startling admission that he had "no clear idea of his story" as it unfolded on the page before him, and that he was at work on "a tale which he [was] not acquainted with," takes rise from a sensibility deeply if perforce unknowingly invested in the idea of its own lack of conscious control. The complacent dreamer and the blithely self-effacing "jack leg" novelist relinquish authority in their writing as the unacknowledged price of freedom from moral responsibility for what that writing reveals. There is perhaps no better measure of Clemens's guilty suffering than his readiness to embrace the blind incomprehension evidently requisite to its relief.

Such relief was fleeting, as we have seen, because while Clemens's bad-faith denial rendered him temporarily insensible to manifestations of guilt, it did nothing to reduce the deeper, perdurable authority of his conscience. In fact, the conspicuous absence of guilt where we most expect to find it—in a dream about a "negro wench," for example, or in a novel about the diabolical cruelty of slavery—is the surest sign that the apposite sentiment is virtually "present" in the palpable tension produced by its strenuous suppression. This is to say that the reality of Clemens's guilt about slavery, and of his conflicted need to confess it, forms one pole of an alternating moral current that has denial as its antipode. The movement back and forth between the poles at once gives rise to and drives the alternating impulses to reveal and conceal compromising elements in the dream and in the strangely divided novel. The result in the latter, extended narrative, where wide-ranging variations on such impulses are regularly at play, is predictably rather complex. Most notably perhaps, several of the novel's most arresting images and utterances bear testimony to an underlying, potently informing tension. As I have already suggested, the reaction in Dawson's Landing to the arrival of the Siamese twins—"that prodigy, that uncanny apparition . . . that weird strange thing that . . . had shaken them up like an earthquake with the shock of its grewsome aspect" (*PW*, 131)—is a manifestation of submerged local anxieties on the score of race-slavery. But the image of two independent selves in one body is of course a startling prefiguration of the model of mind Clemens would outline in his diary just a few years later. In both instances, I hasten to add, the gravitation to the idea of a radical division within the self is geared directly to suppressed, conscience-driven misgivings about the peculiar institution. Thus even as it speaks to bad-faith denial in Dawson's Landing, the earth-shaking "apparition" is also a self-reflexive figuration of the deep division between conscious and unconscious domains in Clemens's psyche, and of his secretly doubled relationship to the accusing inhumanity that the novel strains at once to reveal and to conceal.

Other, kindred images are similarly legible as uncanny recapitulations of Clemens's bad-faith denial of agency in the shaping of what he describes as his self-written mystery story. In tracing her son Tom's contemptible cowardice to the tiny fraction of black blood that secretly flows through his body—"It's de nigger in you, dat's what it is"—Roxy clearly anticipates Clemens's recourse to an independent "other self" as the hidden source of what is morally unaccountable in his own outward behavior. Evidence that the novel is secretly mined with equally volatile, racially inflected secrets is obliquely on display in the pink and scarlet cravats worn by the twins, whose colors clash so violently that they break "all the laws of taste known to civilization. Nothing more fiendish and irreconcilable than those shrieking and blaspheming colors could have been contrived." Thanks to the spread of an especially vivid breed of geranium, the same highly combustible color combination appears in profusion on the cottages of Dawson's Landing. The flowers' "intensely red blossoms accented the prevailing pink tint of the rose-clad house-front like an explosion of flame." Quite appropriately, such florid testimony to the submerged threat of inflammatory eruptions achieves its fullest, most explicit expression in the "new Sunday gown—a cheap curtain-calico thing, a conflagration of gaudy colors and fantastic figures," and the "blazing red" shawl that Roxy wears when she switches the babies. Later on, when Tom learns that he is Roxy's son, the sudden disclosure of that hidden knowledge has the impact of "a gigantic irruption like that of Krakatoa . . . with the accompanying earthquakes, tidal waves and clouds of volcanic dust" (*PW*, 70, 127, 3, 13, 44). Shock-waves produced by deep racial fault-lines are a constant threat to the stability of St. Petersburg society, as they are to the coherence of the novel and the moral equanimity of its troubled author.

Tom is temporarily jarred by what he has learned, but soon withdraws in consciousness to the morally less challenging *status quo ante*. In this, he is caught up in the all-informing pattern of recognition and retreat clearly discernible in Clemens's sharply divided relationship to the "tragic" moral drift of his narrative. At several points along the way, Clemens gives rein to flashes of ironic insight that betray a much deeper penetration into the novel's heart of darkness than anything ventured in the interstitial commentary of the strangely baffled "jack-leg" novelist. Judge York Leicester Driscoll, one of the masters, is described as "a fairly humane man, toward slaves and other animals." Meanwhile, in routinely pilfering food "from the man who daily robbed him of an inestimable treasure—his liberty," a member of the slave community takes assurance that "he was not committing any sin that God would remember against him in the Last Great Day." We are in company with the same ironist at the novel's conclusion, when Tom, who has been identified as Roxy's son and convicted of murder, is pardoned in order that he may be sold down the river in partial payment of his former owner's debts. All agree that were he "white and free it would be unquestionably right to punish him—it would be no loss to anybody; but to shut up a valuable slave for life—that was quite another matter." This intermittent assault on the moral hypocrisy of race slavery culminates in what Clemens describes as the "fiction of law and custom" by which Roxy and her son, both "as white as anybody," are rendered black and delivered into bondage (*PW*, 9, 12, 115, 9). Striking though they are, such ironies are easily overlooked and forgotten, both because they are so few and far between, and because the narrative is otherwise so conspicuously in denial of their accusing moral thrust.

Hershel Parker's important study of the composition of *Pudd'nhead Wilson* demonstrates that the novel's internal lapses and disjunctions radically diminish the weight of the race-slavery plot. "At no time," Parker argues, "neither in the process of inscription in the manuscript at its fullest form nor in the book, did the ending truly 'close' a unified, carefully structured work of art." Instead, "the immorality of slavery is not a serious issue any more, nor man's inhumanity to man, nor heredity versus training; and Tom's being sold down the river is a throwaway joke." There can be no serious dissent from Parker's facts, or from his characterization of the ending of the novel. Yet his critical dismissal of *Pudd'nhead* inadvertently duplicates the very act of suppression that Clemens's narrative itself performs. It is true that Pudd'nhead's concluding courtroom theatrics are "gaudy and thrilling," and that they let "the reader close the book dazzled," and thus distracted from the much graver moral issues raised by Tom's sale down the river.[30] But in condemning such developments as meaningless, Parker fails to recognize that dazzled distraction at the level of reception duplicates the bad-faith denial driving Clemens's relationship to his narrative. The reader who loses sight of the book's dark implications has simply joined Clemens in the moral evasion that may be said to constitute the "meaning" of *Pudd'nhead Wilson*.

It remains to observe that Clemens's all-informing retreat from the moral truth of his fiction is itself multiply—and uncannily—re-enacted in the course of the narrative. Consider, for example, that Clemens introduces Tom's father, Colonel Cecil Burleigh Essex, in the first chapter of *Pudd'n-head Wilson*, but then immediately dismisses the character from the narrative, insisting that "with him we have no concern" (*PW*, 4).[31] There is "concern" aplenty, of course, else why mention Essex in the first place? As it is, he is no sooner revealed than concealed, an act of narrative denial that recapitulates Essex's refusal to acknowledge paternity of his illegitimate "black" son. Later in the story, when he discovers that Tom's adult fingerprints don't tally with those taken when he was a child, Pudd'nhead is on course for a similarly shattering insight into the fictions of law and custom at the foundation of the town's leading institution. His brain begins to "clog" at the threshold of a profoundly disruptive insight, but after "a troubled and unrestful" nap, he awakens to the knowledge that Roxy long ago switched the babies (*PW*, 104). This discovery is so dazzling that it distracts him altogether from his dream's much more earthshaking revelation that the foundational distinction between black and white cannot be sustained. This is the morally subversive truth about race-slavery to which the fingerprints and his dream give Pudd'nhead access, and from which he retreats into the courtroom melodrama and the blind reaffirmation of the unjust *status quo* with which Clemens draws his putative murder mystery to a close.

Roxy is herself quick to observe that the infants cannot be told apart, though she has no sooner recognized the "lie" of the color line than she reasserts its authority by surreptitiously removing her own child to the privileged "white" side of the boundary. This is of course a boundary that

Clemens himself deconstructs in *Pudd'nhead Wilson*, but it is a fleeting insight from which he, like the slave mother in his novel, almost immediately draws back. Once she switches the babies, Roxy is so profoundly committed to the fiction of her son's whiteness that she takes special steps to insure that she will not inadvertently betray her secret.

> With all her splendid common sense and practical every-day ability, Roxy was a doting fool of a mother. She was this toward her child—and she was also more than this: by the fiction created by herself, he was become her master; the necessity of recognizing this relation outwardly and of perfecting herself in the forms required to express the recognition, had moved her to such diligence and faithfulness in practicing these forms that this exercise soon concreted itself into habit; it became automatic and unconscious; then a natural result followed: deceptions intended solely for others gradually grew practically into self-deceptions as well; the mock reverence became real reverence, the mock obsequiousness real obsequiousness, the mock homage real homage, the little counterfeit rift of separation between imitation slave and imitation-master widened and widened, and became an abyss, and a very real one—and on one side of it stood Roxy, the dupe of her own deceptions, and on the other stood her child, no longer a usurper to her, but her accepted and recognized master. (*PW*, 19)[32]

Roxy is moved to this definitive act of bad faith not only by an explosive secret about her son's identity, but also by the knowledge that in saving her child she has condemned another child to slavery, and that she has thereby taken a long step into the heartless, inhumane world of the slaveholders. The "fiction created by herself" thus works for Roxy, as the "fiction of law and custom" works for the masters, and as *Pudd'nhead Wilson* may be said to work for the jack-leg novelist, as a twisted avenue of retreat from an unbearable sense of complicity in the crime of slavery.

There is yet another uncanny recapitulation of Clemens's generative bad faith in the figure of Pudd'nhead Wilson himself. As James Cox has observed, Pudd'nhead is a "Yankee stranger" who "enters Dawson's Landing, drolly observes the community, taking its fingerprints until he alone can disclose the crime which lies hidden at the heart of the society."[33] He can, perhaps; but of course he doesn't. Instead, he makes drama out of a murder mystery that pleases the crowd, completes his rise to respectability and power, and distracts everyone—Clemens included—from the deeper wrong that the fingerprints open to view. This is the same shrewd manipulator who slyly ridicules the local blockheads with his famous joke about the dog. It is integral to the jest's design that it repays the jester with the status of a pudd'nhead, a rank outsider whose social marginality confers seeming immunity from complicity in—and from the consciousness of—the inhumanity to which he is witness in Dawson's Landing. There is evidence of a similarly "knowing" incomprehension in Pudd'nhead's calendar, which expresses—what its author seems outwardly to deny, perhaps even to himself—that he knows enough about humans and their lives to despise them, and to long for the oblivion of the grave. The conspicuous omission of race-slavery from the topics addressed in the calendar is the surest sign that it figures centrally, if not fully consciously, in Pudd'nhead's misanthropy and self-contempt. Like Clemens himself, the putative author of these bitter maxims is torn between competing impulses to reveal and to conceal what he has discovered at the dark heart of Dawson's Landing, and not least of all his own unlooked-for complicity in it.[34]

Students have a debt to Susan Gillman for her thorough and penetrating treatment of Clemens's attempts to construct a model of the human mind. Drawing principally on the notebook entry discussed above, and on closely parallel materials in "My Platonic Sweetheart," Gillman very usefully profiles the contemporary intellectual context in which Clemens speculated about hypnosis, thought transference, and dream analysis. She gives proper emphasis to the importance of the unconscious in his "theorizing," most especially as it contributes to his sense of his creativity as "a threatening uncontrollable power." Gillman directly links what she describes as Clemens's "obsession with identity" to the "frantic outpouring of a distinctly different kind of writing" that he produced "during the last two decades of his life"—works such as the so-called "dream writings," and the cognate narratives edited by William M. Gibson as *The Mysterious Stranger*, which foreground "the instabilities of a divided psyche via an unstable relationship of author to text to reader."[35]

At their most fascinating, these stories are wildly imaginative, formally anarchic, often bizarre, sometimes obscure, but almost invariably a window on Clemens's desperate attempt to find relief from the intolerable moral burden of being himself. The effort was ongoing because permanent relief was unfailingly elusive. (It is altogether telling in this regard that not one of these projects was completed or published in the novelist's lifetime.) In the course of things, Clemens ranged widely into metaphysics, ontology, epistemology, and moral philosophy. He obsessed about God and the devil, time and space, the origins and status of knowledge, free will, determinism, and what he took to be the inherent perversity of human nature. He approached these topics, I emphasize, not with philosophical detachment, but as a man driven to find a justifying explanation for the terrible thing he knew he was. Though a professed atheist, he seldom missed a chance to denounce God as a cruel and immoral hypocrite who "created man without invitation, then tries to shuffle the responsibility for man's acts upon man, instead of honorably placing it where it belongs, upon himself" (*MS*, 405). The moral correlative to this construction of the Christian deity is of course crystal clear: "Man is not to blame for what he is. He didn't make himself."[36]

Theological explanations for mortal degradation hardly diminished the humorist's contempt for human nature, which grew sharper in his later years as he became more than ever convinced of its unchanging influence at all times and places in history. As he bitterly complains in "Man's Place in the Animal World," "Hypocrisy, envy, malice, cruelty, vengefulness, seduction, rape, robbery, swindling, arson, bigamy, adultery, and the oppression and humiliation of the poor and helpless in all ways, have been and still are more or less common among both the civilized and uncivilized peoples of the earth" (*WIM*, 80). Roger B. Salomon is surely correct that such grave universalizing spelled the end of Clemens's always uncertain faith in progress.[37] The same blanket skepticism informs his belief that humans everywhere recoil from the knowledge of their essential depravity into all varieties of evasion and denial. As Satan puts it in *The Mysterious Stranger*, "our race lived a life of continuous and uninterrupted self-deception" (*MS*, 164).

Even as he inveighed tirelessly against universal moral hypocrisy, Clemens continued to elaborate philosophical arguments on the side of ultimate human freedom from responsibility for "sin." Yet the authority of guilt was always much greater with him than the authority of innocence, as his "gospel," *What Is Man?*, well illustrates. Written and revised over a period of several years, the little treatise, which its author regarded as potently subversive, was published in a small, anonymous edition in 1906. Clemens insists centrally that virtue is a fond illusion that fails to conceal the invariable selfishness of human behavior, and, more narrowly, that the unyielding need for moral self-assurance is at the root of all motivation. Though "we ignore and never mention" it, he observes, "the Sole Impulse which dictates and compels a man's every act" is "the imperious necessity of securing his own approval, in every emergency and at all costs. To it we owe all that we are. It is our breath, our heart, our blood" (*WIM*, 147). Humans are thus perforce as hopelessly selfish as they are hopelessly self-deceived about their true degradation. Behavior will vary as temperament, circumstances, and training dictate, but the compulsive need to deny pervasive guilt, and thereby to maintain the illusion of moral rectitude, is the engine driving it all.

Clemens acknowledges that *What Is Man?* espouses "a desolating doctrine" that "takes the glory out of man," and wonders how a person committed to such ideas could ever "be cheerful again, [as] his life would not be worth living." As an answer to this perfectly reasonable question he settles rather lamely for an appeal to temperament: "If a man is born with an unhappy temperament, nothing can make him happy; if he is born with a happy temperament, nothing can make him unhappy." Yet the more philosophically consistent response, surely, is that humans retreat in horror from the "desolating" truth of their natures into consoling illusions of innocence. Such, indeed, is the reflex response of *What Is Man?* itself, which commences in, and constantly reiterates, the argument that humans are machines "moved, directed, COMMANDED, by *exterior* influences—*solely*. [Man] *originates* nothing, himself—not even an opinion, not even a thought." It is the emphatic implication of this "law" that humans are exempt, as machines are, from moral responsibility. In one variant of Clemens's determinist position, God is the outside force governing human behavior: "He is unquestionably responsible for every foreknown or unforeknown crime committed by man, his creature" (*WIM*, 208, 211, 128, 481–82). Of course, logical consistency requires that we reject this argument as yet another evasion of guilt in the service of obligatory self-approval. Yet it is something more urgent than logic that restores us to a sense of the affective primacy of guilt in Clemens's moral universe. "We know very well what Man is," he declares, in a section of the treatise that he thought better of publishing, doubtless because it reveals so clearly the anguish in his heart: "Man hides himself from himself during most hours of the day, and in books and sermons and speeches calls himself by fine names; but there is one hour in the twenty-four when he does not do that. . . . It is when he wakes out of sleep, deep in the night. You know the bitterness of that hour; we all know it. The black thoughts come flocking through our brain, they show us our naked soul, our true soul, and we perceive and confess that we are despicable" (*WIM*, 486–87).

What Is Man? is quite evidently one among the many daytime "books and sermons and speeches" that Clemens wrote in order to hide "himself from himself" in fine-sounding self-justification. Just as clearly, the effort failed to vanquish guilt, and would require repeating, though it provided no little distraction along the way. So viewed, *What Is Man?* is testimony to a process of auto-therapy to which Clemens resorted constantly in his late writing. Jennifer L. Zaccara has usefully linked the humorist's autobiographical dictations to the Freudian "talking cure." "Working with stream of consciousness, free association, memories, and dreams, Twain aimed to tell stories that would enable him to cope with loss: financial bankruptcy followed by the deaths of his daughter Susy and wife, Livy."[38] Writing—and most especially the fiction writing to which we will return in a moment—afforded him even greater therapeutic benefits, for it freed him entirely from the demands of realism and historical accuracy—freed him, that is, from the guilty thoughts, memories, and reflections that so weighed on his mind. On May 9, 1904, Clemens dwelt guiltily on the fact that he had been denied his daily, 2-minute visit to Livy's sickroom because his presence was judged a strain on her fragile health. "So I will give up waiting for the call," he wrote to a friend, "& get me to the work which sweeps this world away & puts me in one which no one has visited but me—nor will, for this book [*The Mysterious Stranger*] is not being written for print, & is not going to be published."[39] Seven years earlier, during the painful August anniversary of Susy's death, he confided to Wayne MacVeagh: "I have mapped out four books this morning, & will begin an emancipated life this afternoon, & shift back & forth among them & make them furnish me recreation & entertainment for three or four years to come, if I last so long."[40] "The Secret History of Eddypus," Paine observes, "was not publishable matter, and really never intended as such. It was just one of the things which Mark Twain wrote to relieve mental pressure" (*MTB*, 3:1188).[41]

The therapy worked up to a point because the fictions to which Clemens gave his attention seemed to promise daytime relief from nighttime demons. And yet, in a paradox that I have already drawn, that promise triggered a relaxation of the censors that eased the way for the return of the repressed and thereby brought an end to the cure. This was writing, as Peter Messent has quite rightly observed, that could not be finished.[42] Such was quite clearly the case with *The Mysterious Stranger*, a collection of fragments in which the innocent young nephew of the Devil comes to the earth bearing liberating insights into the human condition. In the version of the story most often read, "The Chronicle of Young Satan," which Clemens worked on at intervals between 1897 and 1900, the divine stranger advances a philosophy of strict moral determinism. It follows, he insists, that mortals are fools to blame themselves for what they mistakenly regard as their sins.

As I have elsewhere argued at much greater length,[43] the consolations of determinism elude the principal actors in *The Mysterious Stranger* because Clemens was never fully acquiescent in a conception of human nature that excludes some measure of freedom to choose. It was for this reason that he found it difficult to restrain the impulse to blame his characters for their fallen condition, and to heap contempt on their baseless illusions of innocence. In his eyes, as in young Satan's, the human race "duped itself from cradle to grave with shams and delusions which it mistook for realities, and this made its entire life a sham" (*MS*, 164). To illustrate his point, Satan inveighs against the Moral Sense, the putative foundation in human nature for distinctions between right and wrong. In fact, Satan contemptuously observes, the Moral Sense brutalizes mortals by opening an array of moral distinctions to the play of their constitutional selfishness and bad faith, thus permitting them to rationalize their most perfidious crimes as specimens of virtue. Universal habituation to self-deception in matters of right and wrong is the mother to a host of mortal woes, all of them involving enslavement of some sort, most cruelly of humans to one another, and most painfully of the hapless sinner to his conscience. But even as he condemns the Moral Sense, Satan is himself given to outbursts of anger against man and God that betray his own failure to achieve inner equanimity. As James Cox has observed, the divine stranger must himself "forego the emotion of indignation if he is to be free of the Moral Sense."[44]

Satan's inconsistency opens a wide window on Clemens's inability to reconcile the competing claims of determinism and free will. Determinism, which he embraced in theory, promised freedom from guilt at the price of obliterating choice; moral indignation, which he indulged constantly in practice, entailed an assumption of free will that led inevitably for Clemens to the shackles of conscience. Neither version of freedom yielded the complete moral autonomy and unrestraint that the writer longed for, and that he labored in vain to confer on young Satan. The same may be said for the procession of alternative moral palliatives that Clemens advances and then retreats from in his fragmentary narrative. Theodor Fischer imagines that travel will restore him to serenity, only to find, as Clemens surely does in *Following the Equator*, that there is no escape from complicity in the slavery that everywhere follows the rule of "civilization." Insanity seems to promise relief from an intolerable reality until Satan observes that only the very few among the deranged—those who are able to "imagine themselves kings or gods"—arrive at happiness. "The rest," he concludes, "are no happier than the sane." Laughter is also advanced as a solution to human suffering, but Satan's characterization of humor as a "weapon" of destruction is ominous, especially in a narrative as humorlessly misanthropic as "The Chronicle of Young Satan." Against the "colossal humbug" of civilized life, Satan argues, most human resources are virtually powerless. "Only Laughter can blow it to rags and atoms at a blast. Against the assault of Laughter nothing can stand." Yet humor does not expose abuses that they may be reformed; rather, it flattens everything in its path. Laughter is volatile and violent, and its pleasures are those of explosive rage fully indulged (*MS*, 164, 166).

Clemens's inability to finish "The Chronicle of Young Satan" was directly the result of his inability to construct a fictionally satisfying resolution to the vexed moral issue at the heart of his narrative.[45] It is a heart of darkness both in its view of human enslavement to sin and guilt, and in its marked inclination to link man's moral predicament to the scourge of slavery that everywhere accompanies the global spread of "civilization." The same elements resurface in the much briefer "Schoolhouse Hill" version of the story, which Clemens worked on for a few weeks and then abandoned toward the end of 1898. Young Satan, now renamed Forty-four, suddenly appears in St. Petersburg and charms the local children with his miraculous exploits in and out of school. The generally sunny tone of the fragment, as William M. Gibson has observed, strongly suggests that Clemens had set the dark and intractable "Chronicle of Young Satan" aside in order to make "a fresh start in a mood of comedy" (*MS*, 8). Yet from the very outset the levity is crossed and shaded with traces of familiar trouble. Forty-four's principal antagonist in St. Petersburg is the school bully, Henry Bascom, "whose papa was a 'nigger' trader and rich" (*MS*, 176). His warmest support, meanwhile, comes from eccentric, good-hearted Oliver Hotchkiss, a fervent abolitionist (modeled quite evidently on Orion Clemens) who welcomes the fascinating stranger into his home. The perdurable problem of slavery is thus foreground and center right from the start.

Young Satan soon reveals his true identity to his host, and announces that he has come to earth to help mortals live with the burden of original sin, which conferred not merely the knowledge of good and evil, but "also the passionate and eager and hungry *disposition to* DO *evil.*" Allowing that he is powerless to correct the fundamental depravity of human nature, Forty-four nonetheless commits himself "to ameliorating the condition of the race in some ways in *this* life." As Clemens's copious "Schoolhouse Hill" notebook entries clearly reveal, Young Satan's benevolence toward humans centers on finding "a way to rid them of the Moral Sense," which engenders "*insanity* of mind & body," deprives them of all "freedom of thought," and renders them the "slaves" of corrupting conscience. Yet none of this ever found its way into the text, which ends just after Satan's announcement of his earthly mission. The fragment that comes down to us, with its attention to race-slavery and the sham morality of conscience, was caught virtually from the start in the gravitational pull of the very moral issues that Clemens had set out half-consciously to avoid. "Everything is insane—upside down," he observes in his notebook, alongside a reminder that Young Satan has plans for "starting an Anti-Moral Sense church" (*MS*, 216, 217, 437, 442, 441, 446).

"Boys and girls are ignorant," Clemens observes in the first paragraph of "Schoolhouse Hill," for they "do not know trouble when they see it" (*MS*, 175). Perhaps he caught a glimpse of himself here as he set pen to paper in what he hoped in vain would be a comic redaction of Young Satan's adventures. It would be several years before he felt moved to essay a final version of the story, "No. 44, The Mysterious Stranger," to which I will turn momentarily. Meanwhile, he seems to have resumed work on "Tom Sawyer's Conspiracy,"⁴⁶ another initially humorous installment on the matter of Hannibal that soon transformed itself, quite in the manner of *Pudd'nhead Wilson*, from a farce into something too darkly troubled to finish. The plot for the story first surfaced in an extended notebook entry in which Clemens's childhood reminiscences pitch headlong into horrific memories of sex, cruelty, and violence, akin in tone to the contemporary "Villagers of 1840–43," but focused exclusively on the monstrous injustice of slavery.⁴⁷ Here once again the idyll of youth forms a threshold on troubling intimations of moral complicity in the sins of the antebellum South. From the midst of the horror, the plot that Clemens finally settled on must have seemed relatively benign. Huck and Jim are to steal Tom, who is disguised as a slave, from the local slave-trader, Pat Bradish, and then to enjoy the chase and climactic torchlight parade that will surely follow. Quite predictably, however, the plot takes a number of improbable turns, among them the discovery that Bradish is already holding a white man disguised as a slave; Jim's incarceration for Bradish's subsequent murder; and the last-minute revelation that the King and the Duke are the real villains. As the result, what begins as a vintage Tom Sawyer prank is transformed into a narrative of greed, exploitation, and bloody racial violence. The seeming idyll thus collapses back into the guilty memories from whose midst it was extracted, and which it strains quite unsuccessfully to displace.

In a kind of self-reflexive mimicry of his own habits of retreat from morally tight places, Clemens makes much of Providence in the opening pages of the story. Pursuing a brilliantly intuitive antinomian line, Tom persuades Jim that we conform best to the foreordained scheme of things by simply doing what we please. And what pleases Tom most is a plan to stage a civil

war. "That'll just make the summer buzz," he declares. Jim objects strenuously, insisting that Providence would never permit God-fearing white people to engage in such barbaric behavior. When Tom finally relents, Huck is
moved to comment on "what a good heart he had; he had been just dead
set on getting up a civil war, and had even planned out the preparations for
it on the biggest scale, and yet he throwed it all aside and give it up to
accommodate a nigger" (*HH&T* 165–66). Quite clearly, a story this heavily
freighted with historically inflected ironies—all of them turning on the
theme of race-slavery, and not the least of them bearing on the artist's conflicted memories of his own wartime experience—could not for long sustain
the ostensibly comedic impulse which first gave it rise.

As it happens, playing at slave-stealing turns out to be at least as violent
as the game of civil war, and even more accusing in its moral implications.
This was the inescapably tragic racial theme, and its staging as a summertime
diversion hatched in the minds of children opens an especially grave perspective on the origins of such recurrent scourges as slavery and violent war-
fare. In one mood, as we have seen, Clemens did not hesitate to assign
blame for all the world's woes to the designs of a malign creator. In another,
however, he was inclined to reject such theological arguments as contemptible moral evasions. "There are many scapegoats for our blunders," he observes in his notebook, "but the most popular one is Providence" (*MTN*,
347). Clemens fell into this latter mood as he composed "Tom Sawyer's
Conspiracy," with the result that the story invites interpretation as a darkly
ironic recapitulation of the famous "evasion" at the end of *Huckleberry Finn*.
The plot similarities are numerous and striking: Jim, now a legally free man,
is once again in bondage, and once again offers only feeble resistance to
Tom's grandiose—and very dangerous—schemes for his liberation; Huck is
also skeptical, but—characteristically—goes along; the King and the Duke
figure prominently as villains; and a "happy ending," though unwritten, appears imminent. But Tom is much changed in this version of the story. Not
content merely to exploit the adventurous potential of Jim's predicament,
he is now delighted to learn that the black man has been falsely accused of
murder, and takes active steps to confirm the charges and to have the captive
sent downriver for sale into slavery. Through it all, he is callously indifferent
to Jim's suffering, and rapturous over the happy alignment of providential
designs with his own.

The effect of Tom's transformation is to obliterate entirely the impression
proffered by *Huckleberry Finn* that his scheming is only so much boyish good
fun. For now, unmistakably, Tom's "design" is uncannily of a piece with

the worst of the inhumanity spawned by the callous, brutal, self-serving culture of race-slavery. This reality is brought home most emphatically in the discovery that Tom's conspiracy is precisely duplicated in the fraud perpetrated at Pat Bradish's cabin by the King and the Duke. "Ain't it curious?" Tom reflects; "They got in ahead of us on our scheme all around." There is a similarly mordant irony at play in a detective's surmise that Tom's schemes are the creations of "a gigantic intelleck . . . prob'ly the worst man alive," the dread Murrell himself (*HH&T* 211, 230). True, toward the very end of the narrative, Tom is brought to a reckoning at Jim's courtroom conviction for murder. In the nick of time, however, the King and the Duke are shuffled on stage to take the blame. Jim is freed, Tom is a hero once more—but then, just as the happy ending rounds toward a climax, Huck falls silent, leaving the story unfinished. This time around, Clemens knew better.

Conceived as a humorous variation on the familiar matter of Hannibal, "Tom Sawyer's Conspiracy" rapidly, almost perversely transforms itself into a meditation on the twisted logic of American race-slavery. In suggesting that the narrative somehow does this to itself, I am echoing Clemens's acknowledgment in *Pudd'nhead Wilson* that his stories were habitually prone to such unaccountable behavior, and that in telling themselves they invariably progressed from comedy to tragedy. This mysterious process is at intervals obliquely invoked in "Tom Sawyer's Conspiracy," most notably when Huck compares "Tom's idea to plan out something to do" with his own "much easier and more comfortable" inclination to "to set still and let [things] happen their own way" (*HH&T* 164). Here as elsewhere, Clemens was evidently of Huck's persuasion, though with predictably grave results, both for the boy in the story, and for the author in its telling. Such denials of agency obviously echo the evasive arguments from providential design scattered through the narrative. Those arguments fail as a stay against Clemens's evident moral indignation, just as the evasive impulse which gave rise to the story fails to contain restive intimations of complicity in the tragic realities his narrative seems bound to disclose. Yet such gestures toward moral clarity are brought up short because the uncanny resurfacing of elements repressed in *Huckleberry Finn* yields no cathartic resolution. Clemens could not finish "Tom Sawyer's Conspiracy" because he could not fully face his story's clear implication that harmless boyish fun was in fact deeply entangled in the crime of slavery, and that Providence had nothing to do with it.

The guilty knowledge imperfectly evaded in "Tom Sawyer's Conspiracy" resurfaces in the series of late, unfinished "dream writings" in which Clemens sought relief from his own nightmarish reality by construing it fictionally as a terrible dream from which he would eventually awaken. In the earliest of these fragmentary therapeutic experiments, "Which Was the Dream?" he attempts to submerge his own life in a fictionalized portrait of his friend and great moral hero, Ulysses S. Grant, and thereby to earn a kind of absolution for his own failures in war and business. But once the nightmare of personal ruin has commenced, there is no return; instead, the narrative is left unfinished, as if to concede that the moral acquittal of an awakening into Grant's reality is imaginatively beyond reach. The fictional fragment "Indiantown" is similarly drawn off-course into a transparently autobiographical portrait of a moral hypocrite, David Gridley, all sham gentility on the outside, hopelessly degraded within (*WWD*, 166–76). And the unfinished "Three Thousand Years Among the Microbes"—written in 1905, according to Paine, as relief from the guilty brooding and loneliness that overtook Clemens after Livy's death—imagines a universe in which all moral positions are so utterly relativized that cannibalism and the wholesale slaughter of innocents are guilt-free activities (*WWD*, 512–13, 526–27; *MTB*, 3:1238–39).[48]

The longest and most revealing of the unfinished dream narratives is "Which Was It?" Written at intervals between 1899 and 1903, and drawn from the same mold as "Which Was the Dream?" the story centers on the life of George Harrison, who is blessed by fortune with wealth, reputation, and a happy home, all of which are lost when he falls into a guilt-ridden nightmare of debt and family disgrace. Once again, the narrative is drawn ineluctably into darkness, where it ends quite inconclusively, and without restoring Harrison, as originally planned, to his happy "waking" reality. Clemens's commitment to his story of descent and recovery was evidently quite superficial; the deeper, sub-intentional motive driving his seemingly errant narrative was a guilty sense of personal failure from which, once it had taken hold, there was no turning back.

"Which Was It?", though a fiction, is manifestly autobiographical. George Harrison's waking world is closely modeled on the novelist's life with his family in their famous Hartford mansion in earlier, much happier times. Unlike Clemens, Harrison "has never had any troubles or sorrows or calamities to rouse up the literary fires that are slumbering in him and make them burst their bonds and find expression." Soon enough, though, in his terrible dream, he will learn from bitter personal experience that there is "something fearfully disintegrating to character in the loss of money." Guilty self-loathing and hatred of life will overtake him, and with them the impulse to take pen in hand—"for the easement it may give me," he reflects, "to look myself in the face and confess whither I have lately drifted, and what I am become!" Clemens's writing cure, his remorseful sense of financial failure, and his need to confess are here clearly projected. Yet nothing quite prepares us for the stunning self-revelation that follows. "But I cannot do it in the first person," Harrison insists, in a manner clearly reminiscent of Clemens's frustration with formal autobiography.

> I must spare myself that shame; *must* is the right word; I could not say in the first person the things I ought to say, even if I tried. I could not say "*I* did such and such things;" it would revolt me, and the pen would refuse. No, I will write as if it were a literary tale, a history, a romance—a tale I am telling about another man, a man who is nothing to me, and whose weak and capricious character I may freely turn inside out and expose, without the sense of being personally under the knife. I will make of myself a stranger, and say "George Harrison did so and so" (*WWD*, 179, 195, 183).

Clemens of course shared Harrison's need to confess, just as he shared his sense that the truth would elude him so long as he attempted to tell it directly. Did Clemens recognize himself in this most self-revealing portrait? There is no certainty in such matters, though I am inclined to think that this most unconscious of writers may well have missed what seems so very obvious to readers a century later. If I am correct in my surmise, then Harrison's shrewdly evasive literary strategy uncannily mirrors the one that his creator has repressed; the story that results is uncanny in precisely the same way.

Harrison's memories unfold in a series of movements comprised of personally compromising plot complications accompanied by compensating moral reflections. More simply, he is ever on the defensive against what his story may reveal. The first movement finds Harrison entangled in a dizzyingly complex web of murder and deception that ensnares leading members of the entire community, and illustrates that human beings, no matter how principled and compassionate, are in thrall to the perversities of circumstance and temperament. "It's a rotten world!" Harrison concludes, and "we are all rotten together, and the most of us don't suspect it." The majority live in ignorance of their degradation, and of the guilt it spawns, because they take shelter in plausible evasions. One especially greedy character uses what she regards as justified revenge "as a pretext-salve for her conscience's protesting dignity." Harrison takes refuge in kindred moral evasions, but they are not proof against the inward gnawing of guilt. "Ah, Moral Law," he complains, as his own guilt grows heavier, "you are a hard trader." Here, quite clearly, we are in company at one remove with the Clemens who had suffered terrible personal losses, and even more terrible guilt as the result. At the end of the first movement, where Clemens set the manuscript aside late in 1899, Harrison is bitterly resigned to a life of ceaseless moral anguish. Because he is too much a coward to come clean with the world or to commit suicide, there is no hope in him. "Just for that one departure from rectitude," he complains, "I am to swim chin-deep in shames and sorrows the rest of my days" (*WWD*, 223, 236, 260).

It seems likely that this first phase of composition ended as it did because Harrison's straining after relief from remorse had reached such an emphatic dead-end. Variations on the same pattern recur in subsequent movements of the narrative. When Clemens resumed composition, he turned, through his protagonist, to the question whether there can be "worse luck than *death*." The question is of special urgency for Harrison, who finds that he cannot clear his mind of accusing memories. "They flocked to the front as fast as they were banished, and with every return they seemed to come refreshed and reinforced for their bitter work upon his conscience." So painful is his suffering that he longs for the imagined relief of the grave, and reflects bitterly, when his wish is denied, "that charity is not for me" (*WWD*, 262, 267, 273). Clemens was of course regularly prey to similar, guilt-laden longings for death. "How lovely is death," he wrote in 1896, "& how niggardly it is doled out."[49]

Harrison commences his final descent into complete self-loathing when Jasper, a twice-enslaved, twice-self-liberated free black surfaces abruptly, as if out of nowhere, into the narrative. Jasper's advent is sudden and shocking because he is the possessor of carefully guarded evidence that Harrison is guilty of murder. This is his leverage on the white man. Even more significantly, Jasper is a stubborn reminder of the guilt for the crime of slavery deeply repressed in the white psyche. His principal motive is to seek a just reprisal for the generations of brutal mistreatment and injustice endured by his people. "Dey's a long bill agin de lowdown ornery white race," he lectures Harrison, "en you's a-gwyneter to *settle* it" (*WWD*, 415). Harrison's penalty is to change places with a lowly slave, and thus to experience first-hand the pain and humiliation that he once imposed, with unruffled moral complacency, on other human beings. When Jasper forces his white hostage

to change places, he gives outward expression to yet another subversive secret, the much deeper interchangeability of their identities. As the son of a
slave woman and her master, Harrison's uncle, Jasper is blood kin; and as
a party to Harrison's most guardedly guilty secrets, he is the white man's
psychological double.

Clemens could not finish "Which Was It?" because the morally evasive
impulse driving his narrative reaches an absolute impasse in the discovery,
quite imperfectly grasped, that the personal guilt haunting his protagonist is
the expression at one remove of his own remorseful memories of slavery.
Just as Jasper is the final, insurmountable obstacle to Harrison's achievement
of moral repose, so slavery carried the greatest weight in Clemens's burden
of guilt. Beneath all the other personal and collective moral failures there
persists the memory, at once unbearable and irrepressible, of the terrible
crimes against humanity gathered up and given voice by the former slave.
This is a nightmare so real that Harrison cannot awaken from it. Nor could
Clemens, as its persistent resurfacing in his work, and most especially in the
late writing, clearly demonstrates.

At one stage in his ultimately futile flight from conscience, Harrison enjoys an interval of especially blissful denial. "If I could only feel like this, all
the time," he exclaims.

> And why shouldn't I? Troubles are only mental; it is the mind that manufac-
> tures them, and the mind can forget them, banish them, abolish them. Mine
> shall do it. Nothing is needed but resolution, firmness, determination. I will
> exert it. It is the only wisdom. I will put all these goblins, these unrealities
> behind me, I have been their slave long enough; if I have done wrong I have
> atoned for it, I have paid the cost and more, I have sweated blood, I have
> earned my freedom, I have earned peace and a redeemed and contented
> spirit, and why should I not have them? (*WWD*, 406–7)

In Harrison's rather desperate straining after moral self-acquittal we cannot fail to be reminded of Clemens's equally urgent longings. The passage
faithfully captures the spirit of one whose resolute skepticism did nothing to
dampen his enthusiasm for contemporary mind-cure, and who wrote (in
"Three Thousand Years Among the Microbes") that "there was no such
thing as substance—substance [is] a fiction of Mortal Mind, an illusion"
(*WWD*, 492). The *locus classicus* among many kindred pronouncements in
Clemens's work is Satan's declaration, toward the end of *The Mysterious
Stranger*, that "*Nothing* exists; all is a dream. . . . And You are but a

Thought—a vagrant Thought, a useless Thought, a homeless Thought, wandering forlorn among the empty eternities!" This is saving news, Satan insists, for it releases humans from the tragedy of history, and frees them to create realities of their own choosing. "Dream other dreams," he counsels, "and better!" (*MS*, 404–5).

As William M. Gibson has shown,[50] Satan's liberating solipsism had its origins in the desperate need for relief from guilt that overtook Clemens at moments of family tragedy. His consciousness was at times so heavily laden with remorse that he recoiled into alternative realities. On the first anniversary of Susy's death he took refuge in the thought that the "calamity [was] not a reality, but a dream, which will pass,—*must* pass."[51] Similar sentiments turn up regularly during the next several years in Clemens's notebooks, correspondence, and—as we have seen—in the early dream writings. Livy's death in 1904 prompted the retreat to variations on the same consoling theme, most movingly expressed in a letter to Joseph Twichell in which Clemens explains that during substantial periods of each day he regards the world "as being NON-EXISTENT. That is, that there is *nothing*. That there is no God and no universe; that there is only empty space, and in it a lost and homeless and wandering and companionless and indestructible *Thought*. And that I am that thought." Only when they are viewed in this light, he goes on, do

> the absurdities that govern life and the universe lose their absurdity and become natural, and a thing to be expected. It reconciles everything, makes everything lucid and understandable: a God who has no morals, yet blandly sets Himself up as Head Sunday-school Superintendent of the Universe; Who has no idea of mercy, justice, or honesty, yet obtusely imagines Himself the inventor of those things; a human race that takes Him at His own valuation, without examining the statistics; thinks itself intelligent, yet hasn't any more evidence of it than had Jonathan Edwards in his wildest moments; a race which did not make itself nor its vicious nature, yet quaintly holds itself responsible for its acts.

A merciless brute of a God who adds intolerable guilt to the terrible burden of human suffering—all of this makes sense only when "taken as the drunken dream of an idiot Thought, drifting solitary and forlorn through the horizonless eternities of empty Space."[52] Nowhere is the extremity of Clemens's rejection of the human lot more clearly on display than in this outpouring to his friend, and nowhere is the preeminence of guilt among the insults of life more manifest. Human suffering was terrible in Clemens's eyes; human guilt for that suffering even worse.

Here, then, was Clemens's ultimate cure for insupportable remorse: self-removal to eternal solitude in infinite space, and the deliverance of those he mourned to the safety—in good part from himself—of nonexistence. Translated almost verbatim to the conclusion of "No. 44, The Mysterious Stranger"—the last and longest version of young Satan's adventures, written at intervals between 1902 and 1908—and there supplemented with the injunction to "dream other dreams, and better," this famous passage is the surest evidence of Clemens's profound personal investment in the evasive moral thematics of his unpublished late writing. "I am that thought," Clemens insists in his letter to Twichell, straining desperately, and perfectly in vain, for release from his enslavement to conscience into a dream of eternal moral repose. A similar impulse drives the fragmented narratives that comprise "No. 44, The Mysterious Stranger," which may be read as a series of three groping attempts to achieve imaginative closure with oppressive personal guilt. Composition on each of the sections was terminated inconclusively as elusive moral resolution fell further and further from Clemens's grasp.

The first phase of composition, undertaken between November 1902 and October 1903, introduces the mysterious stranger, No. 44, a mild, rather Christ-like boy into a company of printers working in an abandoned castle. Most of the characters cruelly and irrationally abuse the innocent child; a few take his side, but are generally ineffectual in their efforts to protect him. The struggle between good and evil has its focus in the interior life of the youthful narrator, August Feldner, whose friendship for the strange outsider leads to tormented self-reckoning. "Privately my heart bled for the boy, and I wanted to be his friend," August reflects, "but I had not the courage, for I was made as most people are made, and was afraid to follow my own instincts when they ran counter to other people's." The lesson here is one that Clemens would draw at greater length in *What Is Man?*—that humans invariably abandon their principles in order to achieve the self-approval that comes with conformity. Like Clemens himself, August is terribly "ashamed" of his moral failures, which leave him feeling "shabby and mean." Like Clemens again, he warms to the moral consolations of determinism. "Why do you reproach yourself?" No. 44 obligingly inquires, when August acknowledges his grave moral failings. "You did not make yourself; how then are you to blame?" August is moved to observe "how perfectly sane and sensible," and how "intelligent and unassailable" his friend's advice is (*MS*, 244, 247, 250). Yet relief is short-lived. The craven August once again denies No. 44, only to suffer humiliating public exposure. And here Clemens left him, hopelessly awash in bad-faith denial.[53]

Clemens's moral engagement in the first phase of "No. 44" is rather coolly abstracted from his immediate personal concerns; we associate him more with August's moral sensitivity and anguish than with the specific issues that burden the youthful narrator. The moral temperature rises quite considerably in phase two, by far the longest section of the novel, which occupied the aging humorist during the first six months of 1904. August tries to find ways to shield No. 44 from the wrath of the printers, who threaten to go out on strike if the strange outsider is not fired. When various expedients fail to ease the crisis, No. 44 creates exact "duplicates" of the inhabitants of the castle who complete the work, thus infuriating the "originals." When blame is directed to No. 44, he suddenly appears, and then just as suddenly expires in a "dazzling white fire" that reduces him to ashes. August is "full of sorrow, and also of remorse" for his many "failings of loyalty [and] love" to the departed boy. "There were more of these sins to my charge than I could have believed," he laments; "they rose up and accused me at every turn, and kept me saying with heart-wearying iteration, 'Oh, if he were only back again, how true I would be, and how differently I would act.'" August seeks release from guilt in various rationalizations, but then wearily concedes, "I was trying to excuse myself for my desertion of him in his sore need . . . but in every path stood an accusing spirit and barred the way; solace for me there was none" (*MS*, 309–10).

Forty-Four soon returns from the dead—"it is nothing," he declares, "I have done it many a time!"—but his miraculous resurrection yields scant relief for the conscience-stricken August. Little wonder that he is impressed with the duplicates, who are strangely exempt from remorse of any kind. Forty-Four explains that a duplicate is an embodied manifestation of the "Dream-Self," which is ordinarily invisible and asleep during the waking hours of the "Workaday-" or "Waking-Self." "It has far more imagination than has the Workaday-Self," he adds, "and a much wider range of pleasures." The waking and dreaming selves are joined by the unconscious—identified by No. 44 as the "Soul"—to form a tripartite division of the self modeled quite closely on the earlier version outlined in Clemens's 1897 notebook entry on *Dr. Jekyll and Mr. Hyde*. Relations between the three selves are integral to the unfolding romantic plot involving August Feldner and Marget Regen, the master's niece, which displaces the print-shop conflict at about the midpoint of the second phase of the narrative. Meanwhile, No.

44 is prompted to reflect on the degradation of the human race—"I have always felt more sorry for it than ashamed of it," he tells August—with special attention to the pervasive injustice of life, and to an all-defining determinism ("What is written must happen") that encompasses the mind itself, which "is merely a machine, that is all—an *automatic* one," over which we have "no control." These are of course the familiar features of Clemens's by now weary wrestling with the riddle of life's misery, and with his special incubus, guilt (*MS*, 313, 315, 342, 320, 326, 333).

The romance plot, which seems to take shape as a reflexive retreat from the intractable moral challenges facing August in the print shop, is itself soon overtaken by the protean specter of guilt that haunts *The Mysterious Stranger.* This should come as no surprise, especially as Clemens's ongoing attempts to define the self are part and parcel with his ambition to somehow explain, and thereby to harness, his conscience. Recall that it is the duplicates' wondrous exemption from guilt that first catches August's attention. Later on, when he has mastered the elaborate psychic scheme of things, his confident approval—"It seemed to me that I had now ciphered the matter out correctly"—clearly mirrors Clemens's own. Even so, August recognizes almost immediately that correctly ciphering the mind affords him scant protection from its errant ways, and least of all from guilt. "And now a sorrowful thought came to me," he laments; "all three of my Selves were in love with the one girl, and how could we all be happy? It made me miserable to think of it, the situation was so involved in difficulties, perplexities and unavoidable heart-burnings and resentments." In their competition to win the love of Marget's multiple selves, August's corresponding selves are hopelessly divided against one another in their pursuit of the elusive prize. The boy soon finds that he has the power to manipulate Marget to his will, but only by keeping her in ignorance of what he has done. Should he tell her the whole truth? "No," he decides, "I couldn't bring myself to it, I couldn't run the risk. I must think—think—think. I must hunt out a good and righteous reason for the marriage without the revelation. That is the way we are made; when we badly want a thing, we go to hunting for good and righteous reasons for it; we give it that fine name to comfort our consciences, whereas we privately know we are only hunting for plausible ones" (*MS*, 343, 348–49).

August resigns himself to his bad-faith scheme—"I seemed to find what I was seeking," he observes, "and I urgently pretended to myself that it hadn't a defect in it"—and decides to use hypnotism to bring Marget to the altar. He is drawn even deeper into deception and betrayal, however, when he is caught prowling around Marget's boudoir, but contrives to shift the blame for the indiscretion onto his duplicate Dream-Self, Emil Schwarz, who, in a startling turn of events, is then "forced" to marry Marget. "Good heavens!" August exclaims, when his "injurious lies" completely backfire, "I had only ruined myself" (*MS*, 349, 353). It was at this moment of complete moral defeat that Clemens terminated the second phase of composition on "No. 44."

The final phase, undertaken in June and July 1905, illustrates at its most desperate Clemens's late-life attempt to conceive and execute a fictional narrative that avoids the unaccountable slide from the comic into the tragic, and from innocence into the grip of conscience. This last attempt commences with August longing for the relief from his life's misery that he knows will come with the return of No. 44. "I *was* so glad to see him again!" he exclaims, when his divine friend suddenly materializes in his midst; "the very sight of him was enough to drive away my terrors and despairs and make me forget my deplorable situation." Forty-four "blandly" suggests that the solution to August's problem is perfectly simple and obvious: kill Emil Schwarz, and with him kill Marget's maid, who was witness to August's heedless indiscretion. When the morality of his approach is challenged, No. 44 insists that "human beings aren't of any particular consequence," but agrees nonetheless "to turn the maid into a cat, and make some *more* Schwarzes, then Marget would not be able to tell t'other from which" (*MS*, 356, 357, 358).

August acquiesces in his friend's "solution" not because it is morally defensible— quite obviously it is not—but because it serves as a sop to his conscience; guilt is not so much addressed and resolved as it is temporarily swept from sight and mind. But only temporarily. When a chance encounter with Emil Schwarz triggers "a little prod" from his conscience, August once again retreats to bad-faith denial, beguiling himself with the thought that because his betrayal of Schwarz led to the loss of Marget, it was no offense at all. "Having reached solid ground by these logical reasonings," he gloats, "I advised my conscience to go take a tonic, and leave me to deal with this situation as a healthy person should." Once again, however, the ruse fails to yield moral equanimity. "I hadn't intended to do the handsome thing," August is forced to concede. He then consoles himself that "it was natural for me to take the credit of it and feel a little proud of it, for I was human." But consolation is in turn quickly dissipated in the acknowledgment that "being human accounts for a good many insanities." Not surprisingly, moral tergiversation at this hectic pace soon precipitates a rupture in August's sense of himself. He is startled to find that he no longer recognizes his own voice, and his image in the mirror is "*merely* a resemblance" of himself, "nothing more" (*MS*, 363–64). This unsettling split in his identity is of course linked directly to the precarious division that has opened in his moral nature. Increasingly drawn to comforting expedients on one side, and the slave of a relentless conscience on the other, August's sense of self is strained to the point of near-fragmentation.

Clemens initial attraction to the notion of multiple selves was quite characteristically driven by the dual impulses to acknowledge conscience and, at the same time, to neutralize its moral significance. Though this approach afforded him a certain theoretical leverage on the problem, his helpless subjection to guilt was the insuperable obstacle to permanent relief. Just so, although August's "logical reasonings" yield a brief respite, conscience proves the more powerful pole of his painfully divided moral nature. Like Clemens, he is compelled by the very intensity of his guilty suffering to seek such shreds of comfort as he can find on the "innocent" side of his tripartite identity. Thus August is fascinated by his Dream-Self Schwarz's declaration of complete indifference to the charges that have been leveled against him. "Why, you are as indifferent about this as you are about everything else," the boy observes; "Come! surely, you've got a heart hidden away somewhere." But no sooner has August's tone of reproach begun to gather momentum than he is suddenly brought up short by the spontaneous admission, "Land, I wish I were in your place!" (*MS*, 368) Wouldn't it be grand, we can hear Clemens exclaim, to live free from guilt!

Sensing that his outburst has somehow exposed him, August tries to turn the tables by putting Schwarz on the defensive. You have come here, he declares aggressively, "to reproach me for—for—"; but the self-incriminating words simply won't come, and he lapses into guilty silence. "These things were of no sort of consequence," Schwarz reassures him, and then reveals that he has come not to heap blame on August, but to plead for release from the "bonds of flesh—this decaying vile matter, this foul weight, and clog, and burden, this loathsome sack of corruption" in which his "spirit is imprisoned, her white wings bruised and soiled." Schwarz implores August to intercede for him with No. 44, who alone can restore him to his "natural" condition as a disembodied dream. "Oh, this human life," he complains, sounding very much like Clemens himself, "this earthly life, this weary life! It is so groveling, and so mean; its ambitions are so paltry, its prides so trivial, its vanities so childish." August can take scant pleasure in all of this, as it is of course his own degraded mortal condition that his

Dream-Self describes with such horror and contempt. Worse still, in contrasting the lives of waking and dreaming selves, Schwarz places almost exclusive emphasis on the oppressive weight of conscience in the first, and on its blissful absence in the second. "To think you should think I came here concerned about those other things—those inconsequentials!" he exclaims, referring to August's lingering guilt and fear of reproach.

> Why should they concern me, a spirit of air, habitant of the august Empire of Dreams? *We* have no morals; the angels have none; morals are for the impure; we have no principles, those chains are for men. We love the lovely whom we meet in dreams, we forget them the next day, and meet and love their like. They are dream-creatures—no others are real. Disgrace? We care nothing for disgrace, we do not know what it is. Crime? we commit it every night, while you sleep; it is nothing to us.

Life without guilt, Schwarz goes on, is integral to a host of other freedoms enjoyed by his kind. "We have no character, no *one* character, we have *all* characters; we are honest in one dream, dishonest in the next; we fight in one battle and flee from the next. We wear no chains, we cannot abide them; we have no home, no prison, the universe is our province; we do not know time, we do not know space—we live, and love, and labor, and enjoy, fifty years in an hour, while you are sleeping" (*MS*, 368–70).

August offers no resistance to the notion that it is guilt above all things that makes mortal life "odious." Once it is taken out of play, Schwarz reveals, all other forms of constraint fall away, and the unfettered reign of the pleasure principle commences. That he speaks for Clemens in all of this goes without saying. Little wonder that August is "powerfully stirred" by his Dream-Self's message, and that he is "moved" to set aside "the scoffs and slurs which he had flung at my despised race," and to intercede on his behalf when No. 44 next appears in their midst (*MS*, 370). While they wait, August's attention is irresistibly drawn to the idea of life without guilt. He is fascinated by the independence and resourcefulness of Marget's former maid, who has now been transformed into a cat. Clemens was especially fond of cats because they were a mirror in which he caught sight of an idealized image of himself. "They don't give a damn for discipline," he observes admiringly in "The Refuge of the Derelicts"; "And they can't help it, they're made so. . . . [A cat] is the only creature in heaven or earth or anywhere that don't have to obey *somebody* or other, including the angels. . . . He is the only independent person there is" (*MTFM*, 180).[54] The focus then shifts to Schwarz himself, whose description of "his life and ways as a dream-sprite" perfectly exemplifies the "methodless method" of diminished moral resistance that kept Clemens coming back to session after session of his autobiographical dictations. Schwarz carries on "in a skipping and disconnected fashion. . . . He would side-track a subject right in the middle of a sentence if another subject attracted him, and he did this without apology or explanation." Such was the discursive ideal of a man who loved to talk and write, but whose subjects, no matter how seemingly benign, invariably drew him into unanticipated bouts with conscience. Schwarz is blissfully exempt from such moral liabilities, for there is "*nothing* permanent about a dream-sprite's character, constitution, beliefs, opinions, intentions, likes, dislikes, or anything else; all he cares for is to travel, and talk, and see wonderful things and have a good time" (*MS*, 376, 378). Here, quite clearly, was Clemens's beau ideal of moral perfection.

No. 44 suddenly materializes and relieves the grateful Schwarz of his earthly bonds. He then engages August in amiable conversation. True to form, however, this happy trend soon takes its own inevitable turn toward darkness when the cat arrives to announce that the conflict in the castle has grown violent and that No. 44 and August are in grave danger. In a manner altogether reminiscent of Tom Sawyer—and, indeed, of Clemens himself—No. 44 seizes upon the occasion as an opportunity to take center stage. "I love shows and spectacles, and stunning dramatics," he says, "and I love to astonish people, and show off, and be and do all the gaudy things a boy loves to be and do." He first contrives to appear before the crowd in a flood of brilliant light—"it beat Barnum and Bailey hands down," he exults—and then, in what August describes as "the very greatest marvel the world has ever seen," he reverses time. This stupendous feat produces some stunning effects, and it affords August the opportunity to undo the indiscretion in Marget's boudoir that brought on his latest bout with conscience. Quite characteristically, Clemens's imagination is drawn to the idea of freedom from guilt, a state achieved in this instance by reverse time-travel to the sites of past misdeeds. Such seemingly promising developments are no sooner set in motion, however, than their moral liabilities come to view. For August finds that in glancing backward over time his eye invariably falls on the myriad heartbreaks and catastrophes of the past. "In every city funerals were being held again that had already been held once, and the hearses and the processions were marching solemnly backwards; where there was war, yesterday's battles were being refought, wrong-end first; the previously killed were getting killed again." Caught off-guard yet once more by his unaccountable gravitation to the nightmare of history—to that in the past which he could neither forget nor endure—Clemens set his manuscript aside, this time more or less for good (*MS*, 386, 391, 396, 400).

William M. Gibson, the editor of the Mysterious Stranger manuscripts, appends two final chapters to his reconstruction of *No. 44, The Mysterious Stranger*. The first, Chapter 33, was written last, in 1908, and "may have [been] intended," Gibson speculates, "as an alternate ending to the whole" (*MS*, 11). The brief narrative features another of No. 44's brilliant "effects," the Assembly of the Dead, a ghoulish procession of the skeletons of legendary figures from the past, extending backward to the remote beginnings of time. Quite characteristically, August is initially quite taken with things: "To me the Procession was very good indeed," he says, "and most impressive." But before long he begins to recognize "skeletons whom I had known, myself, and been at their funerals, only three or four years before." Here, we may confidently surmise, Forty-Four's extravaganza precipitates an entirely unanticipated descent into guilt-laden memories of Livy's death and funeral, just four years earlier. "But to think how long the pathos of a thing can last," August reflects, "and still carry its touching effect, the same as if it was new and happened yesterday!" (*MS*, 400, 402).

Just hours after Livy's passing, Clemens wrote to Howells of his gratitude "that her persecutions are ended. I would not call her back if I could" (*MTHL*, 2:785). Yet it is the clear implication of the Assembly of the Dead that life persists in some form after death. August's eye falls on the "slim skeleton of a young woman, and it went by with its head bowed and its bony hands to its eyes, crying, apparently. Well, it was a young mother whose little child disappeared one day and was never heard of again, and so her heart was broken, and she cried her life away." Adam and Eve stagger by in rags, along with Moses and Pharaoh and Caesar and Cleopatra, and a host of others extending all the way back to the Missing Link, and all the way forward to the recent, personal present. The precious consolations of oblivion are thus cancelled in a vision of perdurable human misery on the other side of the grave. "For hours and hours the dead passed by," August recalls with horror, "and the bone-clacking was so deafening you could hardly hear yourself think." And here, borne down yet once more by the perverse gravity of his memory and imagination, Clemens thrust the offending vision from his consciousness. "All of a sudden," the fragment abruptly concludes, "44 waved his hand and we stood in an empty and soundless world" (*MS*, 402, 403).

But of course it is the irresistible implication of this remarkable chapter that there is no safe haven of retreat from intolerable human reality, no blissful vacancy at the terminus of mortal existence. Thus the Assembly of the Dead, like all of Clemens's essays into the untried dimensions of time, space and identity, failed to provide the moral respite for which he was so desperately groping. All such avenues, no matter how remote and extreme, brought him back to the anger and misery and loneliness—and guilt—at the dark center of his inescapable self. Such is the larger significance of the chapter that Gibson places at the very end of *No. 44, The Mysterious Stranger*, which features the familiar declaration that life is nothing more than a solipsistic dream, and that the key to happiness therefore is simply to "dream better dreams." This is of course a version of the 1904 letter to Joseph Twichell (discussed above) in which Clemens acknowledges that he regularly retreats from the unbearable fact of Livy's recent death into the consoling illusion that his beloved wife, and all the world with her, exist only in the precincts of a solitary thought wandering forever in infinite space. Taking refuge in solipsism worked fairly well at intervals, Clemens explained to his friend: "And so, a part of each day Livy is a dream, and has never existed." But during the rest of the day, he adds, "she is real, and is gone. Then comes the ache and continues."[55]

Clemens's pain, we know, was a species of grief made unbearably heavy by the guilt that invariably went with it. Livy's loss was keenly felt; the self-accusing sense of responsibility for her suffering and death, and for the suffering and death of all those close to him, and for all the other real and imagined errors of his long life—this relentless, accumulating guilt was keenly felt, and grew worse with time. Clemens's late fiction, like all of his fiction, only more so, is the record of his desperate need, never satisfied, to ease that "ache." The consolations of determinism were a slender stay against the potent, morally perilous instinct of freedom and the reflex refusal to relinquish choice. Doubling and trebling of the personality into regions, conscious and unconscious, of light and dark, failed utterly as a restraint on ubiquitous, Argus-eyed conscience. The retreat to dreams yielded temporary relief, but no permanent defense against shattering relapses into waking anguish. Flights outward into the remoteness of space and time invariably circled back to the familiar, morally compromised places and memories from which they sprang. Solipsism and nihilism on self-approving terms were unsustainable. There was simply no escape from the confines of his imperial ego. On one side, he took moral responsibility for virtually everything that fell within range of his consciousness; on the other, he was incapable of acquiescing in any of the self-limiting psychological and philosophical schemes that tempted him with the promise of relief from the intolerable weight of his commitments. Himself was hell.

Epilogue

The fourth and final volume of Albert Bigelow Paine's *Mark Twain: A Biography* is much more detailed than the other three. This is because it records the last few years of Clemens's life, when Paine, now the "official" biographer and trusted member of the humorist's household, enjoyed the privileged access of a friend and confidant. As Paine proudly announces at the very beginning of volume 4, "We have reached a point in this history where the narrative becomes mainly personal" (*MTB*, 4:1257). Given what we know of Paine's awe of Clemens, and of his assiduous commitment, after his subject's death, to the myth of his largely uncomplicated respectability, the narrative is remarkable for what it reveals about the darkness of the final phase.[1] Clemens's life-weariness is everywhere on display. "Why can't a man die when he's had his tragedy?" he complains. "I ought to have died long ago." "I have been thinking it out," he declares on another occasion; "if I live two years more I will put an end to it all. I will kill myself" (*MTB*, 4:1336, 1337).[2] The reiterated longing for death is quite manifestly the reflex of remorseful self-loathing. "He still had violent rages now and then," Paine concedes, brought on by guilty memories of "some of the most notable of his mistakes." He tormented himself with anguished reruns of Livy's death. "If I had been there a minute earlier, it is possible—it is possible that she might have died in my arms. Sometimes I think that perhaps there was an instant—a single instant—when she realized that she was dying and that I was not there." Paine draws our attention to Clemens's marginal observation in a copy of Charles C. F. Greville's *Journal of the Reigns of George IV and William IV* (1873): "What a man sees in the human race is merely himself in the deep and honest privacy of his own heart. Byron despised the race because he despised himself. I feel as Byron did, and for the same reason" (*MTB*, 4:1529, 1350, 1539). How much graver the portrait would be, we surmise, if the biographer had been inclined to tell the whole truth!

Paine is clear and unequivocal, however, in his treatment of Clemens's accelerating attraction to varieties of determinism. "We are automatic machines which act unconsciously," his subject observed in July, 1909. "All day long our machinery is doing things from *habit & instinct*, & without requiring any help or attention from our poor little 7-by-9 thinking apparatus." It is equally clear that bondage to necessity frees human beings from moral responsibility for their iniquity. "The several temperaments constitute a law of God, a command of God," Clemens insisted, and "whatsoever is done in obedience to that law is blameless." He "repeatedly emphasized this doctrine," Paine relates, "and once, when it was suggested to him that it seemed to 'surround everything, like the sky,' he answered: 'Yes, like the sky; you can't break through anywhere.'" Taking a cue from a lecture by Bernard Shaw, Clemens declared that "there is no such thing as morality; it is not immoral for the tiger to eat the wolf, or the wolf the cat, or the cat the bird, and so on down; that is their business. . . . It is not immoral for one nation to seize another nation by force of arms, or for one man to seize another man's property or life if he is strong enough and wants to take it" (*MTB*, 4:1511, 1296–97, 1322, 1335).[3] This from the sometime anti-imperialist, for whom the release from the intolerable burden of personal guilt had its price in surrender to the inevitability of cruelty and injustice.

The persistence of Clemens's resort to determinism is the measure, I would suggest, of his late-life unhappiness with himself and the world. This said, I am far from suggesting that he was permanently in thrall to anger, bitterness, and self-loathing. He was, Paine makes it clear, notably resilient. He had to be. His moods swung back and forth between pleasurable elation and repose at one pole, and stinging self-hatred and misanthropy at the other. This affective divide informs Paine's seemingly contradictory characterizations of his subject as a man who, "more than anyone I ever knew . . . lived in the present," and as one living "curiously apart from the actualities of life . . . not in the actual world, but in a world within his consciousness, or subconsciousness" (*MTB*, 4:1479, 1519). I hasten to emphasize, however, that the aging Clemens embraced life's pleasures—writing, society, and endless day- and night-long billiards matches—principally as stays against the assaults of anguish. By this emotional calculus, pleasure is inversely proportional to the quantum of pain it displaces. It is also fragile, and vulnerable to sudden, shattering reversals. Writes Paine: "I sometimes thought of his inner consciousness as a pool darkened by his tragedies, its glassy surface, when calm, reflecting all the joy and sunlight and merriment of the world, but easily—so easily—troubled and stirred even to violence" (*MTB*, 4: 1336). The same precarious volatility stands out in the biographer's observation that Clemens's moods of remorse seemed to overwhelm him at times. He spoke of Henry's death and little Langdon's, and charged himself with both. He declared that for years he had filled Mrs. Clemens's life with privations, that the sorrow of Susy's death had hastened her own end. How darkly he painted it! One saw the jester, who for forty years had been making the world laugh, performing always before a background of tragedy. "But such moods were evanescent," Paine assures us. "He was oftener gay than somber" (*MTB*, 4:1300).

Poor Clemens was constantly prey to emotional descents, even in the midst of the prophylactic pleasures with which he filled so much of his time. Paine quickly learned to keep a low profile at those explosive intervals when "the risk of getting struck by lightning" was particularly acute. Thunderbolts were especially "apt to fly" during the interminable billiards games that commenced right after lunch and often continued, with a break for dinner, until well past midnight (*MTB*, 4:1302). Clemens insisted on winning, and often bent the rules to ensure victory. "He was not an even-tempered player," Paine admits.

> When the balls were perverse in their movements and his aim unsteady, he was likely to become short with his opponent—critical and even fault-finding. Then presently a reaction would set in, and he would be seized with remorse. He would become unnecessarily gentle and kindly—even attentive—placing the balls as I knocked them into the pockets, hurrying the length of the table to render this service, endeavoring to show in every way except by actual confession in words that he was sorry for what seemed to him, no doubt, an unworthy display of temper, unjustified irritation. . . . Once, when he found it impossible to make any of his favorite shots, he became more and more restive, the lightning became vividly picturesque as the clouds blackened. Finally, with a regular thunder-blast, he seized the cue with both hands and literally mowed the balls across the table, landing one or two of them on the floor. (*MTB*, 4:1327–29)

Quite in spite of Paine's attempt to cast this episode as a kind of Olympian drama, we are in fact witness here to a deeply troubled old man in the throes of a childish temper tantrum. In the immediate sequel, he is overtaken by a characteristic agony of remorse at the spectacle he has made of himself, and reduced to reluctant, servile gestures of apology. Reporting on yet another game spoiled by Clemens's rule changes and bickering, Paine notes that "sometimes when I had let a questionable play pass without comment, he would watch anxiously until I had made a similar one and then

insist on my scoring it to square accounts. His conscience was always repair-
ing itself" (*MTB*, 4:1366).

In a letter of April, 1903, Clemens describes to a friend one of his frequent nightmares about the "black days when I was buried under a mountain of debt." His gratitude for the relief that comes when he awakens from
the familiar, accusing dream is substantially enhanced by his awareness that
"there is a blistering & awful reality about a well-arranged *un*reality." Indeed, he adds, the horror of the thing is so shattering "that two or three
nights like that of mine could drive a man to suicide."[4] Conscience was a
constant in Clemens's experience. It was the resistless agent of the anguish
in his dreams, in his memories, in the unaccountable turn toward darkness
in his unfinished fictions, and even in what passed for recreation. Remorse
was especially heavy in family matters, where he felt the weight of responsibility for the suffering and death of his brother, Henry, his son, Langdon, his
daughter, Susy, and his wife, Livy. His feelings surface clearly, if obliquely,
in *No. 44, The Mysterious Stranger*, when August Feldner recounts the advice
of his Dream-Self, Emil Schwarz, "not [to] get married, because a family
brought love, and distributed it among many objects, and intensified it, and
this engendered wearing cares and anxieties, and when the objects suffered
or died the miseries and anxieties multiplied and broke the heart and short-
ened life" (*MS*, 379).

Better, then, to avoid the anguish of family life; better still, Clemens argues in "The Turning Point of My Life," which he composed late in 1909,
never to have lived at all. Insisting that his vocation as a writer was a prede-
termined outcome driven by the forces of circumstance and temperament,
he allows that there is "no great difference between a man and a watch,
except that the man is conscious and the watch isn't." Quite characteristically, however, absenting himself in theory from responsibility for his life
hardly reconciles Clemens to his consciousness of what that life has entailed.
Such is the implication of the essay's concluding regress to the Garden of
Eden, and to God's all-determining decision to outfit Adam and Eve with
temperaments that made them easy prey for the serpent. "What I cannot
help wishing," Clemens declares, is

> that Adam and Eve had been postponed, and Martin Luther and Joan of Arc
> put in their place—that splendid pair equipped with temperaments not made
> of butter, but of asbestos. By neither sugary persuasions nor by hellfire could
> Satan have beguiled *them* to eat the apple. There would have been results!
> Indeed yes. The apple would be intact to-day: there would be no human

race; there would be no *you*; there would be no *me*. And the old, old cre-
ation-dawn scheme of ultimately launching me into the literary guild would
have been defeated. (*WIM*, 463–64)

How very poignant that in the last words of the last essay published in his
lifetime, Clemens should have cast such a cold eye on human history, and
on his own illustrious part in it.

On Christmas Eve 1909, Clemens's daughter Jean suffered an epileptic
seizure and died in her bath. Almost as a matter of reflex, the stricken father
retreated to his writing desk, where he did what he could with words to
shape and contain a complex array of intolerable feelings. The essay that
emerged, "The Death of Jean," which was published posthumously in
1911, was his last, anguished grappling with the linked themes of family,
remorse, and the imagined comforts of oblivion. "Would I bring her back
to life if I could do it?" he asks. "I would not. If a word would do it, I would
beg for strength to withhold the word. And I would have the strength; I
am sure of it. In her loss I am almost bankrupt, and my life is a bitterness,
but I am content: for she has been enriched with the most precious of all
gifts—that gift which makes all other gifts means and poor—death."[5] But
Clemens's resignation was more wish than reality, for—quite predictably—
his mourning was immeasurably complicated by guilt.

Jean's epilepsy, which at times flared into violent behavior, grew worse
after her mother's death in 1904, and placed an increasingly great strain on
her surviving parent's very limited tolerance for the responsibilities and potential discord she brought into his life. He dealt with the problem by sending his daughter—very much against her will—to a series of sanatoriums,
where she was safely outside of sight and mind; and by delegating responsibility for the details of her care to his devoted secretary, Isabel Lyon, who
read, screened, and responded to Jean's letters home, consulted with her
physicians, and often visited her in Clemens's place. When Jean complained
that the truth about her unhappiness in exile was being kept from her father,
he replied without hesitation: "Evidently, there is something that has been
kept from me—but that is right, and as it should be, unless it is something
that I could remedy. Clara, Miss Lyon and Mr. Paine keep all sorts of distresses from me, and I am very thankful for it—distresses which they are
aware I could not remedy, I mean. They know I desire this; for I am taking
my holiday, now after 60 years of work and struggle and worry and
vexation."[6]

But making time for his children had never been easy for Clemens. On
the day after Susy's death in 1896, he confessed to Livy: "I neglected her as

I neglect everybody in my selfishness."[7] Ten days later, he came back to the same guilty theme. "My remorse does not deceive me. I know that if she were back I should soon be as neglectful of her as I was before—it is our way."[8] It was more of the same with Jean, only much worse, because her needs were so painfully exigent, and because his willingness to meet them was so very limited. Quite tragically for both of them, he denied his daughter what Hill describes as "the most effective medicine [she] could have had . . . the presence of her father."[9]

Belatedly, Clemens came to recognize the terrible damage that his abdication of parental responsibility had wrought, and brought Jean home for the last few months of her life. But even his most resolute defender, Karen Lystra, concedes that he was "appallingly selfish" in his treatment of his daughter, and that he strained to conceal from himself "the enormity of his failure as a father."[10] So understandably great was Clemens's guilt that he sought to disburden himself by heaping blame on Isabel Lyon, whom he accused of engineering Jean's banishment in order to advance her selfish ambition to become his wife. Quite abruptly, the trusted intimate became "a liar, a forger, a thief, a hypocrite, a drunkard, a sneak, a humbug, a traitor, a conspirator, a filthy-minded and salacious slut pining for seduction."[11] This utterly improbable demonizing, which goes on at much greater length in the Ashcroft-Lyon manuscript—Clemens's bilious, 429-page 1909 assault on his secretary—protests much too much, and reveals above all else the guilt-stricken father's desperate groping for relief from the sting of conscience. Virtually all of the evidence indicates that Clemens, exploiting to the full his formidable power and charisma, persuaded the adoring Miss Lyon to serve full time in loco parentis, and then used her as a scapegoat when the guilt for his own admitted derelictions became too heavy to bear.[12]

Such behavior was hardly unprecedented. As Charles H. Gold has recently demonstrated in *"Hatching Ruin," or Mark Twain's Road to Bankruptcy*, Isabel Lyon suffered virtually the same unjust treatment that Clemens had earlier inflicted on James W. Paige—who labored for years on the typesetter bearing his name—and Charles L. Webster—who managed Clemens's publishing company during the mid-1880s. Both men initially enjoyed their employer's complete confidence, but then fell totally from favor when—thanks in good part to Clemens's neglect and poor decision-making—their enterprises failed. Clemens's hatred of both was vastly disproportionate to their actual offenses against him, and had its hot core in his suppressed guilt for the suffering and humiliation he had brought on himself and his family.

Gold traces much of the trouble to Clemens's headlong greed, his notorious impatience with business details, and the guilt that drove his cruelty toward helpless scapegoats, whose "failures represent[ed] his own worst failures, the ones that struck hardest at his sense of self, his security, his aspirations for his family, and his reputation." Gold highlights the many parallels between the treatment accorded Charles L. Webster and Isabel Lyon. "Both were, at the outset, praised and valued. Both met cruel and quick rejection and were vilified when they could not defend themselves. . . . Both were family members of a sort who came to misunderstand their roles, to regard their relationship with Clemens as closer than it really was. Both were dependent on Clemens, and he turned savagely on them." Like Lear, Gold observes, Clemens "saw himself as 'more sinned against than sinning,' and also like Lear, he brought it on himself."[13]

Jean was the last of a long procession of family members and close friends who died during the final years of Clemens's life. In almost every case, his reaction to such passages was a grief which mingled bereavement with a large measure of guilt. This was especially the case with Jean, whose suffering was indeed exacerbated and prolonged by her father's admitted failures as a parent. Viewed in this light, Clemens's ready acquiescence in Jean's death gives clear if rather troubling expression to his painfully tangled feelings. "O, Clara, Clara dear," he wrote to his surviving daughter, "I am so glad she is out of it and safe—safe! I am not melancholy, I shall never be melancholy again, I think" (*MTL*, 2:835). Freed at last from that poor thing, her life, Jean in death was also safely removed from the paternal rejection which had contributed so sharply to her misery, and to her father's unbearable remorse.

Notes

Chapter 1

Never Quite Sane in the Night

1. Samuel Clemens to Miss Kate Staples, 8 October 1886, as cited by Dixon Wecter, *Sam Clemens of Hannibal* (Boston: Houghton Mifflin, 1952), 65.

2. William Dean Howells, "My Mark Twain," in *Literary Friends and Acquaintances*, ed. David F. Hiatt and Edwin H. Cady (Bloomington: Indiana University Press, 1968), 274.

3. Ron Powers, *Dangerous Waters: A Biography of the Boy Who Became Mark Twain* (New York: Basic Books, 1999), 141. For a similar emphasis on the emotional gravity of Clemens's childhood, and on its importance for his work, see the relevant chapters of Pamela A. Boker's *The Grief Taboo in American Literature: Loss and Prolonged Adolescence in Twain, Melville, and Hemingway* (New York; New York University Press, 1996)

4. Dixon Wecter, *Sam Clemens of Hannibal* (Boston: Houghton Mifflin, 1952), 82.

5. Ibid., 67.

6. Ibid., 51.

7. *Mark Twain's Notebooks & Journals, Volume 1 (1855–1873)*, ed. Frederick Anderson, Michael B. Frank, and Kenneth M. Sanderson (Berkeley: University of California Press, 1975), 21–23. The editors provide a detailed analysis of Clemens's adjustments to his source, the Reverend George Sumner Weaver's *Lectures on Mental Science According to the Philosophy of Phrenology* (1852).

8. See also 253: "He was in the grip of a compulsion to think and act always in terms of exploitation and profits."

9. Andrew Hoffman, *Inventing Mark Twain* (New York: William Morrow and Company, 1997), 122, 276.

10. Hamlin Hill, *Mark Twain: God's Fool* (New York: Harper & Row, 1973), ix, 118, 9, xvi, 212–13.

11. Ibid., 269–73. For the cogent elaboration of a closely related theme, see Everett Emerson's essay, "Mark Twain and Humiliation," *Mark Twain Journal* 29 (1991): 2–7.

12. Ron Powers, *Mark Twain: A Life* (New York: Free Press, 2005), 43. Powers makes the same general point in *Dangerous Waters*, 135.

13. Clara Clemens, *My Father, Mark Twain* (New York: Harper and Brothers, 1931), 6–7. See also Lawrence I. Berkove, "Poe, Twain, and the Nature of Conscience," *ESQ*, 46 (2000): 239–53.

14. John Milton, *Paradise Lost*, 4:75.

15. Wecter, *Sam Clemens of Hannibal*, 142–48.

16. Wecter, *Sam Clemens of Hannibal*, 262. Pamela A. Boker observes that Clemens's mother "repeatedly reminded young Sam of his inherently dishonest character" (*The Grief Taboo in American Literature*, 75).

17. See also 98. Philip Ashley Fanning's *Mark Twain and Orion Clemens: Brothers, Partners, Strangers* (Tuscaloosa: University of Alabama Press, 2003) substantially augments our understanding of the troubled relationship between the humorist and his older brother.

18. *Mark Twain's Letters, Volume 2: 1867–1868*, ed. Harriet Elinor Smith and Richard Bucci (Berkeley: University of California Press, 1990), 2: 50, 58.

19. As cited in *MCMT*, 149.

20. Howells, *My Mark Twain*, 262.

21. Clara Clemens, *My Father, Mark Twain*, 251.

22. Hill, *Mark Twain: God's Fool*, xxvii.

23. "The Death of Jean," *Mark Twain's Own Autobiography*, ed. Michael J. Kiskis (Madison: University of Wisconsin Press, 1990), 249.

24. *Mark Twain's Letters, Volume 1: 1853–1866*, ed. Edgar Marquess Branch, Michael B. Frank, and Kenneth M. Sanderson (Berkeley: University of California Press, 1988), 324.

25. Los Angeles *Times*, 15 April 1951, 1:40; as cited in Hill, *Mark Twain: God's Fool*, 224.

26. Susan Gillman, *Dark Twins: Imposture and Identity in Mark Twain's America* (Chicago: University of Chicago Press, 1989), 11.

27. Lawrence Clark Powell, "An Unpublished Mark Twain Letter," *American Literature* 13 (1942): 406–7.

28. Sir John Adams, *Everyman's Psychology* (Garden City: Doubleday, Doran & Company, 1929), 204.

29. "An Unpublished Mark Twain Letter," 407. For an illuminating treatment of the scientific context of Clemens's mechanistic determinism, see Thomas D. Zlatic, "Mark Twain's View of the Universe," *Papers on Language and Literature* 27 (1991): 338–53.

30. George Orwell, *Nineteen Eighty-Four* (New York: Harcourt Brace Jovanovich, 1982), 142–43. My brief overview of self-deception is indebted throughout to *Self-Deception and Self-Understanding: New Essays in Philosophy and Psychology*, ed. Mike W. Martin (Lawrence: University Press of Kansas, 1985). I have also been edified by Herbert Fingarette's now classic study, *Self-Deception* (New York: Humanities Press, 1969).

31. Larzer Ziff—in *Mark Twain* (New York: Oxford University Press, 2004)—observes that Clemens shared with Henrik Ibsen a penetrating view of "the capacity of an entire society to live and enforce a lie" (104).

32. See my *In Bad Faith: The Dynamics of Deception in Mark Twain's America* (Cambridge: Harvard University Press, 1986), 211.

33. "An Unpublished Mark Twain Letter," 407.

34. For evidence of young Clemens's support for slaveholders and contempt for abolitionists, see Robert Sattelmeyer, "Did Sam Clemens Take the Abolitionists for a Ride?" *The New England Quarterly* 68 (1995): 294–99.

35. Elements of the argument set forth in this chapter derive from my earlier writings on Clemens, specifically: *In Bad Faith*, 211–15; *Having It Both Ways: Self-Subversion in Western Popular Classics* (Albuquerque: University of New Mexico Press, 1993), 112–13; and "Mark Twain's Travel Writing," *Cambridge Companion to Mark Twain*, ed. Forrest G. Robinson (New York: Cambridge University Press, 1995), 43–46. St. George Tucker Arnold, Jr. observes—in "Mark Twain's Birds and Joel Chandler Harris's Rabbit: Two Modes of Projection of Authorial Personality in Comic Critters," *Thalia: Studies in Literary Humor* 11 (1989): 37—that the Indian Crow "struck Twain as the perfect image of himself."

36. As cited in *MCMT*, 380.

37. Ibid., 381.

38. Howells, *My Mark Twain*, 316.

39. Michael J. Kiskis provides a useful summary of Clemens's "Experiments in Autobiography" in his edition of *Mark Twain's Own Autobiography*, 253–54.

40. For more detail on Clemens's experience with dictation, and on the 1906–9 sessions, see Michael J. Kiskis, "Mark Twain and Collaborative Autobiography," *Studies in the Literary Imagination* 29 (1996): 27–40.

41. "Down the Rhone," *Europe and Elsewhere*, in *The Writings of Mark Twain*, Definitive Edition (New York: Harper and Brothers, 1922–25), 29:129, 139.

42. For a full elaboration of this critical position, see my *In Bad Faith*, 111–211.

43. *Mark Twain: The Fate of Humor* (Princeton, N.J.: Princeton University Press, 1966), 302.

44. See *MCMT*, 378; Hill, *Mark Twain: God's Fool*, 136–38; and G. Thomas Couser, *Altered Egos: Authority in American Autobiography* (New York: Oxford University Press, 1989), 91. For a more general literary assessment, see Pavel Balditzin, "Mark Twain's *Autobiography* as an Aesthetic Problem," *Russian Eyes on American Literature* (Jackson: University of Mississippi Press, 1992), 71–84.

45. Hill, *Mark Twain: God's Fool*, 136.

46. *Mark Twain's (Burlesque) Autobiography and First Romance* (New York: Sheldon & Company, 1871), 18.

47. For contemporary responses, see *Mark Twain's Letters, Volume 4: 1870–71*, ed. Victor Fischer and Michael B. Frank (Berkeley: University of California Press, 1995), 381.

48. "An Autobiography," *Aldine* (April 1871): 58. For background, see *Mark Twain's Letters, Volume 4: 1870–1871*, 337.

49. *Mark Twain's Own Autobiography*, ed. Kiskis, xxx–xxxi.

50. Ibid., 242.

51. Howells, *My Mark Twain*, 316.

52. *Mark Twain, Business Man*, ed. Samuel Charles Webster (Boston: Little, Brown, 1946), 143–44.

Chapter 2
The General and the Maid

1. Angus Fletcher, *Colors of the Mind: Conjectures on Thinking in Literature* (Cambridge: Harvard University Press, 1991), 3–4, 9.

2. Ibid., 5.

3. Ibid., 8.

4. Clemens to William Bowen, 6 February 1870, *Mark Twain's Letters, Volume 4: 1870–1871*, ed. Victor Fischer and Michael B. Frank (Berkeley: University of California Press, 1995), 50.

5. Dixon Wecter, *Sam Clemens of Hannibal* (Boston: Houghton Mifflin, 1952), 140.

6. There is reference in the published version to the power of circumstance, but it appears after the measles episode, and without allusion to the irresistible inner promptings of temperament. Albert Bigelow Paine noted on the first page of the typescript of the discarded version that Clemens "read it aloud to Jean and me. We did not approve and it brought on one of his heart attacks" (*WIM*, 521). However, Paine's account in *MTB* (4:1528) indicates that it was not the discussion of temperament and the measles that brought on the attack. In *Tom Sawyer's Conspiracy*, the young hero purposely gets himself sick in order to promote one of his adventures, only to learn that he has contracted scarlet fever, and not the measles (see *HH&T*, 184–88).

7. *My Father Mark Twain* (New York: Harper and Brothers, 1931), 6–7.

8. For a full account of the *Pennsylvania* disaster, see Ron Powers, *Dangerous Water* (New York: Basic Books, 1999), 265–89.

9. Quoted in Fred W. Lorch, "Mark Twain and *The Pennsylvania* Disaster," *The Twainian* 9 (1950): 2. For a fuller analysis of Clemens's reaction to Henry's death, see my essay, "Why I Killed My Brother: An Essay on Mark Twain," *Literature and Psychology* 30 (1980): 168–81, from which I draw here.

10. *Mark Twain's Letters, Volume 1: 1853–1866*, ed. Edgar Marquess Branch, Michael B. Frank, and Kenneth M. Sanderson (Berkeley: University of California Press, 1988), 80–81.

11. See, for example, *MTB*, 1:142; Bernard DeVoto, *Mark Twain's America* (Boston: Little Brown, 1932), 103–4; Dixon Wecter, *Sam Clemens of Hannibal*, 256; Henry Nash Smith, *Mark Twain, The Development of a Writer* (Cambridge: Harvard University Press, 1962), 132; *MCMT*, 194; and Edgar Marquess Branch, "Men Call Me Lucky: Mark Twain and the *Pennsylvania*" (Oxford, Ohio: Friends of the Library Society, Miami University, 1985), 49–50.

12. "The Devil and Samuel Clemens," *The Virginia Quarterly Review* 23 (1947): 584–86. Ron Powers is equally emphatic in declaring that Clemens suffered "a lifetime of guilt over his role in guiding his brother toward his doom, a guilt

compounded by the excruciating luck of his own survival" (*Mark Twain: A Life* (New York: Free Press, 2005), 89.

13. *The Standard Edition of the Complete Psychological Works of Sigmund Freud*, 24 vols. (London: Hogarth Press, 1953–74), 14:246.

14. Ibid., 14:248.

15. Ibid., 14:256.

16. Ibid., 14:251. Drawing directly on Freud's "Mourning and Melancholia," Pamela A. Boker elaborates fully and quite plausibly on the biographical and literary implications of Clemens's reaction to Henry's death. There was, Boker generalizes, "a strong pathological element in his response to loss and grief" (*The Grief Taboo in American Literature* [New York: New York University Press, 1996], 102.).

17. Ibid., 14:251.

18. In a 25 April 1880 letter to her son, Orion, Jane Lampton Clemens recalls that "Henrys nurse was a negro boy they were playing in the yard. Henry was high enough to hold the top of the kettle and peep over. This time there was hot embers he ran into the hot embers bare footed. I set on one chair with a wash bowl on another & held Henry in my armes & his feet in the cold water or he would have gone in to spasems before your father got there from the store with the Dr" (MTP), I am grateful to Robert Hirst and Victor Fischer of the Mark Twain Papers for bringing this letter to my attention.

19. *Mark Twain's Letters*, ed. Branch et al., 1: 81.

20. Ibid.

21. *Mark Twain's Notebooks & Journals, Volume 2 (1877–1883)*, ed. Frederick Anderson, Lin Salamo, and Bernard L. Stein (Berkeley: University of California Press, 1975), 454; see also 470 and 555.

22. Ibid.

23. Ibid.

24. *Mark Twain, Business Man*, ed. Samuel Charles Webster (Boston: Little, Brown and Company, 1946), 37.

25. While recounting Henry's death in *Life on the Mississippi*, Clemens recalls that the doctors wanted to administer morphine to the chief mate of the *Pennsylvania*. Although he was in terrible pain, the patient refused the medicine on the grounds that his wife had been killed by it. Instead, he endured the agony and "lived to be mate of a steamboat again" (*LM*, 245). While the two stories overlap in obvious ways, the precise bearing of this incident on the later account of Henry's death is unclear. It is tempting to speculate that Henry's rather implausible overdose is fabricated out of materials provided by the chief mate's example.

26. James M. Cox, *Mark Twain: The Fate of Humor* (Princeton, N.J.: Princeton University Press, 1966), 162.

27. Ibid., 164. In "'Good Rotten Material for Burial': The Overdetermined Death of Romance in *Life on the Mississippi*," *Literature and Psychology* 36 (1990), Stephen Cooper traces "Twain's relentless obsession with death in *Life on the Mississippi*" (78) to guilt over Henry's demise on the *Pennsylvania*.

28. Smith, *Mark Twain: The Development of a Writer*, 82.

29. Branch, "Men Call Me Lucky," 49–50.

30. See the detailed discussion of "proleptic guilt" in my essay, "The Silences in *Huckleberry Finn*," *Nineteenth-Century Fiction* 37 (1982): 50–74.

31. *Mark Twain's Letters: Volume 4, 1870–1871*, ed. Victor Fischer and Michael B. Frank (Berkeley: University of California Press, 1995), 51.

32. Sieur Louis de Conte is similarly moved by the fiery execution that concludes his *Personal Recollections of Joan of Arc*: "All these things I saw, albeit dimly and blurred with tears; but I could bear no more" (*JA*, 456). I am indebted to Dixon Wecter's useful discussion of many of these materials in *Sam Clemens of Hannibal*, 253–56.

33. See *Mark Twain's Notebooks & Journals*, ed. Robert Pack Browning, Michael B. Frank, and Lin Salamo (Berkeley: University of California Press, 1979), 3:105; and *MCMT*, 296–97.

34. Robert Underwood Johnson to Clemens, 22 August 1885, *MTP*.

35. Robert Underwood Johnson to Clemens, 13 November 1885, *MTP*.

36. Cox, *Mark Twain: The Fate of Humor*, 196.

37. *Mark Twain's Letters, Volume 1: 1853–1866*, 160.

38. Ibid., 165.

39. *Early Tales and Sketches, Volume I: 1851–1864*, ed. Edgar Marquess Branch and Robert H. Hirst (Berkeley: University of California Press, 1979), 391.

40. "Luck," in *Merry Tales*, The Oxford Mark Twain (New York: Oxford University Press, 1996), 67.

41. Clemens was sufficiently pleased with this version of the story to include it among the chapters of his autobiography published during his lifetime in the *North American Review*. See *Mark Twain's Own Autobiography*, ed. Michael J. Kiskis (Madison: University of Wisconsin Press, 1990), 214.

42. Compare the second, published account in *WIM*, 461.

43. *My Mark Twain*, in Howells, *Literary Friends and Acquaintances*, ed. David F. Hiatt and Edwin H. Cady (Bloomington: Indiana University Press, 1968), 302–3.

44. *New York Times*, 12 February 1901; as cited in Paul Fatout, *Mark Twain on the Lecture Circuit* (Bloomington: Indiana University Press, 1960), 276.

45. *Mark Twain's Own Autobiography*, ed. Kiskis, 21.

46. *Early Tales and Sketches,* ed. Branch and Hirst, 1:319.

47. Clemens sets out a version of the same argument in the autobiography (see *MTE*, 360).

48. "The Private History of a Campaign That Failed," in *Merry Tales*, 42, 45; for Kaplan's analysis—and his confident assertion that the battlefield fatality was "almost surely invented"—see *MCMT*, 275–77.

49. See also *MTA*, 1:21, 21; and *MTHL*, 1:340, 394–95.

50. See *MTHL*, 2:545.

51. *JA*, xxxix.

52. Cox, *Mark Twain: The Fate of Humor*, 261–64.

53. Brooks D. Simpson, in his *Ulysses S. Grant: Triumph over Adversity 1822–1865* (Boston: Houghton Mifflin, 2000), 459–60, emphasizes that Grant was an untutored

military genius, well known for having read little military history and giving scant weight to elaborate strategy.

54. As quoted in ibid., 462.

55. On Grant, see Geoffrey Perret, *Ulysses S. Grant, Soldier and President* (New York: Random House, 1997), 283; and Simpson, *Ulysses S. Grant*, 460, 463–64.

56. Compare Simpson, *Ulysses S. Grant*, who notes that Grant was known as "the American Sphinx" (xvii), and Perret, *Ulysses S. Grant, Soldier and President*, 277.

57. Lyman, a union officer who knew Grant, is quoted in Simpson, *Ulysses S. Grant*, xix.

58. Randal Knoper, *Acting Naturally: Mark Twain in the Culture of Performance* (Berkeley: University of California Press, 1995), 9–10, 171, 172.

59. Cox, *Mark Twain: The Fate of Humor*, 263.

60. *Mark Twain's Speeches* (New York: Harper and Brothers, 1923), 137; *MTA*, 1:48.

Chapter 3
My List of Permanencies

1. Autobiographical dictation, September–December 1909, MTP.

2. *Mark Twain: The Development of a Writer* (Cambridge: Harvard University Press, 1962), 99–100. For a full reconstruction of the Whittier dinner and its aftermath, see Henry Nash Smith, "'That Hideous Mistake of Poor Clemens's,'" *Harvard Library Bulletin* 9 (1955). 145–80.

3. For Howells's detailed account of the event, see *My Mark Twain*, in *Literary Friends and Acquaintances*, ed. David F. Hiatt and Edwin H. Cady (Bloomington: Indiana University Press, 1968), 293–97.

4. Ibid., 296.

5. *Mark Twain to Mrs. Fairbanks*, ed. Dixon Wecter (San Marino, Ca.: Huntington Library, 1949), 217.

6. Autobiographical dictation, 11 January 1906, MTP.

7. Ibid.

8. Ibid.

9. Ibid.

10. Autobiographical dictation, 23 January 1906, MTP.

11. Ibid.

12. Isabel Lyon, Daily Reminder, 22 May 1906, MTP.

13. See *Mark Twain's Own Autobiography*, ed. Michael J. Kiskis (Madison: University of Wisconsin Press, 1990), 230–37.

14. Notebook 38 (May–July 1896), MTP.

15. For a much fuller elaboration of this critical argument, see my "Patterns of Consciousness in *The Innocents Abroad*," *American Literature* 58 (1986): 46–63.

16. Roger Salomon, *Twain and the Image of History* (New Haven: Yale University Press, 1961), 205.

17. My summary of the composition history of *Roughing It* follows the account in *MCMT*, 120–28.

18. *Mark Twain's Letters, Volume 4: 1870–1871*, ed. Victor Fischer and Michael B. Frank (Berkeley: University of California Press, 1995), 230.

19. Henry Nash Smith, "Mark Twain as an Interpreter of the Far West: The Structure of *Roughing It*," in *the Frontier in Perspective*, ed. Walker D. Wyman and Clifton B. Kroeber (Madison: University of Wisconsin Press, 1965), 21.

20. Gilman M. Ostrander, *Nevada: The Great Rotten Borough, 1859–1864* (New York: Knopf, 1966), 13.

21. See especially the letters written between September 1861 and September 1862, in *Mark Twain's Letters, Vol. 1: 1853–1866*, 124–237.

22. *Mark Twain's Letters, Volume 4: 1870–1871*, 195, 348.

23. William R. Gillis, *Gold Rush Days with Mark Twain* (New York: Albert and Charles Boni, 1930), 75.

24. Dixon Wecter, *Sam Clemens of Hannibal*, 235–36.

25. *As I Remember Them* (Salt Lake City, 1913), as quoted in Edgar Marquess Branch, *The Literary Apprenticeship of Mark Twain* (Urbana: University of Illinois Press, 1950), 108.

26. *Gold Rush Days with Mark Twain*, 72–75, 98–101, 103–7, 109–16, 153–56, 173–74.

27. See *MTB*, 1:224–27, 297–302; and Ivan Benson, *Mark Twain's Western Years* (Palo Alto: Stanford University Press, 1938), 151.

28. See also *AMT*, 103, 311–13.

29. As reprinted in *The Mining Frontier*, ed. Marvin Lewis (Norman: University of Oklahoma Press, 1967), 186.

30. Dan DeQuille, *The Big Bonanza* (New York: Knopf, 1967), 54–61, 212–14, 270–71, 309–15, 331–39, 347–51, 415–27.

31. Howells's remarks appeared in the *Atlantic Monthly*, June 1872, as cited in *MCMT*, 148. For an analysis that runs parallel in important ways with mine, see Lawrence I. Berkove, "The Trickster God in *Roughing It*," *Thalia: Studies in Literary Humor* 18 (1998): 21–30. Berkove appears to be unaware of my earlier essay, "Seeing the Elephant: Some Perspectives on Mark Twain's *Roughing It*," *American Studies* 21 (1980): 43–64.

32. Ostrander, *Nevada: The Great Rotten Borough*, 58–59.

33. For more detail on Wiegand, see the very helpful notes in The Works of Mark Twain edition of *Roughing It*, ed. Franklin R. Rogers and Paul Baender (Berkeley: University of California Press, 1972), 620–26, and Lawrence I. Berkove, "'Assaying in Nevada': Twain's Wrong Turn in the Right Direction," *American Literary Realism 1870–1910* 27 (1995): 64–80.

34. *Mark Twain of the "Enterprise,"* ed. Henry Nash Smith (Berkeley: University of California Press, 1957), 193. All of the evidence bearing on the episode is usefully assembled in this volume.

35. Ibid., 29.

36. Ibid., 204–5.

37. Cox, *Mark Twain: The Fate of Humor*, 17.

38. Leland Krauth, "Mark Twain Fights Sam Clemens' Duel," *Mississippi Quarterly* 33 (1980): 146. From the midst of dozens of brief references to and treatments of the duel, Krauth neglects to mention two others of more substantial interest: in the unpublished, first version of "The Turning Point of My Life" (*WIM*, 528); and in Samuel E. Moffett's "Mark Twain: A Biographical Sketch," *McClure's Magazine* 13 (1899): 523–29. Ron Powers agrees that "the affair continued to vex him long afterward, and he treated it with careful levity in his writings" (*Mark Twain: A Life* [New York: Free Press, 2005], 141).

39. Ibid., 146, 141, 150.

40. *Mark Twain's Own Autobiography*, ed. Kiskis, 71.

41. *Mark Twain of the "Enterprise,"* ed. Smith, 196.

42. Ibid., 190.

43. Herman Melville, *Moby-Dick* (New York: Norton, 1967), 195–96.

44. *Mark Twain's Notebooks and Journals, Volume I: (1855–1873)*, ed. Frederick Anderson, Michael B. Frank, and Kenneth M. Sanderson (Berkeley: University of California Press, 1975), 15.

45. Clemens wrote again the following March: "That most infernally troublesome book is at last hidden from sight & mind in the jaws of three steam presses" (*MTHL*, 1:290).

46. *Mark Twain's Letters to His Publishers*, ed. Hamlin Hill (Berkeley: University of California Press, 1967), 109.

47. Ibid.

48. James M. Cox (*Mark Twain: The Fate of Humor*, 13–24) is characteristically penetrating in his treatment of Clemens's adoption and deployment of his famous pseudonym. If, as Paul Fatout has argued, Sellers did not in fact take "Mark Twain" as his nom de plume (*Mark Twain in Virginia City* [Bloomington: Indiana University Press, 1964], 34–39) Clemens's claim that he did so merely supplements the already ornate self-indictment submerged in this passage from *Life on the Mississippi*.

49. Clemens refers to a riot among striking laborers in a letter home from St. Louis in late February, 1855 (*Mark Twain's Letters, Volume 1: 1853–1866*, 50).

50. In his very useful edition of *Life on the Mississippi* (New York: Penguin Books, 1984), James M. Cox notes that "this brief, humorous account of Mark Twain's 'desertion' from the army is a forerunner of his more elaborate and serious account of his war experience in 'The Private History of a Campaign that Failed' " (449).

51. *Mark Twain's Correspondence with Henry Huttleston Rogers*, ed. Lewis Leary (Berkeley: University of California Press, 1969), 309.

52. On the provenance and thematics of the maxims, see William M. Gibson's useful account in *The Art of Mark Twain* (New York: Oxford University Press, 1976), 158–76.

53. Hunt Hawkins argues persuasively that "Twain's anti-imperialism was . . . gradually undermined by his pessimism" ("Mark Twain's Anti-Imperialism," *American Literary Realism 1870–1910* 25 [1993]: 34). See also Peter Messent's discerning

"Racial and Colonial Discourse in Mark Twain's *Following the Equator*," *Essays in Arts and Sciences* 22 (1993): 67–83.

54. Howells, *My Mark Twain*, 277.

Chapter 4
Telling Fictions

1. Afterword to the *GA*, 24.

2. *Mark Twain's Letters, Volume 4: 1870–1871*, ed. Victor Fischer and Michael B. Frank (Berkeley: University of California Press, 1995), 50.

3. SLC to Mrs. Bowen, 6 June 1900, MTP.

4. *The Adventures of Tom Sawyer* (Berkeley: University of California Press, 1982), 270.

5. SLC to Charles B. Dillingham, 2 August 1902 and 9 November 1902, MTP.

6. *My Mark Twain*, in *Literary Friends and Acquaintances*, ed. David F. Hiatt and Edwin F. Cady (Bloomington: Indiana University Press, 1968), 288, 257.

7. See also *MCMT*, 379–80, and Louis J. Budd, *Our Mark Twain: The Making of His Public Personality* (Philadelphia: University of Pennsylvania Press, 1983).

8. Hamlin Hill, *Mark Twain: God's Fool* (New York: Harper and Row, 1973), 147.

9. SLC to Olivia L. Clemens, 31 May 1902, MTP.

10. Miscellaneous autobiographical note, DV #243, MTP.

11. Autobiographical dictation, 10 August 1907, MTP.

12. For another, powerfully developed understanding of simulation, burlesque, and impersonation in Clemens's humor, see Cox, *Mark Twain: The Fate of Humor* (Princeton, N.J.: Princeton University Press, 1966), *34–62 and passim*. For more on Clemens's youthful encounter with the mesmerist, see Powers, *Dangerous Water* (New York: Basic Books, 1999), 74–8. See also Boker, *The Grief Taboo in American Literature* (New York: New York University Press, 1996), 87–89, 95.

13. Cox, *Mark Twain: The Fate of Humor*, 154–55.

14. *Twain and the Image of History* (New Haven: Yale University Press, 1957), 158–59.

15. Ibid., 150.

16. In one of the notes appended to the novel, Clemens describes the plan for Norfolk's execution, and identifies Hume as his source. See *P&P*, 405, note 3.

17. Ibid., 406, note 7.

18. Clara L. Clemens to Samuel E. Moffett [1902?], MTP.

19. Clemens to Charles B. Dillingham, 9 November 1902, MTP.

20. Notebook 35, MTP. For further discussion, see Wecter, *Sam Clemens of Hannibal* (Boston: Houghton Mifflin, 1952), 147–50, and *HH&T*, 344–45.

21. Ibid.

22. Ibid.

23. Arthur G. Pettit, *Mark Twain & the South* (Lexington: The University Press of Kentucky, 1974), 5, 9.

24. SLC to Karl Gerhardt, 1 May 1883, MTP.

25. Pettit, *Mark Twain & the South*, 73.

26. Ibid., 15.

27. Terrell Dempsey, *Searching for Jim: Slavery in Sam Clemens's World* (Columbia: University of Missouri Press, 2003), 221–24, 280, 279.

28. Clemens to Charles B. Dillingham, 2 August 1902, MTP.

29. As the editors of the California edition (ed. Victor Fischer and Lin Salamo [Berkeley: University of California Press, 2003], 443) observe, "Clemens was similarly unable to forget the grief caused by the separation of slave families when they were sold. He wrote about it in 'A True Story' (1874), chapter 21 of *A Connecticut Yankee* (1889), and chapter 3 of *Pudd'nhead Wilson* (1894)."

30. See my essay, "The Silences in *Huckleberry Finn*," *Nineteenth-Century Fiction* 34 (1982): 50–74.

31. Henry Nash Smith, *Mark Twain, The Development of a Writer* (Cambridge: Harvard University Press, 1962), 132–33.

32. Ibid., 130.

33. Ibid., 124.

34. James M. Cox, "A Hard Book to Take," in *One Hundred Years of Huckleberry Finn: The Boy, His Book, and American Culture*, ed. Robert Sattelmeyer and J. Donald Crowley (Columbia: University of Missouri Press, 1985), 391. For an ingenious elaboration on Cox's critical argument, see Gerry Brenner, "More than a Reader's Response: A Letter to 'De Ole True Huck,'" *The Journal of Narrative Technique* 20 (1990), 221–34. In "On the Nature and Status of Covert Texts: A Reply to Gerry Brenner's 'Letter to "De Ole True Huck,'"" *The Journal of Narrative Technique* 20 (1990), 235–44, James Phelan recapitulates Brenner's position and comments upon it. See also Victor A. Doyno, "Huck's and Jim's Dynamic Interactions: Dialogues, Ethics, Empathy, Respect," *The Mark Twain Annual* 1 (2003), 19–29, where a very similar critical position is advanced.

35. Spencer Brown seems to have been the first to make this point. See his "*Huckleberry Finn* for Our Time," *The Michigan Quarterly Review* 6 (1967): 45.

36. On audience reception of *Huckleberry Finn*, see my *In Bad Faith*, 118–22, 134–38, 238–41.

37. The editors note (*HF*, 375–76) that "Mark Twain's manuscript did not include the phrase, 'persons attempting to find a Moral in it will be banished,' which he added in revision, probably on the typed printer's copy."

38. *How to Tell a Story, and Other Essays*, The Oxford Mark Twain (New York: Oxford University Press, 1996), 220.

39. In my essay "An 'Unconscious and Profitable Cerebration': Mark Twain and Literary Intentionality," *Nineteenth-Century Literature* 50 (1995): 357–80, I argue that Clemens's "scattered observations on the writer's craft tend strongly to confirm our impression that he usually set to work with a few characters and episodes in mind, but with no clear, fully developed format or thematic structures. Thus we are obliged to concede that much of the apparent design in his writing is probably unconscious in origin" (358). There has been little intellectually compelling dissent

from this general view, though in *Mark Twain in the Margins: The Quarry Farm Marginalia and A Connecticut Yankee in King Arthur's Court* (Tuscaloosa: University of Alabama Press, 2000), 1–28, Joe B. Fulton strenuously disagrees.

Chapter 5
Dreaming Better Dreams

1. *Inventing Mark Twain*, 415. See also Harold K. Bush, Jr., " 'Broken Idols': Mark Twain's Elegies for Susy and a Critique of Freudian Grief Theory," *Nineteenth-Century Literature* 57 (2002) 237–68.

2. Joseph H. Twichell to Mark Twain, 9 December 1901, MTP.

3. *Mark Twain at Work* (Cambridge: Harvard University Press, 1942), 116.

4. *Mark Twain: God's Fool* (New York: Harper and Row, 1973), xvii.

5. William R. Macnaughton, *Mark Twain's Last Years as a Writer* (Columbia: University of Missouri Press, 1979); Bruce Michelson, *Mark Twain on the Loose* (Amherst: University of Massachusetts Press, 1995); Karen Lystra, *Dangerous Intimacy: The Untold Story of Mark Twain's Final Years* (Berkeley: University of California Press, 2004).

6. " 'Well, My Book Is Written—Let It Go . . . .': The Making of *A Connecticut Yankee in King Arthur's Court*," *Biographies of Books: The Compositional Histories of Notable American Writings*, ed. James Barbour and Tom Quirk (Columbia: University of Missouri Press, 1996), 50.

7. "Afterword" to the Oxford Mark Twain edition of *A Connecticut Yankee in King Arthur's Court*, 4.

8. *Mark Twain's Fable of Progress: Political and Economic Ideas in "A Connecticut Yankee"* (New Brunswick: Rutgers University Press, 1964), 105. In his Introduction to The Works of Mark Twain edition of *A Connecticut Yankee* (Berkeley: University of California Press, 1979), Smith leans to the view that "Hank Morgan is at bottom Clemens himself" (p. 4).

9. *Twain and the Image of History* (New Haven: Yale University Press, 1961), 114, 105, 108.

10. *Sentimental Twain: Samuel Clemens in the Maze of Moral Philosophy* (Philadelphia: University of Pennsylvania Press, 1994), 151.

11. Baetzhold ("Well, My Book Is Written," 63) argues that Charles Ball's *Slavery in the United States*, a slave narrative published in 1837, and pictures of Siberian exiles in *Century* magazine, were "important sources" for the descriptions of the slaves in *A Connecticut Yankee*.

12. Terrell Dempsey, *Searching for Jim*, 221–24.

13. See Camfield, *Sentimental Twain: Slavery in Sam Clemens's World* (Columbia: University of Missouri Press, 2003), 151–64, for a thoughtful discussion of the philosophical context in which *A Connecticut Yankee* was written.

14. Peter Messent, "Afterword" to *AC*, 1. See also Susan Gillman, *Dark Twins: Imposture and Identity in Mark Twain's America* (Chicago: University of Chicago Press, 1989), 149–56; Gregg Camfield, *Sentimental Twain*, 164–73; and Lawrence

Howe, *Mark Twain and the Novel: The Double-Cross of Authority* (New York: Cambridge University Press, 1998), 174–82. Roger B. Salomon's earlier treatment (*Twain and the Image of History*, 127–31), though brief, is still valuable.

15. The enforced auction of Dan'l and Jinny also turns up in chapter 7 of *The Gilded Age*, though in that version they disappear into "the remote South to be seen no more by the family" (*GA*, 78).

16. Clemens's views of mind-cure are widely discussed. See especially K. Patrick Ober, *Mark Twain and Medicine* (Columbia: University of Missouri Press, 2003), 210–22; Hoffman, *Inventing Mark Twain*, 337; Fred Kaplan, *The Singular Mark Twain* (New York: Doubleday, 2003), 487; and Lystra, *Dangerous Intimacy*, 22–23. For broader historical perspectives, see Gail Thain Parker, *Mind Cure in New England* (Hanover, N.H.: University Press of New England, 1973) and Eric Caplan's excellent *Mind Games: American Culture and the Birth of Psychotherapy* (Berkeley: University of California Press, 1998), especially chapter 4.

17. "My Mark Twain," in *Literary Friends and Acquaintances*, ed. David F. Hiatt and Edwin H. Cady (Bloomington: Indiana University Press, 1968), 310.

18. *The Love Letters of Mark Twain*, ed. Dixon Wecter (New York: Harper and Brothers, 1949), 333. Hill (*Mark Twain: God's Fool*, 41) speculates that the letter may have been written in early 1902.

19. See *AMT*, 122 and 123.

20. See *AC*, 93.

21. I am grateful to Lin Salamo for her help in locating this reference.

22. *Mark Twain and the Novel*, 182.

23. *New York American*, May 26, 1907; in *Mark Twain: Life As I Find It*, ed. Charles Neider (Garden City, N.Y.: Hanover House, 1961), 388. In his "Reply to the Editor of 'The Art of Authorship,'" published in 1890, Clemens generalizes from his own experience that the "training most in use" among writers is of an "unconscious sort, and is guided and governed and made by-and-by unconsciously systematic, by an automatically-working taste—a taste which selects and rejects without asking you for any help, and patiently and steadily improves itself without troubling you to approve or applaud" (in *CTSSE*, 1:945).

24. Frederick Anderson, Introduction to the facsimile of the first American edition of *Pudd'nhead Wilson/Those Extraordinary Twins* (San Francisco: Chandler, 1968), xviii.

25. *Mark Twain's Letters to His Publishers, 1867–1894*, ed. Hamlin Hill (Berkeley: University of California Press, 1967), 354.

26. From the Textual Introduction to *PW*, 176.

27. "My Platonic Sweetheart," 48, MTP.

28. Kaplan adduces as evidence young Sam Clemens's admiration for Wales McCormick, who made no secret of his designs on an attractive slave girl. Despite protests from the girl's mother, it was "quite well understood," Clemens recalls, "that by the customs of slaveholding communities it was Wales's right to make love to that girl if he wanted to" (*AMT*, 88).

29. "My Platonic Sweetheart," 9, MTP. For analysis along similar lines, see Susan Gillman, *Dark Twins*, 51–52; and Suzi Naiburg, "Negro Wench and Platonic Sweetheart: Images of Splitting and Integration in Samuel Clemens's Dreams," *Essays in Arts and Sciences* 232 (1994): 67–84.

30. Hershel Parker, *Flawed Texts and Verbal Icons: Literary Authority in American Fiction* (Evanston: Northwestern University Press, 1984), 141.

31. Essex's death is also mentioned in passing at the end of chapter 4 (*PW*, 22).

32. Susan Gillman (*Dark Twins*, 73–75) insightfully incorporates this passage into her discussion of identity and the law in slave culture.

33. "*A Connecticut Yankee in King Arthur's Court*: The Machinery of Self-Preservation," in *Mark Twain: A Collection of Critical Essays*, ed. Henry Nash Smith (Englewood Cliffs: Prentice-Hall, 1963), 128.

34. Barbara Ladd's view (in *Nationalism and the Color Line in George W. Cable, Mark Twain, and William Faulkner* [Baton Rouge: Louisiana State University Press, 1996], 137) that "*Those Extraordinary Twins* and *Pudd'nhead Wilson* are constructed around questions of the extent and nature of one's complicity with one's history," speaks in an obvious way to my understanding of these texts. See also Robert Moss, "Tracing Mark Twain's Intentions: The Retreat From Issues of Race in *Pudd'nhead Wilson*," *American Literary Realism 1870–1910* 30 (1998): 43–55; Stephen Railton, "The Tragedy of Mark Twain, by Pudd'nhead Wilson," *Nineteenth-Century Literature* 56 (2002): 518–44; and Christopher Gair, "Whitewashed Exteriors: Mark Twain's Imitation Whites," *Journal of American Studies* 39 (2005): 187–205.

35. *Dark Twins*, 31, 48–50.

36. Autobiographical dictation, June 25, 1906, MTP.

37. *Mark Twain and the Image of History*, 126.

38. "Mark Twain, Isabel Lyon, and the 'Talking Cure,'" *Constructing Mark Twain: New Directions in Scholarship*, ed. Laura E. Skandera-Trombley and Michael J. Kiskis (Columbia: University of Missouri Press, 2001), 101.

39. SLC to Muriel Pears, MTP.

40. SLC to Wayne MacVeagh, 22 August 1897, MTP.

41. See also *MTHL*, 2:664, 670, 689.

42. *Mark Twain*, 159. See also Shelley Fisher Fishkin, "False Starts, Fragments and Fumbles: Mark Twain's Unpublished Writing on Race," *Essays in Arts and Sciences* 20 (1991) 17–31.

43. See *In Bad Faith* (Cambridge: Harvard University Press, 1986), 228–37.

44. *Mark Twain: The Fate of Humor* (Princeton, N.J.: Princeton University Press, 1966), 283.

45. The "Conclusion of the book," which was composed in 1904 as the projected ending for "No. 44, The Mysterious Stranger," and later tacked on to "The Chronicle of Young Satan" in a posthumous, bowderlized edition of *The Mysterious Stranger*, had no part, so far as we know, in Clemens's conception of the earliest version of his story. We will come back to this important fragment in due course. For more detail on textual history, see William M. Gibson's fascinating Introduction to his edition of *The Mysterious Stranger*. For a critical reading of the "Conclusion of

the book" as an "ending" for "The Chronicle of Young Satan," see *In Bad Faith*, 223–24.

46. William R. Macnaughton draws this very plausible inference in *Mark Twain's Last Years As a Writer*, 111–12.

47. Notebook 41 (January–July 1897), 57–58, MTP.

48. For readings differently focused but entirely compatible with my own, see Messent, *Mark Twain* (Basingstoke: Macmillan, 1997), 169–74, and Gillman, *Dark Twins*, 172–76. Gillman notes in passing that "there can be no guilt" (176) in the world of "Three Thousand Years Among the Microbes."

49. SLC to Olivia Langdon Clemens, 19 August 1896, MTP. The letter was written to notify his wife of the death of their daughter, Susy.

50. See Gibson's very thorough and revealing discussion in *MS*, 26–33, which I summarize in this paragraph.

51. SLC to Wayne MacVeagh, 22 August 1897, as cited by Gibson, *MS*, 28.

52. SLC to Joseph Twichell, 28 July 1904, as cited by Gibson, *MS*, 30.

53. Gibson indicates (*MS*, 9–10) that the first phase of composition carried Clemens through either chapter 7 or chapter 8. My interpretation proceeds on the assumption that he broke off at the end of chapter 7, though the argument applies just as well a chapter later.

54. Tuckey indicates that the unfinished novel was written in 1905–6.

55. SLC to Joseph Twichell, 28 July 1904, as cited by Gibson, *MS*, 31.

Epilogue

1. Hamlin Hill, in *Mark Twain: God's Fool* (New York: Harper and Row, 1973), 268, emphasizes that "Paine, as the literary editor of the Mark Twain Estate, was a willing participant in the suppression of . . . unpleasant facts." As late as 1926, Paine wrote to Harper and Brothers: "I think on general principles it is a mistake to let any one else write about Mark Twain, as long as we can prevent it. . . . As soon as this is begun (writing about him at all, I mean) the Mark Twain that we have 'preserved'—the Mark Twain that we knew, the traditional Mark Twain—will begin to fade and change, and with that process the Harper Mark Twain property will depreciate" (as quoted in Hill).

2. "'The country home I need,' he said fiercely, 'is a cemetery . . . I think I have had about enough of this world, and I wish I were out of it'" (*MTB*, 4:1337). He kept a print of Saint-Gaudens' somber "Adams Memorial"—which reminded him of his failures with Livy—on his mantelpiece (*MTB*, 4:1350–51).

3. See also *MTB*, 4:1270, 1363, 1469.

4. Clemens to John MacAlister, 7 April 1903, MTP.

5. "The Death of Jean," *Mark Twain's Own Autobiography*, ed. Michael J. Kiskis (Madison: University of Wisconsin Press, 1990), 249.

6. Clemens to Jean Clemens, 21 May 1908, MTP (as cited in Hill, *Mark Twain: God's Fool*, 198).

7. Clemens to Olivia Langdon Clemens, 19 August 1896, MTP.

8. Clemens to Olivia Langdon Clemens, 29–30 August 1896, MTP.

9. Hill, *Mark Twain: God's Fool*, 169.

10. Karen Lystra, *Dangerous Intimacy: The Untold Story of Mark Twain's Final Years* (Berkeley: University of California Press, 2004), 86, 191.

11. Clemens to Clara Clemens, 6 March 1910, MTP (as cited in *MCMT,* 386).

12. I am not persuaded by Karen Lystra's recent indictment of Isabel Lyon in *Dangerous Intimacy*. Lystra builds her case almost exclusively on the widely discredited Ashcroft-Lyon manuscript, which Hamlin Hill rightly condemns as "a geyser of bias, vindictiveness, and innuendo" (Hill, *Mark Twain: God's Fool*, 231). To the very considerable extent that it mirrors the sentiments and tone of its major source, Lystra's book is similarly flawed. For a more balanced treatment, see Laura E. Skandera-Trombley, "Mark Twain's Last Work of Realism: The Ashcroft-Lyon Manuscript," *Essays in Arts and Sciences* 23 (1994): 39–48. "One cannot help but be struck by how improbable his accusations are," Skandera-Trombley observes, "and by how terribly petty he sounds. Twain's charges are consistently contradictory and for every accusation there is an implied admission of guilt" (41). See also Jennifer L. Rafferty, " 'The Lyon of St. Mark': A Reconsideration of Isabel Lyon's Relationship to Mark Twain," *Mark Twain Journal* 32 (1994): 43–55. Rafferty's thorough, sympathetic, and entirely plausible assessment includes testimony from Henry Nash Smith, who describes Lyon as "truly one of the most remarkable people I have ever met," and who declares that "Mark Twain did Mrs. Lyon an injustice at the time she left his employ" (54). Fred Kaplan concurs. The Lyon-Ashcroft Manuscript, he concludes, "was petty, sanctimonious, and self-demeaning, and as a factual account egregiously unreliable" (*The Singular Mark Twain* [New York: Doubleday, 2003], 647.

13. Charles H. Gold, *"Hatching Ruin," or Mark Twain's Road to Bankruptcy* (Columbia: University of Missouri Press, 2003), 15, 61, 156. "In all of his woes," Guy Cardwell observes, "Clemens characteristically vacillated between expressions of guilt and efforts to find scapegoats" (*The Man Who Was Mark Twain* [New Haven: Yale University Press, 1991], 79).

Index

Huckleberry Finn, 117, 134
  bad faith in, 18
  evasion at end of, 193
  Jim's appearance in, 131
  Jim's treatment in, 117
  moral imperative of, 153
  moral issues in, 29
  personal investment of, 133
  race/slavery in, 136
  reputation of, 74
  slavery implications of, 153
Hudson, Laura K., 81
human nature, 186
Hume, David, 129
hyperbole, 45
hypnotism, 202
hypocrisy, 24, 89, 108, 126, 169, 183,
    187, 195, 214

Ibsen, Henrik, 218*n*31
imperialism
  European, 107
  in *Following the Equator,* 106
  global, 109
  Old World, 23
Indian crow, 24
Injun Joe, 43, 57, 125–26
innocence, 93
The Innocents Abroad, 84
The Innocents Adrift (Paine), 28
irresponsibility, 15
Ishmael, 99

Jack-leg novelist, 185
Jackson's Island, 120, 142, 219
James, William, 14
Janet, Pierre, 180
Jim *(Huckleberry Finn)*
  disclosure of, 155
  on Finn, 149
  power of, 143
  vigilance of, 148
Jim Crow, 110

Joan of Arc, 73. *See also Personal Recollections of Joan of Arc*
Johnson, Robert Underwood, 64
Journal of the Reigns of George IV and William IV (Greville), 209
juvenile fiction, 117

Kaplan, Justin, 12, 31, 61, 69, 87, 179
King's Ward, 131
Kiskis, Michael J., 32
Knoper, Randall, 76
Krauth, Leland, 97, 225*n*38

Laird, James L., 96, 98
Lamentations, 46
Lampton, James, 114
Langdon, Jervis, 11, 87
Langdon, Olivia, 40, 59, 86, 158
Life on the Mississippi, 53, 59, 106
  autobiographical significance in, 106
  childhood memories in, 59
  Henry Clemens in, 58
  emotion in, 53
  guilt in, 62
  Pennsylvania explosion and, 50
literary discourse, 38
locus classicus, 198
"Lucretia Smith's Soldier", 66
Luther, Martin, 212
Lyman, Theodore, 76
lynching
  hatred and, 153
  horrors of, 110
Lyon, Isabel, 83, 214
Lystra, Karen, 159, 232*n*12

Macnaughton, William R., 159
MacVeagh, Wayne, 189
"Man's Place in the Animal World", 187
Mark Twain: A Biography (Paine), 209
"Mark Twain Fights Sam Clemens' Duel" (Krauth), 225*n*38
Mark Twain: God's Fool (Hill), 6